301. 16 (417)

UNDERSTANDING CONTEMPORARY IRELAND

Understanding Contemporary Ireland

State, Class and Development in the

Republic of Ireland

Richard Breen
Senior Research Officer
The Economic and Social Research Institute
Dublin

Damian F. Hannan
Research Professor
The Economic and Social Research Institute
Dublin

David B. Rottman
Senior Staff Associate
National Center for State Courts
Williamsburg

Christopher T. Whelan
Senior Research Officer
The Economic and Social Research Institute
Dublin

GILL AND MACMILLAN

First published 1990

Published by
THE MACMILLAN PRESS LTD
Houndmills, Basingstoke, Hampshire RG21 2XS
and London
Companies and representatives
throughout the world
and by
GILL AND MACMILLAN LTD
Goldenbridge, Dublin 8

Printed in Hong Kong

ISBN 0–333–42368–2 (Macmillan hardcover)
ISBN 0–333–52496–9 (Macmillan paperback)
ISBN 0–7171–1741–3 (Gill and Macmillan paperback)

Contents

Contents

List of Tables

List of Figures

ix

Preface

During the 1950s, when most of the rest of Europe was enjoying the fruits of post-war reconstruction and unprecedented growth, the Republic of Ireland was suffering chronic economic depression and massive levels of emigration. At the close of that decade, and faced with the manifest failure of the policies it had pursued since securing independence from Britain almost forty years previously, the Irish State embarked on a programme of development which rapidly transformed the economy and with it Irish society. This book is about that transformation and its effects. In particular we focus on the relationship between the policies pursued by the Irish State, beginning in the late 1950s, and the class structure of Ireland. We shall argue that, despite promises of general prosperity, the benefits of Ireland's belated economic development have been very unevenly distributed, leading to a growing polarisation between social classes. At first sight this seems paradoxical, given that the task of distributing economic rewards has lain primarily with the State, which has come to play a central role in underpinning the distribution of economic opportunities. Some indication of this is given by the fact that total annual State expenditure now exceeds 60 per cent of GNP. We shall argue, however, that the State's role has been such as to make it unable either to ensure sustained economic growth or to moderate inegalitarian tendencies in the class structure.

We develop the background to this argument in the first two chapters of the book. While our concern is with the post-1958 period, we have found it necessary to present a brief account of the Irish State and the class structure over the period since independence. This provides the essential background against which the depth of the 1958 watershed must be gauged and also serves the function of introducing the non-Irish reader to what we believe to be, for our purposes, the salient points in Ireland's post-independence history. For this material, most of which appears in Chapter 2, we have drawn heavily on the work of a number of modern Irish historians. In Chapter 3 we chart the overall patterns of change in the Irish class structure between the 1950s and the present day. In Chapters 4 to 9 we look in some detail at the role of the State in a number of areas – the distribution and redistribution of income via taxes and transfers; educational policy; the family; industrial policy and industrial relations; and agricultural policy. In each of these we seek to demonstrate the effects of the policies pursued by the State on the class structure and, as far as possible, we explain why these policies have neither secured sustained growth nor led to an amelioration of the unequal distribution of privilege and opportunity. Chapter 10 concludes with a summary of our argument and a discussion of the light it sheds on the current crises of the Irish State.

Our perspective treats Ireland as a country which industrialised late and rapidly. Consequently it shares much with other countries on the European periphery, such as Greece and Spain – not least the sometimes uneasy intermingling of elements of tradition and modernity. Thus our study can stand as a source of comparative material within that context. But unlike other European countries, Ireland has a long history of political and economic domination by a colonial power. So, in some respects, its experience can fruitfully be compared with those of the developing countries of the Third World. These dual parallels make Ireland unique as a testing ground for ideas concerning the development process and its consequences.

We take social class as the core for our explanation of social change. However, in Ireland, to a degree rarely found in Western democracies, the State has played a dominant role in shaping the class structure and ultimately, therefore, in determining the allocation of life chances of individuals. This requires us to present an integrated account of the State's role, not only through industrial, economic and social policies, but as a medium through which parties to the distributional conflicts of modern capitalism seek to exert their influence. This entails both efforts to establish a corporatist approach to resolving those conflicts and the remarkable susceptibility of Irish governments to the pressures of organised interests.

In the course of some ten years of sociological research on Irish society our work has led us to a shared view of how the transformation of Irish society took place. The results have appeared in research monographs and articles. This book is a synthesis of that empirical work and the theoretical perspective which informed it. We view the central concern of sociology, as a discipline, to be the study of the processes by which social forms are produced and reproduced. So while our central task is to provide a description of the social structure, our emphasis is on social process: the sequence of development that has shaped modern Ireland and the dynamics for future change implicit in the structure of contemporary Irish society.

The bulk of the underlying research on which this book is based was undertaken by the four of us at The Economic and Social Research

Institute. We would like to thank Professor Kieran Kennedy, Director of the Institute, and our colleagues for the support we have consistently enjoyed in our efforts to contribute to a sociological understanding of modern Irish society.

1 Introduction: The Transformation of Ireland's Social Structure

THE RISING TIDE

Few societies have changed so rapidly and so radically as has the Republic of Ireland since 1960. The resulting transformation is particularly striking given Ireland's image as a rural, conservative and Catholic backwater of post-war Europe. Moreover, there was substance to the image. The first 40 years of independence – from the 1920s to the 1960s – were notable for institutional continuity rather than change, and for an isolation which, by 1950, had become acute. As the rest of Europe basked in a sustained period of economic growth and implemented basic Welfare State principles, Ireland slumbered, unable or unwilling to cope with its considerable economic and social problems. In the late fifties, however, crisis led to innovation in the form of State initiatives to promote industrialisation. Success in those initiatives brought a more general promise that the fruits of independence would finally be realised, vindicating the long nationalist struggle. The associated expectations and excitement were captured in the catch phrase of the 1960s, 'the rising tide that would lift all boats' by setting a new universal standard and ignoring old restrictions.

This chapter begins with an outline of the main features of the post-1960 transformation and the underlying dynamic in the form of the interaction between the State's new economic and social policies and a changing social class structure.

It was the link between those State policies, which initiated late industrialisation, and the class structure that gave Ireland's transformation its distinctiveness. The inter-relationship is complex, however, since many of what we regard as the most important consequences of State action were clearly unintended. Subsequent sections of this chapter introduce the sociological concepts through which we intend to construct our explanation for the distinctive course contemporary Ireland has taken since 1960.

As one of the first nations to achieve independence from a colonial power in the twentieth century, Ireland seemed destined to mark out a

1

new course. The signing of the Anglo-Irish Treaty on 6 December 1921 heralded the imminent demise of British rule and its replacement by an independent Irish State. It had been evident since 1919 that Home Rule would not suffice as an expression for Irish nationalist aspirations. Dail Eireann over the 1919–21 period succeeded in establishing itself as a State *in potentia,* a national parliament whose decrees, law courts and local governments sapped the final legitimacy of the British administration. Yet independence proved a bitter triumph. The new State emerged in 1922 only to slide immediately from revolution into civil war over the issue of partition. By the terms of the Treaty, six of the island's 32 counties remained within the United Kingdom. The new 26-county State was, both administratively and economically, an artificial creation. Its territory had never previously been treated as a unit and partition excluded the bulk of the island's industrial base: 'It was as if Scotland had obtained self-government with Glasgow and the Clyde left out' (O'Brien, 1962, p. 11). Political independence, therefore, did not alter the marginal economic position within the United Kingdom[1] which Ireland had filled since the beginning of the previous century. If anything, that marginality was increased.

Economic marginality and Civil War wounds left limited scope for innovation. Even that limited scope, however, was not pursued. The members of the first Government of the Free State vigorously adopted the orthodoxy of the 1920s – free trade – and proudly styled themselves the most conservative revolutionaries in history.[2] With their political opponents adopting an abstentionist stance towards Parliament, the Government's main struggle was to establish order in the economy and its authority in the cities, towns and villages. Partition facilitated this effort by removing one of the more likely bases for contention. Roman Catholics initially constituted 90 per cent of the new State's citizens, a share that rose gradually to 95 per cent. Religious homogeneity reflected more than nominal allegiances: 'Ireland is unusual in having a large majority not just of Catholics, but of committed and practising Catholics' (Whyte, 1980, p. 4). The Catholic Church emerged from the nationalist struggle with enhanced authority and prestige. Although its hierarchy had never been in the vanguard of that struggle, the Church had served as a counterweight to the power of London for generations, while individual clergy had assumed a more activist role. The Church placed its considerable influence at the disposal of the first Government. It was a natural alliance. Both Church and State saw the potential for chaos everywhere, a perception that is perhaps understandable in the immediate aftermath of the Civil War. Once an Irish government administering Irish law had become established, the Catholic Church in Ireland altered its stance to the continental pattern of wholehearted support for the State and unrelenting opposition to those who would undermine it (see Fanning, 1983, pp. 53–60).

The potential for divisiveness in the economic arena also failed to materialise. Agriculture remained the dominant economic interest, despite the nationalist commitment to industrialisation. A series of reforms between 1905 and 1922 had established most farmers as owner-occupiers, definitively settling the main issue underlying the Land War of the 1880s. Although the size and commercial value of farm holdings varied greatly, these inequalities were simply not on the agenda for debate in the State's early years. The attainment of security of tenure and, later, ownership had, by the 1920s, made rural Ireland deeply conservative. Independence had been achieved by a generation of farmers who had realised their ambitions, and they (together with their family members who were also recorded as working on the land–so-called 'relatives assisting') represented some 44 per cent of the work force (Rottman and Hannan, 1982, p. 46). The sporadic agitation toward breaking up larger landholdings that had preceded independence was not sustained during the first decade of the new State. Class divisions were strong and manifest but did not translate into the most significant cleavages in defining party politics.

So the Irish Free State was characterised by stability and continuity, despite the vicissitudes of a harsh economic climate, first at home and later internationally. A clear strategy evolved to cope with Ireland's economic vulnerability as a small and open participant in the world economy. Free trade policies which favoured substantial farmers prevailed – although their initial success did not outlast the world Depression. Yet, when the 1932 election brought the anti-Treaty party under de Valera to power, the new State was sufficiently established to effect a smooth transition.

De Valera's Ireland was dominated by a re-awakened search for economic and cultural sovereignty. The new Government aggressively reversed policies favouring the large, commercial farm sector. Free trade was abandoned and replaced by a formidable protectionist wall built out of some of the highest tariffs in the world. National self-sufficiency, not the farmer's profit, was the touchstone that guided de Valera's government.[3] The desire to assert economic independence and to stimulate native industry brought a return to nationalist orthodoxy, and in the 1937 Constitution de Valera succeeded in vesting sovereignty in the people of Ireland, not in their Parliament within the British

Commonwealth, as had been the case in the 1922 Constitution. The Free State became Eire in Irish, Ireland in English.

Sovereignty was immediately expressed by remaining neutral during World War II, a period termed in Ireland 'The Emergency'. 'The Emergency' required an expansion of State powers and activity to a level that had previously been neither possible nor desired. Economic orthodoxy, Catholic social teaching, and the doctrine of self-sufficiency had proved inhospitable soil for anything but a minimal State. Initiatives towards economic planning, for example, were abandoned with celerity when the war ended. Yet the war years demonstrated possibilities beyond a nationalism based on impoverished self-sufficiency[4], and the values underlying de Valera's Ireland were subjected to sceptical scrutiny and found wanting by a new generation of intellectuals and civil servants.

Still, societal change was postponed. Ireland initially shared in the post-war economic boom and in the enthusiasm for the Beveridge Welfare State but neither could be sustained into the 1950s. While most of the industrial democracies were enjoying unprecedented economic growth, Ireland's economy was stagnant, suffering through a series of balance of payments crises which were exacerbated by the conservative responses of the Government. All impetus toward social progress had foundered as early as 1951, when a proposal to introduce free health care for pregnant women and newborn infants met implacable opposition from the Catholic Church. The proposal was withdrawn and the government that sponsored it collapsed.

The 1950s marked the end of the post-independence search for a national identity and economy rooted in conceptions of traditional, rural Ireland. The tentative questioning of the war years gave way to open despair of the nation's ability to survive. Rural Ireland was characterised, by a Government Commission, as having descended into 'a psychological and economic malaise'.[5] The policy of self-sufficiency had, to an extent, shored up the urban working class, but at a low standard of living compared with other European countries. The vocabulary and politics of economics had already begun to supplant that of nationalism – a shift which was perhaps facilitated by the decision in 1948 to break with the Commonwealth and declare a Republic.

Despite that declaration, after four decades of independence, Ireland in 1960 could be characterised economically as one of the peripheral regions of the United Kingdom. British capital was the major source of foreign investment. Two-thirds of all exports went to the British market. Entry into the labour market for each new generation often meant emigration to Britain. For the one half of new workers who remained in Ireland, their main expectation was inheriting a family business, mainly in low-productivity small-scale farming. Within a ten-year period, however, State-induced economic development industrialised Irish society. Growth in the manufacturing and service sectors offered the prospect of full employment within Ireland for a generation of young people. Membership of the European Community (EC) in 1973 solidified an economic, as well as cultural, re-orientation away from Britain. It also marked the emergence of a class structure in which advantage was allocated increasingly on the basis of educational credentials and less through family property. One marker of the change was Ireland's inclusion as one of the eighteen industrial market economies recognised by the World Bank in the 1970s.[6]

It is in this context that 1958 has a claim to be one of the significant milestones in the evolution of Irish society and Irish nationalism. Publication of the *Programme for Economic Expansion* in that year had installed Keynesian economic principles as the main items on the national agenda. This effectively abandoned the assumptions that had guided the nationalist movement since the Land War of the 1880s: that Ireland would prosper by promoting the interests of the small farmers and of native industry serving the local market. According to this view, Ireland's impoverishment could be attributed to its being governed for the benefit of Britain; self-government in the national interest would inevitably bring employment opportunities and, in their train, an end to emigration and the resumption of population growth. Nineteen fifty-eight marked the formal recognition that this old agenda was not tenable.[7] Henceforth, the primary objective of national policy would be to reap the full benefit from participation in the world economy. Economic planning and the associated State initiatives in the economy represented a new 'strategic policy choice' by which a basis was sought for coping with Ireland's economic openness (see McCormack 1979).

So 1958 marks a turning point in the nature and rule of the Irish State. More significantly, it also marks the point at which the various strands of societal change within Irish society fused. From then onwards, State and class structure evolved in tandem. Though historians may dispute the depth of the watershed, sociologically 1958 dates the beginning of the contemporary period in Ireland.

That is clear from the consequences that followed the change in policy direction. The swiftest of these was Ireland's ability to benefit from the buoyancy of international trade during the period of the First

Programme: 1959–63. Ireland's GNP grew at an annual rate of four per cent in those years and 'economic growth during the 1960s was faster and more sustained than at any previous period in Irish history' (Walsh, 1979, p. 33). Economic expansion produced a boom in opportunities for white collar and skilled manual employment, and accentuated the long-standing trends towards a declining agricultural labour force and the marginalisation of smallholders. The underlying processes of class formation were sufficient to engineer a new class structure that was firmly implanted by the end of the 1960s.

Another strand of the development process was a refocused and strengthened commitment to corporatist endeavours. Corporatist thinking in Ireland had previously been associated with Catholic social teaching, inspired by a Papal Encyclical of 1931 (Whyte, 1980, pp. 67–95). After 1958 the emphasis was on facilitating the implementation of economic planning through the use of consultative bodies and institutionalised negotiation between the 'social partners': trade unions, employers and the State, with farmers' interests also generally represented; the Catholic Church has not been a participant.

Economic growth in Ireland was State inspired and directed. State expansion outpaced even the rate of economic growth in the 1960s and 1970s, with public expenditure absorbing an ever increasing share of a rising national product. In 1960, total public expenditure stood at the equivalent of 32 per cent of GNP; in 1980 it stood at 64 per cent. The central Civil Service doubled in size over those same years. An expanding State sector was also fuelled by the social problems created by the sheer intensity of economic development and the demand for social services in the long neglected areas of health, education and housing. So decisions taken in 1958 within a limited range of economic policy areas led to changes in the role of the Irish State that were revolutionary. The timing of the changes intensified their impact. Ireland had not participated in the spurt of State activism that had characterised the 1950s in the rest of Europe. It had considerable catching up to do (King, 1986).

An expanding economy, rising public expenditure, the end of emigration, and massive shifts in the occupational structure all promised that the 1960s would bring Ireland's long postponed social revolution. After all, with the shackles of traditionalist ideologies and economic conservatism broken, it seemed safe to assume that the egalitarian objectives of Irish nationalism could be realised and realised fairly painlessly: the rising tide, in other words.[8] It is our contention that they were not realised, even in part. Ireland in 1972, the last year included in a formal economic plan, remained a rigidly class-bound society. The rest of that decade brought home the material consequences of a stable distribution of privilege, without the salve of an expectation that renewed economic progress would provide a way out of the malaise. Indeed, Irish political and social life in the 1980s harkens back to the disillusionment of the 1950s. That disillusionment ultimately paved the way for the breakthrough of the post-1958 periods.[9] Certainly, a similar level of discontent is evident today. The difference is that Ireland's current predicament is no longer atypical. Disillusion with the efficacy of State expenditure, the fragility of corporatist arrangements, and recent economic recession are the common plight of the advanced capitalist societies.

The most marginalised classes in Ireland today are residual categories, strongly rooted in the pre-1958 economy. In the rapidity of change, the families in those categories were subjected to deep cultural as well as economic dislocations. State interventions ignored or downplayed the cultural dimension, except in the case of small farmers. Some boats had remained stranded even in the course of the strong tides of the 1970s. The politicians had misunderstood the structure of the society that they governed.

CLASSIFYING CONTEMPORARY IRELAND

Sustained economic growth in the years immediately after 1958 represents a watershed in Ireland's societal development. The significance is comparable to what the end of World War II meant for other European countries. So in our view the contemporary period of Irish society dates back only to about 1960. From then onwards, the dynamic elements in the society's social structure were those characteristic of the advanced capitalist societies: industrialisation and urbanisation. Our assertion is based on the nature of the processes in Irish society by which social institutions are produced and reproduced. After, 1960, those processes took a form that approximates to that of other industrial capitalist societies. Discontinuities within Irish society from 1960 are more important than the quite considerable structural and cultural continuity that we can still identify, though the impact of that continuity is one reason for our highlighting the diverse structural forms that advanced capitalism can assume. Advanced capitalism is a category that embraces a range of societies. There is no inherent developmental logic that acts to make these societies more similar over time. Indeed, as Giddens (1973, p. 17) notes 'industrial societies unquestionably introduce a rate of social change previously unparalleled in history'. That change enhances the importance of the distinctive bases from which countries embark. So the label itself merely delineates some general characteristics of contemporary Ireland.

A more precise label would specify Ireland's place in the world economy and political order. Ireland is one of the small peripheral societies of capitalist Europe. Here, size is accurately expressed in a variety of units: population, national income, natural resources or manufacturing output. On all of these yardsticks, the Republic of Ireland is tiny by Western European standards. Classifying contemporary Ireland requires that we weigh equally Ireland's past as a post-colonial society that achieved independence only within this century, and its present status as a member of the European Community.

Contemporary Ireland is not simply a poacher turned gamekeeper. It continues to occupy an essentially dependent, if privileged, position within the world economy. Ireland is part of the periphery of the core. Ireland's affinities in the European context are with those societies – like Greece, Portugal, Spain and Finland – that evolved within a sub-region in the shadow of a powerful centre, and for whom economic development remains incomplete. That incompleteness is most concretely expressed in their partial industrialisation; in the retention of a substantial agricultural sector that is only partially commercialised; and in a proportionately large self-employed work-force, urban as well as rural.

Irish economists adopted the 'small open economy' model to describe and then analyse the national situation. By 1977, the label had moved from academic journals into the policy-making process and political discourse (Bristow, 1980, p. 7).[10] 'Small' here is an economic quantity. Ireland's smallness renders it a 'price-taker', and the terms of its trade lie largely outside its control. Its slight contribution to the world economy forces it to accept these as given. 'Openness' refers to the extent to which a country's traded sector is large relative to its 'sheltered', non-traded sector (which includes public service, construction, distribution and utilities activities). Such an economy is strongly affected by external market developments. Ireland's openness is substantial: in recent years the value of exports has been equivalent to more than one half of total GNP, while imports have exceeded 60 per cent of GNP (McCormack, 1979, p. 95). The Irish economy depends heavily on foreign trade and has a free flow of investment capital (Norton, 1980, p. 183). In practice, this means that inflation, unemployment, interest rates and other key economic aggregates are largely externally determined. However, the degree of openness is itself a policy choice, although in the short run it may have to be accepted as a fact of life or constraint on policy autonomy. Governments, by deliberate acts of policy, seek in various ways to insulate their economies from developments abroad (McCormack, 1979, p. 94).

Sociologists use dependency as a basis for classifying societies in a way that brings in criteria other than those of the economic theories from which the concept derived.[11] In this view, the capitalist system evolved as a core which successfully captured the vast bulk of the surplus created by the world economy, leaving areas outside of the core at various levels of underdevelopment. In the model put forward by Wallerstein (1974), competition in such a system is a zero-sum game, with nation-states categorised as core, semi-peripheral and peripheral. Peripheral and semi-peripheral societies are, to varying degrees, so exploited as to be left with both an underdeveloped economy and a distorted social structure. Economically industrialisation is either inhibited or its fruits transferred to the core societies rather than serving locally as the dynamic for national development. The state and class structure of the non-core societies are left incomplete, and fail to evolve in the manner experienced by the core.

The main features of contemporary Ireland lie somewhere within the range represented by the semi-peripheral category. Unfortunately, despite the vast world system/dependency literature, that range is only vaguely demarcated. Classifying countries according to 'world system status' remains very much an act of intuition (Weede and Kummer, 1985). The most empirically sophisticated classification exercise (Snyder and Kick, 1979, p. 1110) resulted in Ireland being clustered with a rather diverse band of countries: Cuba, East Germany, Hungary, Cyprus, Bulgaria, Rumania, the USSR, Kenya, Iran, Turkey, Iraq, Lebanon, Jordan and Israel.[12] Faced with that rich variety, we conclude with Weede and Kummer (1985) that categories such as 'semi-peripheral' are ideal-types; empirically, societies are arranged along a continuum of development and/or dependency.

Mouzelis's (1978a and b) analysis of modern Greece provides a further contrast through which we can clarify the middle ground status which we attribute to Ireland. A colonial past (as part of the Ottoman Empire), a peripheral location and State sponsored, foreign financed industrialisation during the 1960s combine to make Greece a relevant touchstone for our study. Greek industrial capitalism assumed an 'enclave' form, which '... has neither destroyed ... the simple commodity family unit which still prevails heavily in agriculture and small industry, nor has it become articulated with them in an organic positive manner' (Mouzelis, 1978b, p. 254).

This certainly has resonance for the Irish situation, though not for most of Western Europe. So do the consequences that Mouzelis outlines. The first is an overdeveloped State, a product of local capitalism that has not reached the stage of being self-regulatory. A second is a substantial degree of State autonomy, deriving in large measure from a political system whose cleavages do not as yet conform to the basic class divisions within the society. Finally, though over-developed and autonomous, the State remains weak, due to society's dependent position within the world economy (Mouzelis, 1978b, pp. 259–64).

With EC membership, particularly in the recently enlarged EC, Ireland belongs to a very exclusive semi-periphery. Ireland, Greece, Spain and Portugal share some important traits. First, there is a large (by Western European standards) agricultural sector, comprised mainly of small producers whose viability must be underwritten by both the individual State and the European Community. Second, industrialisation has been largely financed by foreign investment, especially that of multinational corporations, and this introduces a distorting effect on the class structure. Poulantzas (1973) observes that such a process of industrialisation promotes a new sector of the bourgeoisie, dependent on foreign capital but defining its interests in national terms. The 'Grand' bourgeoisie is, as a result, more segmented than in either the European centre societies or the 'dependent-indus-trialising' societies of the Third World. A third characteristic is that urban growth has been a relatively late phenomenon. It was only in the 1970s that the urban population in Ireland came to outnumber the rural population, shifting the balance of the nation's political and cultural life. Finally, with urbanisation and industrialisation, the European semi-periphery countries have come to have internal regional imbalances – particularly manifest in average income levels – that are more extreme than those found in the European core. Portugal, Ireland and Finland share a further complicating factor; continued dependency within a larger European economic region, such as the British Isles, the Iberian Peninsula or Scandinavia.

The key to understanding Ireland's recent past and discerning its probable future lies, we believe, in the distinctive relationship between State policy and class formation in the European periphery. We approach that link with a particular perspective as to the structures corresponding to class and State and a definite preference as to how to explore their interrelationship in the Irish context.

STATE AND CLASS: IDENTIFYING SOCIAL CLASSES

The social class structure represents the way in which the distribution of resources for economic participation is organised in a society. A social class thus consists of families that possess similar packages of resources that can be used to generate income. Understanding a social class structure presents two problems: (1) identifying the set of positions that are available for economic participation – the 'empty places' which individuals can fill[13] – and (2) specifying the mechanisms by which individuals are recruited or allocated to places within that set of positions. Our approach to those problems is based on our interpretation of the perspective developed by Giddens in *The Class Structure of the Advanced Societies* (1973). While noting the tendency for the market system of capitalist economies to generate a typical three-tiered social class structure, in this approach the precise shape and resilience of the class structure in any society is a matter for empirical analysis (Giddens, 1973, p. 110).

The 'empty places' represent the economic aspect of the process of class formation. In capitalist societies these can be categorised under one of three basic market capacities: capital in the form of company shares, farmland or business firms; credentials or qualifications earned through the educational system; and labour skills for manual employment. Capital, credentials and skills are attributes with which individuals can bargain in the markets of capitalist society in exchange for an income. A fourth capacity, however, is available to those excluded from the markets and has assumed increasing importance in recent decades. This is entitlement to social welfare income maintenance. It can be thought of as a subsidiary form of economic differentiation, as one's entitlement is often determined by one's past market participation. In Gidden's (1973, pp. 217–9 and 289) analysis, families relying, in whole or in large part, on such a capacity represent the 'underclass' of advanced capitalist society.

The mechanisms for filling these 'empty places' are pre-eminently social and related to families rather than to individuals (see Goldthorpe, 1983). These operate so as to bring together sets of occupational categories – economic classes in Weber's terminology – into a smaller number of cohesive social classes. Social mechanisms build on economic market relationships, translating them into non-economic social structures (Giddens, 1973, p. 165). The result is a social class, a group whose membership is relatively closed with only limited possibility for those born into the group to transfer into another one through educational, occupational or marriage mobility. Where mobility is so restricted, members of a social class are also likely to share common life experiences, similar work patterns and a distinct style of life. More crucially members of a social class have similar life chances for access to the material and cultural goods available in a society. It is because the social processes underlying class formation vary widely across societies that there is no one social class structure associated with advanced capitalist society. Similarly economic change, however deep, within any one society may or may not be associated with alteration to the relative advantages enjoyed by various social classes.

THE MODERN CAPITALIST STATE

The State has been brought back as a central explanatory concept for comparative sociological analyses. As Skocpol (1985, pp. 3–8) notes, from the mid-1970s onwards we witness a steady increase in references to States as the unit of analysis and a corresponding diminution of the emphasis afforded to societies. This book emerged from that reorientation. In particular we share the belief that the role of the modern State cannot be adequately comprehended through abstract theorising. Rather, like 'social class', it is mainly of interest in terms of its manifestations in varying economic and political situations. Our study of the Irish State is informed, however, by a particular understanding of the State, its relationship to other social structures, and the main dimensions by which the modern capitalist State can be characterised.[14]

The State is best understood as a type of organisation. One of its defining characteristics is that only one such organisation can exist in a society at a given time. In practice, of course, we can identify a diversity of organisations as constituting 'the State', These share a common purpose of governing, a monopoly on the use of coercion, and a form of administration based on an executive comprised of individuals who act in the capacity of office holders within carefully specified rules and regulations. The State is the structure that underlies and unites these agencies, offices and individuals, a structure that can be thought of as either a set of organising principles or of regulations.[15] In Skocpol's phrase, 'States are fundamentally administrative and military organisations that extract resources from society and deploy them to maintain order at home and to compete against other States abroad' (Skocpol and Trimberger, 1977, p. 107).

When so defined, the State must be allowed an autonomous influence on society. Though it is not independent of the balance of power among social classes within society and the international environment, neither is the State passive. As the main administrative institution in a society, the State is continuously engaged in the regulation of conflict among the other structures of the society. However, as Peter Hall (1984, pp. 24–5) suggests, the State is best treated not as a reflection of that conflict but as a 'distorting mirror' that puts the final configuration to the resolution of conflicts. Part of the reason for that distorting effect is the pressure on the State from external conditions with which it must contend. Another potential distortion is introduced by the personnel staffing the State apparatus. Administrators, or rather a dominant cadre drawn from their ranks, can pursue their own agenda–or seek to do so (Skocpol, 1985, pp. 11–12).

In stressing the autonomy of the State there is no suggestion of omnipotence. Like social class boundaries, the State's autonomy has a clarity that varies between societies, differentiated empirically by the extent to which the State can formulate goals independently. States also differ in their capacity to implement the goals that they formulate. Our interest is in the extent to which the State can determine societal outcomes, such as the distribution of life chances. The autonomy and capacity of the State are the two main variables that explain such outcomes. But like all organisations, the consequences of the State's goals and activities are frequently unintended.

The converse of the State's autonomy is the autonomy of political institutions and actors. As an organisation, the State has objectives that can be distinguished from, and potentially oppose, those of the other institutions that constitute modern society (Zeitlin, 1985, p. 27). Representative bodies such as parliaments and elected executives are part of the structures that define the modern capitalist State. The process that selects the membership of these institutions results in a distinct connection to the public, one that both transmits public opinion and helps to create it. The State must be brought back in without obscuring the very real autonomy of the political process in advanced capitalist societies (Poggi, 1978, pp. 108–16).

States, then, can be characterised in two main dimensions that range from strong to weak: autonomy and capacity. Those dimensions are obviously linked. Autonomy can be expressed as the ability of the State to set goals that differ from those of the dominant interests in a society. Capacity is a more multifaceted concept. It subsumes the resources available to the State, its ability to raise and then allocate finances, and to recruit competent state managers (Skocpol, 1985, pp. 15–17). Other organisational characteristics affect the State's capacity. In particular, the bureaucratic development, centralisation and depth of the State apparatus can be either strong or weak, and thus frustrate or facilitate the State's ability to realise its goals. Centralisation is generally associated with a more efficacious State. However, it has been noted that there are structural arrangements that States devise to circumvent the diminution of capacity usually found with decentralisation. We use the term 'depth' to represent these aspects of State structure. State-owned enterprises offer a major example of how the State's capacity can expand despite a notional loss of control through decentralised decision making.[16]

Autonomy and capacity interact most crucially in the course of industrialisation. The dynamic of that interaction can be stated as a generalisation, though the outcome will be distinct to each society:

> In advanced industrial countries and in the "semiperiphery", growing state activities and an increasingly deep penetration of economy and society by state interventions seem to have played a critical part in enabling capitalist political economies to foster economic growth and manage socioeconomic conflicts. Yet the internal structure of the state and the state's relation to the class structure of society limit the state's capacity to intervene in civil society in pursuit of the goals of economic growth and income redistribution.   (Rueschemeyer and Evans, 1985, p. 68).

We include Ireland in the ranks of the semi-periphery. Significant State intervention emerged a decade or more after it had become common-place within the European core. The success of the initial intervention suggests that the limitations on the State's ability to intervene had been overcome. Two propositions offer insight into how that occurred:

> First, in order to undertake effective interventions, the state must constitute a bureaucratic apparatus with sufficient corporate coherence. Second, a certain degree of autonomy from the dominant interests in a capitalist society is necessary not only to make coherent

state action in pursuit of any consistent policy conception possible, but also because some of the competing interests in economy and society, even structurally dominant ones, will have to be sacrificed in order to achieve systematically required "collective goods" that cannot be provided by partial interests.

(Rueschemeyer and Evans, 1985, p. 68)

Corporate coherence was a long-standing trait of the Irish State, a legacy of the British administration, preserved by the system's small size. State autonomy was enhanced by the crisis atmosphere of the 1950s. Other competent actors willing or able to respond, were absent. One successful intervention, however, does not necessarily enhance a State's own autonomy and capacity. Indeed, Rueschmeyer and Evans (1985, pp. 68–9) suggest that the more successful the intervention, the more sharply the legitimacy of the State's action will be questioned. That questioning is accompanied by the State becoming ever more of an arena for social conflict. Thus, however successful the intervention, it need not set the stage for more effective future interventions. Indeed, the contrary results may follow.

THE INTERACTION OF CLASS AND STATE

The evolution of the Irish State since Independence is traced in Chapter 2. Chapter 3 turns to change in the class structure, providing an opportunity to assess the extent to which the Irish State since 1958 has been afforded a sufficient 'degree of autonomy from the dominant interests' to build on the success of the late 1950s and early 1960s. State and class were being simultaneously transformed and, it is our contention, contemporary Irish society was forged by the interaction between those two change processes. As the final section to this introductory chapter, we turn therefore to that interaction. Our emphasis is on the diversity of possibilities for industrial development. Large-scale industrial expansion and the accompanying economic growth inevitably reshape a society's social structure. There is no single mechanism however, by which that change occurs: 'in each country it takes place in specific social and economic conditions and is subject to direct and indirect national and international pressures' (Marceau, 1977, p. 4). This variation has been highlighted during the 1980s as we see countries with similar economic structures confront common economic problems with very different strategies and very different results (Hall, 1984).

Comparative analyses by Moore, Giddens and Marceau suggest two factors that combine to determine the path to industrial development taken by particular societies.[17] First, the class structure providing the framework for the decisive period of industrial expansion shapes the consequences that accrue: in England, the framework was a developed and stable bourgeois order; in Germany, industrial growth preceded the emergence of such an order and was undertaken instead through the initiative of a State controlled by the traditional land-owing élite. Second, societies differ in the duration and intensity of the period of decisive industrialisation. England is the archetype of gradual and early industrial growth, and France of a protracted and uneven industrialisation that culminated in a post-Second World War spurt of massive and rapid industrial expansion. Generally, the more recently manufacturing became the predominant force in an economy, the more swiftly that transformation was accomplished.

Ireland, in our interpretation, is an example of a late-industrialising country that adopted a strategy for development based on outward-looking free-market policies that were nevertheless State inspired. We view that strategic choice as one of a series made by Irish governments.

Commentators on the abrupt shift in Ireland's economic policy – and in the agenda of Irish nationalism – stress the ease with which so fundamental a change was accomplished. We note, however, that by the late 1950s there was only a small pool of interests from which opposition could have been recruited. Native industrialists were few in number and the Irish bourgeoisie was divided: between those dependent on foreign capital and indigenous capital, between commercial and productive sectors, and between Catholics and Protestants. Certainly, Irish entrepreneurs were neither sponsors nor beneficiaries of the industrialisation strategy that was implemented. In an economist's assessment (O'Malley, 1985, p. 46), 'Irish indigenous industry suffered a net loss in market share as it lost out in the home market without a compensating increase abroad'. An alternative potential modernising élite, however, had been gathering strength and influence since the 1940s. It consisted of senior civil servants, academic government advisers and a small number of politicians. The success of the intervention precluded opposition or even dissent – at least initially.

However, despite the depth of the transformation Ireland experienced since 1958, in some crucial respects stability rather than change proved to be the chief outcome. It is rare to find a society that so stoutly maintained the basic distinctions among families in terms of advantaged and disadvantaged in the face of sudden and successful economic development. The 'empty places' changed, as did the mechanisms for allocating individuals to those places. Yet the families that enjoyed privileged positions in the old class structure secured comparable positions in the new one. Those families at the bottom of the old class hierarchy have, if anything, drifted downward into a new underclass, dependent on State income maintenance for their livelihood. Such an outcome did not, of course, stem only from State policy, much less from the objectives of that policy. In Ireland, State expansion was registered primarily in the State's growing role of paymaster. Control of key areas affecting the class structure, in education for example, remained in the hands of other institutions, such as the Churches.

CONCLUSION: CONTINUITY AMIDST CHANGE

Change is the dominant theme of this book. Contemporary Ireland is the product of the interaction between State institutional arrangements inherited from Britain but modified after Independence, the policy choices made by the State, international economic developments, and the unanticipated consequences of rapid, State-sponsored industrialisation on the class structure. Ireland, by the 1980s, was truly transformed.

The promise of change, and of the nationalist cause, remained largely unrealised. The 'rising tide' had not sufficed to erase some of the continuities of Irish history, particularly the markedly unequal distribution of life chances. From the 1950s onwards, economic issues and terminology have exercised an extraordinary hold on the national agenda. Ireland's first 'pork barrel' election was fought in 1951, marking economic nationalism as the successor to nationalism based on a self-reliant Irish identity.[18] There is, however, a strong link between those two forms of nationalism. De Valera's Ireland was constructed as an antithesis to the class-bound English society from whose grasp Ireland, or at least the larger portion of it, had been freed. The class basis of Irish society in the 1930s and 1940s went unacknowledged; Republican ideology recognised no class distinctions. When the ideology of economic growth took centre stage, it was easy to adopt the assumption that an expanding economy would perforce spread its benefits widely through multiplier effects. That assumption held sway for several decades without being subjected to critical scrutiny. Today, its failure is transparent. But the obsession with matters economic continues, a testimony both to the exhaustion of conventional political ideologies in contemporary Ireland and to the tenacity of social class boundaries. Economic development was achieved at a price. It required that a particular balance between institutions and between classes be established and then underwritten at State expenses. Retaining that balance today requires all of society's resources. The remaining chapters of the book examine in more detail the origins of that predicament; in the final chapter we look to the prospects for change inherent in contemporary Irish society.

NOTES

1. The most comprehensive treatment of the peripheral regions in the British Isles is Michael Hechter (1975).
2. The claim was made by Kevin O'Higgins, the first Minister for Home Affairs and the 'strong man' of the Free State Government until his assassination in 1927 (McCormack, 1979, p. 103).
3. This contrasts with the first Free State Government, for whom 'the touchstone by which every economic measure must be judged was its effect on the prosperity of the farmer'. The statement is by the economist George O'Brien in his obituary on that Government's Minister for Agriculture (*Studies,* 1936), quoted in David Johnson (1985, p. 22).
4. The significance of the war years is asserted in particular by Terence Brown (1985, Chapter 6) and by Ronan Fanning (1983, pp. 152, 159).
5. The evaluation is from the Commission on Emigration's 1954 Report, quoted in Brown (1985, p. 184).
6. John Blackwell (1982, p. 48); The distinction was awarded in 1978. See Michael Fogarty (1982, p. 25).
7. A succinct summary of the 'mainstream Irish nationalism' programme can be found in Paul Bew and Henry Patterson (1982, p. 191). For a sceptical view of the economic and social forecasting ability of turn of the century Irish Nationalists and of the merits of their grievances against the Union, see James Meenan (1982, pp. 5–12).
8. See the views of the political scientist David Thornley as cited in Brown (1985, pp. 245–6).
9. Some Irish economists have argued that the key to the post-1958 economic growth lies in the rising level of domestic demand and that this could have been achieved without resorting to 'outward-looking' policies of free trade. See Kieran A. Kennedy and Brendan Dowling (1975, p. 248) and the literature review provided by Eoin O'Malley (1980, pp. 15–17).
10. Patrick Honohan (1985, pp. 356–75) offers a critique of the adequacy of the small open economy model as a description of Ireland's economic plight.
11. We associate the Dependency approach with the influential statement by A. G. Frank (1967), as it was reflected in Immanuel Wallerstein's perspective on the world capitalist system – e.g. Wallerstein (1974 and 1975). This approach has been applied to Ireland by, among others, Andrew Orridge

(1983); Richard Stanton (1979); and James Wickham (1980). A critical view of such exercises can be found in Rory O'Donnell (1979).

12. Snyder and Kick (1979) identify three 'blocks' of countries that are then combined into the 'semi-periphery'. That including Ireland is the most clearly semiperipheral in its 'world status'. The other two blocks are more ambiguously located. Snyder and Kick (1979, pp. 1114, 1116) find similarities in the situation of (a) Venezuela, Peru, Argentina, Uruguay, and South Korea and of (b) Finland, Saudi Arabia, Taiwan, India, Pakistan, Burma, Ceylon, Malaysia, and the Philippines. The 'blocks' were determined from 1965 data on 118 countries.

13. The phrase 'empty places' is A. Przeworski's, as cited in Erik Olin Wright and Luca Perrone (1977, pp. 32–55) from whom the distinction between 'places' and 'mechanisms' is adapted. The distinction involves oversimplification since the 'mechanisms' may influence the nature of the empty places – as in the impact of female participation in the labour force on 'the core stratification relations' (Mann, 1986, p. 56).

14. The merit of such an approach is well argued by Benjamin and Duvall (1985, pp. 20–1) and by P. Evans, D. Rueschemeyer and T. Skocpol (1985, p. 363). See also T. Skocpol and E. Amenta (1985, pp. 572–5) bringing 'historical specificity to explanatory debates about the development of public policies in capitalist democracies'.

15. Benjamin and Duvall (1985, p. 28) adopt two distinct conceptions of the State:

> The first is the continually operating (i.e., administering regulating, etc.), relatively permanent institutional aggregate of public bureaucracy and administrative apparatus as an organised whole. This is State 1. The second, State 2, is the more encompassing institutional–legal order, which is the enduring structure of governance and rule in society – the machinery and the means by which conflict is handled, society is ruled, and social relations are governed.

16. This discussion and particularly the importance of State ownership is from Deitrich Rueschemeyer and Peter B. Evans, 'The State and economic transformation: toward an analysis of the conditions underlying effective intervention', in Evans et al. (1985, pp. 50–9).

17. See Giddens (1973, pp. 139–55); Marceau (1977, pp. 14–17); Barrington Moore (1966).

18. Ronan Fanning (1983). The description of the 1951 election as Ireland's first 'pork barrel' election is taken from O'Leary's *Irish Elections,* and is cited by Fanning on page 188. Fanning offers the following quotation from the historian Desmond Williams, writing in 1953: '... one of the most striking features of Irish politics in recent years has been the frequency with which politicians employ economic phraseology. Englishmen perhaps would not regard this as something strange; they have been used to it for many years. In Ireland, however, it is probably only since 1948 that ordinary people have appeared to take an interest in economic debate ... The declaration of the Republic in 1948-49, however, finished a long chapter in modern Irish politics'.

2 The Evolution and Structure of the Irish State

INTRODUCTION: THE AUTONOMY AND CAPACITY OF THE IRISH STATE

The structure of the Irish State and its development after Independence bear the marks of the post-colonial, semi-peripheral experience. Certainly nationalism and economic vulnerability were influential in shaping the role of the State. Of these influences, nationalism was perhaps dominant, as it often directed State policies down paths which economic interest did not justify. Irish nationalism however, was untypically an agent of stability rather than upheaval. Though the new nation drifted immediately into civil war, the split in the nationalist movement served in practice to shore up constitutional democracy, so that by 1926 the early 'crisis of legitimacy' was permanently resolved (Pyne, 1969, p. 50). Such an initial foundation of stability is rare in post-colonial societies and made continuity rather than change the defining characteristic of independent Ireland in its early decades.

In this chapter we assess the changing autonomy and capacity of the Irish State. The main theme in our view is a State that until recently retained substantial autonomy but exercised only a limited capacity. This describes both what we term the 'auxiliary State' that prevailed until the late 1950s and the strongly interventionist State that afterwards aggressively pursued outward-looking economic policies and established a fully-fledged Welfare State. Though the chapter is presented chronologically, there are some structural features which remain influential throughout.

Autonomy refers to the ability of a State to formulate and pursue its own goals. We can identify four main structural features that affected the autonomy of the Irish State:

(a) The main constraints on autonomy were external rather than internal, counterbalanced to varying extents by nationalist aspirations;

20

(b) Class interests were not a substantial constraint on the State, due primarily to the segmented nature of the bourgeoisie;
(c) The political system was locally centred rather than focused on major national economic or social policy issues; and
(d) A well-entrenched civil service apparatus with a tradition of autonomous action was inherited from the British administration and retained after independence.

Capacity indicates the State's ability to implement the policies suggested by its goals. These are obviously linked to, but conceptually distinct from, factors that affect State autonomy. In Skocpol's framework, particular importance is placed on the existence of an effective bureaucratic machinery and its 'means of raising and deploying financial resources' through taxation and borrowing (Skocpol, 1985, p. 17). Here we can identify five factors that affected, largely to restrict, the capacity of the Irish State:

(a) The State was active primarily as the financier, not as the direct provider of services in key areas such as education–actual control remained with non-State institutional structures;
(b) An extensive network of voluntary organisations, charities, and what were termed 'vocationalist' arrangements supplemented or competed with State provision of services and mediation;
(c) The yield from taxation – particularly on income – was deliberately limited to a low level, and State objectives were frequently pursued by the use of 'tax expenditures', that is, by exempting forms of income from tax;
(d) The implementation of many goals was in practice allocated to State sponsored or State owned enterprises. These possessed considerable discretion *vis-à-vis* the central civil service and Parliament but often held an attachment to the specific interests in their field of activity;[1] and
(e) A heavy reliance was placed on expert advisers, official and unofficial, and official commissions were used to review key areas of public policy, sometimes incorporating and other times bypassing the major relevant interest groups as well as the politicians and the civil service.

Generally, these factors have acted over time to lead to a diminution of autonomy even while trends in the levels of taxation and public expenditure have created the illusion of increased capacity. De Valera had sufficient autonomy in the 1930s to pursue economic policies that had disastrous financial consequences for the most powerful interests in Irish society. By the 1960s the choice of goals was far more greatly circumscribed, both through external and internal influences, but the State's capacity to raise tax revenue and, potentially, to redistribute income had vastly expanded. This tradeoff rendered the State capable of greater action in pursuit of an ever diminishing range of options. Also, the State's capacity has not increased uniformly in all arenas of Irish society. This chapter considers the patchy nature of the Irish State as it stands today: 'The very unevenness of a State's existing capacities ... may be the most important structural feature to recognise in understanding how it confronts challenge' (Evans et al., 1985, pp. 351–2).

In Ireland the role of the State has contracted or expanded largely in response to influences from the international environment. But the breadth of that role has also shifted, along with a Church and State relationship that has alternated between harmony and conflict; political allegiances that have, to varying degrees, followed social bases; and the composition of governments, which has alternated between periods of one party dominance and coalitions.

THE AUXILIARY STATE: 1922–1958

The State in independent Ireland initially played an auxiliary role, supplementary, though not necessarily subordinate, to other institutions within the society. Ireland in 1922 was 'essentially an old country setting up for itself as a new state' (Meenan, 1980, p. 125). In reality there were two states. The first was the Republic, established in 1919, whose government was constituted by those Sinn Fein Members of Parliament who were not imprisoned. That State had developed an extensive judicial and administrative presence in the south of Ireland. On 9 January 1922 however, the unity of Sinn Fein disintegrated over the issue of the Anglo-Irish Treaty. The anti-Treaty faction, under de Valera, narrowly lost the vote on the terms of the Treaty and immediately absented itself from the Dail. Three days later, the pro-Treaty supporters met again, this time in their capacity as members of the UK House of Commons. Together with four representatives of Trinity College, they formally agreed to establish the Irish Free State, as specified in the Treaty, and elected a provisional Government. For a brief period, the Republic and the Free State coexisted and the two factions remained nominally under the Sinn Fein rubric.

The June 1922 General Election resulted in a large pro-Treaty majority of deputies. However, civil war intervened before the new Dail could meet and the split became irreversible. The pro-Treaty group remained faithful to the provisional Government and formed a new party, Cumann na nGaedheal. Defeated in two elections (the second in 1923) and in the Civil War, the anti-Treaty forces re-grouped as the Third Sinn Fein Party, adhering to the Republic and thus declining to participate in the Free State Dail. Though splinter groups remained to claim the mantle of the Republic proclaimed in 1919, when de Valera re-entered the Dail in 1927, constitutional democracy within the Free State framework was assured.[2] It was by no means a foregone conclusion. As the historian Joseph Curran argues: 'Whether the state was to be ruled by the people or by a revolutionary junta was the most important question confronting Ireland in 1922 and the underlying cause of the civil war' (Curran, 1980, p. 280).

The blood spilled in answering that question had long-term implications for Irish politics. Its immediate effect was to postpone change to the State apparatus. The main departments of the British administration were retained. By the Treaty terms, the Free State did not come into existence until the last month of 1922 and for most of that period the members of the provisional Government were not responsible to the Dail. Continuity during this awkward transition was provided by the composition and structure of the Civil Service: 'Under changed masters the same main tasks of administration continued to be performed by the same staff on the same general lines of organization and procedure'.[3] Some 98 per cent of the Free State's civil servants had formerly been in the employ of the British administration.[4] Most importantly, the core of the State remained constant. The premier department of government, Finance, 'was closely and consciously modelled upon the British system of financial administration' and remained so for nearly four decades (Fanning, 1978, p. 1). Finance's primacy stemmed from its absolute control of the purse strings. No other government department could expend public funds without Finance approval, nor could draft legislation be sent to the Cabinet before Finance had assented (Fanning, 1983, pp. 63–4).

The turning point, according to the historian Ronan Fanning, was 1958. The 'old' department was steadfastly dedicated to maintaining stability; the 'new' department was seen, and saw itself, as the instrument for change (Fanning, 1978, pp. 626–7). Such change at the core of the State had widespread ramifications. It marked the end of the auxiliary State and the beginning of massive expansion in the State's activities, revenues, expenditures, and staff. That metamorphosis required the abandonment of an ideology of non-State intervention which had guided policy under a succession of governments and which had deep roots in Irish Catholicism and nationalism.

On independence, the balance of influences clearly favoured an auxiliary State. There were, however, pressures on the members of the first Free State government to adopt a substantial interventionist role. Ireland had benefited from the pioneering social welfare legislation enacted by Liberal governments earlier in the century. So Irish citizens had experience of a State that provided old age pensions (enacted in 1908) and compulsory social insurance for manual workers and low-paid white collar employees (National Insurance Act, 1911). Generally, the post-1880 strategy to retain Ireland within the Union had led to State intervention that was 'on, by contemporary British standards, a wide front', with 'a greater propensity to turn to the State to solve social and economic problems'.[5]

The nationalist struggle for independence raised the stakes further. Under the Democratic Programme of 1919, Sinn Fein promised each citizen of the Republic the right to 'an adequate share of the produce of the Nation's labour'. This was a clear commitment to a radical redistribution of resources. The national sovereignty was declared to extend over 'all the wealth-producing processes within the land and . . . all rights to private property must be subordinate to the public right and welfare'.[6] Despite the grand rhetoric, the Democratic Programme was never seriously deployed as a weapon in the struggle for independence. It was directly influential as a way of incorporating the Labour movement into the Sinn Fein cause. But success was secured through a broadly based nationalism that was able to sidestep potentially divisive class issues. The real legacy of the Democratic Programme was perhaps the State-sponsored bodies, established in later decades to pursue the objectives of developing the nation's wealth-producing resources through State initiative (Chubb, 1970, pp. 253–4).

With that exception, whose importance only gradually emerged, the balance of pressures on the new nation argued for a minor rather than a substantial State role. Nationalist grievances formed one such argument. The claim that Ireland was subject to excessive taxation within the United Kingdom had been a prominent feature of agitation first towards home rule and later towards independence (Fanning, 1978, pp. 120–2). This was allied to a belief that a native administration would perforce govern more cheaply than had any British administration. Low taxation and State expenditure kept within the limits of current revenue were central policies guiding the Cumann na nGaedheal government of 1922–32.

Economic exigencies and memories of civil war anarchy reinforced the Government's innate conservatism. The central element of Free State economic policy was the promotion of agricultural exports, anticipating that the resulting profits would in time stimulate more general economic growth. The State's role in that process was to do as little as possible. This view was formed amidst a crisis of declining world agricultural prices which lasted until 1925: 'in the interests of low agricultural costs, taxes and state expenditure were kept down, budgets were balanced, and little was spent on social welfare or on improving the bad housing situation in Dublin or the large towns' (Murphy, 1975, p. 65).[7] The State could intervene to encourage agricultural efficiency or to establish the Irish currency at parity with the UK pound sterling, but tariff protection for native industry was an anathema. A Tariff Commission was established in 1926 and cast its cold eye on all requests for protection. Its endeavours were facilitated by the acquiescence of native industrialists to a policy of free trade. The State's response to the high level of unemployment prevailing in the early 1920s was to stand aloof and allow emigration to transfer the problem elsewhere, notably to America. Emigration in independent Ireland quickly returned to the levels of the century's first decade (Cullen, 1972, pp. 174–5).

The monument to this deeply conservative outlook is the notorious decision in 1924 to lower the weekly old age pension by a shilling–a 10 per cent decrease from the UK level. Ireland's demographic pattern did make the burden of the 1911 legislation greater than in Britain, and indeed the politicians had actually moderated the advice of the Department of Finance officials, who had requested a 20 per cent reduction (Fanning, 1978, p. 111). But the decision entered the lexicon of Irish political abuse as a disastrous political misjudgement: the 'shilling off the old age pension'.

Historians, and especially economic historians, have come to see Cumann na nGaedheal's policies in a more favourable light. Certainly those policies were to the direct benefit of the social class and regional base from which the party drew its most fervent supporters: substantial proprietors in agriculture and commerce – 'ranchers and importers' in the phrase of one disillusioned party member – located mainly in the country's eastern half.[8] The party's electoral successes point to a more diverse base, consisting of those who looked to the Treaty and to Commonwealth membership as the mainstay of stability and prosperity for the new country.[9] The policies of the first Free State government certainly pursued that goal and in doing so followed the economic orthodoxy of the period, which was strongly Free Trade. Given the formidable obstacles facing the new nation, 'to have secured a stable currency and a balanced budget against the background of Civil War was an immense attainment' (Johnson, 1985, p. 9).[10]

And in one important area – the reform of local government – the 1922–32 administration brought to fruition a basic theme of the independence struggle. The welfare and health functions were consolidated into multipurpose local authorities, modelled on the American county. With this reform, Ireland broke with the Victorian approach to social welfare: the workhouse. The changes were equally comprehensive in the area of law. The Courts of Justice Act 1924 swept away the British system of justices of the peace, magistrates and grand juries, and put in their place a fully restructured court hierarchy in which a professional judiciary presided at all levels. Here too the American model was of considerable importance.

Despite its minimalist approach to State activity, it was recognised that extraordinary needs could only be met by State effort. In this, if nowhere else, the Government kept faith with Sinn Fein's avowed policy, as stated in the Democratic Programme, to exploit natural resources in the national interest. This led to a commitment to build a hydroelectric power station on the River Shannon. The agency, established in 1927 to extend electricity nationwide, the Electricity Supply Board and the Sugar Company (to extract sugar from native beet) were the prototypes of the State-sponsored body. The ESB's spectacular success in raising the nation's electricity output tenfold in its first 14 years of existence made such bodies a popular model for locating subsequent major State endeavours outside of the central government apparatus (Johnson, 1985, p. 24).

The willingness to intervene in pursuit of a major objective such as electrification did not mark a softening in the general stance towards State non-intervention. This stance was in full accord with Catholic social teaching of the period. The Catholic Social Movement which had proved influential in providing an alternative to socialism as a base for social class conflict on the European continent, was gathering momentum in Ireland throughout the 1920s. As enshrined in the 1931 Papal Encyclical *Quadragesima Anno,* this viewed State activity with suspicion. The Encyclical put forward the principle of 'subsidiary function': 'It is an injustice and at the same time a great evil and disturbance of right order to assign to a greater and higher association what lesser and subordinate organisations can do'.[11]

The role of the State was thus to be greatly circumscribed. It would oversee the activities of the various subsidiary organisations. But the actual provision of services would be carried out by the subsidiary organisations whose internal affairs would be regulated through vocationalist arrangements. This view of the proper role of the State was espoused in the 1943 *Report of the Commission on Vocational Organisation* and influenced a number of experiments in rural redevelopment and urban social work services that were community rather than State inspired and funded. However, the full programme of the vocationalist movement – a vocational board for each industry and profession – as an administrative network superior to the State was never implemented.

A final strand shaping the emerging Irish State was a deep-seated suspicion of officialdom instilled during the long years of British rule. Moreover, the last experience of self-government had ended with the Act of Union in 1800. Historians argue that the concept of the State as a framework of laws and institutions was not widely held in Ireland at the time of independence. Neither wing of Sinn Fein in 1921 was in fact in favour of constitutional democracy on the British or American model of party politics (Pynne, 1969, p. 32). Hence, careful provision was made in the Constitution of 1922 for legislation by popular referendum as well as by Parliament. Political inexperience, Catholic social philosophy, economic exigencies, and the nationalist tradition, all argued for a State whose role would be less substantial than in most European nations (Lyons, 1973, p. 476).

In 1932, the Free State experienced its first transfer of power. Eamon de Valera and his party had entered constitutional politics in 1927; in the 1932 general election Fianna Fail won sufficient seats to form a majority in the Dail with the support of a small number of Labour deputies. Labour support could not be taken for granted and indeed de Valera's victory had been achieved through an appeal to the less well-off sections of the new nation: small farmers, small businessmen, farm labourers, and the urban working class – all groups that had fared poorly under the policies pursued during Cumann na nGaedheal's years in power.

In response, social reform moved up a notch as a government priority during the 1930s. This was particularly manifest in extensive efforts to provide new housing through local authorities. So vast was the cost of the 132,000 houses constructed in the next ten years that an extensive subsidy from central government funds was required. In practice, the subsidy was as much a form of Depression era public work as it was a programme to replace a largely antiquated housing stock

(Murphy, 1975, p. 87). But the 1930s also brought a more generous pension policy and legislation establishing an Unemployment Assistance Scheme (1933) and a Widows' and Orphans' Pension (1935).

De Valera's vision however, did not include a massive expansion of the State's responsibilities. Three years in office, his St. Patrick's Day message summed up his political philosophy:

> Ireland remained a Catholic nation, and as such set the eternal destiny of man high above the '-isms' and idols of the day. Her people would accept no system that described or imperilled that destiny. So long as that was their attitude none of the forms of state-worship now prevalent could flourish in their land; the state would be confined to it proper functions as guardian of the rights of the individual and the family, co-ordinator of the activities of its citizens … (quoted in Rumpf and Hepburn, 1977, p. 99).

De Valera remained faithful to that philosophy throughout his years as Prime Minister (initially termed 'President of the Executive Council', then, following the 1937 Constitution, Taoiseach): 1932–48, 1951-54, and 1957-59.

His legacy however, was sufficiently flexible to facilitate the post-1958 State expansion. Two aspects of De Valera's leadership in particular paved the way. The first was his aggressive economic policy. In the same month that he assumed power, de Valera announced a policy of protectionism. In doing so his government was conforming to the drift in international economic policy towards protection through high tariffs while at the same time implementing traditional Sinn Fein economic dogma. But de Valera's economic policy sought more than protection; it aimed for self-sufficiency in agriculture and in industry; in investment and in production. Self-sufficiency, above all, meant ending the country's dependence on Britain. Economic self-sufficiency itself, however, was merely an intermediate objective: de Valera's goal was an Irish identity constructed entirely from native cultural resources. The question was not tariffs but 'what kind of Ireland was hoped for' (Meenan, 1967, p. 75). Self-sufficiency downgraded the importance of agricultural exports, as farmers were now to produce for the home market. Wheat replaced cattle in the fields and native industry expanded to serve the domestic market behind massive tariff walls that kept out imports.

These economic consequences were exacerbated by the 'Economic War' with Britain over the 1932–38 period. The conflict arose over the

issue of the land annuities which the first Free State government had
undertaken to collect from Irish tenant purchasers of farm land and
then pay to the mainly British-resident former landowners. De Valera
rejected the legality of that transaction and the UK government
promptly retaliated with high tariffs on Irish imports, justified as a
means of recouping the amount of the annuities. The main casualty of
the war was the profit of large farmers. The main Irish beneficiaries
were manufacturers and industrial workers. Industrial output
expanded, as did the number employed in manufacturing. The exact
magnitude of economic growth during the 1930s is difficult to establish
due to the rudimentary nature of relevant statistics, but the success was
none the less impressive in the context of the world Depression.[12]
Perhaps more importantly, a precedent was set in which the State
intervened fundamentally in the national economy in pursuit of a
vision of what independent Ireland should be.

The 'Economic War' ended with a series of Anglo-Irish agreements
in early 1938. With the onset of a more global war the next year, in
which Ireland maintained neutrality, self-sufficiency became a necessity
not a policy option. Before World War II began however, de Valera's
second legacy was in place: the Constitution of 1937. Bunreacht na
hEireann is an amalgam of Catholic moral principles, nationalist
aspirations, and American precedents, the latter being evident in its
liberal ideas on human rights. In its time, it was notable for the first two
features. The Catholic Church had exercised enormous sway over Irish
governments in the 1920s in all matters of public morality and by 1932,
with old quarrels forgotten, de Valera was prepared to exercise a
similar deference to the Church. Ireland in the 1930s and most of the
1940s can only be understood in terms of what one historian has
described as the underlying 'system of mutually reinforcing political
and episcopal visions', which shunned material progress in pursuit of
an Irish identity based on traditional rural practices and values
(Fanning, 1963, p. 158). The 1937 Constitution embodied that system.
De Valera sought to provide a set of principles that would ensure that
State activities would follow Catholic teaching rather than the alternative views then sweeping across Europe.[13] Articles 40–44 of the Constitution represent a charter of Irish social policy, dealing respectively
with due process of law, the family, education, private property and
religion. Article 45 contains 'directive principles of social policy' for the
two houses of the Oireachtas – thus specifically excluding the judiciary:
'the ownership and control of the material resources of the community
may be so distributed amongst private individuals and the various

classes as best to subserve the common good; and the State pledges itself to safeguard with especial care the economic interests of the weaker sections of the community, and, where necessary, to contribute to the support of the infirm, the widow, the orphan, and the aged'. It is difficult to discern the influence of these worthy statements on government policy in the remaining years of de Valera's Ireland. But their symbolic impact was definitive. Ireland was as self-sufficient economically, spiritually and intellectually as was possible in the twentieth century.

The original Constitution of 1922 was a practical and liberal document that implemented the Treaty with more regard for the symbols than the substance of the British constitutional system. De Valera both influenced the new Constitution with a distinctly Irish Catholic world view and by omissions severed the connections with the British Crown and the Commonwealth. Ireland became a Republic in all but name. Following the American model, the Constitution established a rigid separation of powers between executive, legislative and judicial branches of government, all under popular, rather than parliamentary, sovereignty. This paved the way for judicial activism in the 1960s as the courts began to interpret legislation in the light of the Constitutional provisions. This engaged the State comprehensively in the lives of its citizens to a degree that renders the subsidiary principle void.

That shift did not occur for another 30 years. Attempts during the 1940s and 1950s to copy the advances being undertaken by other countries in health and social welfare provisions were met by sufficiently strong opposition from the Catholic Church to frighten politicians into headlong retreat. The obvious poverty and social distress of the period could not be alleviated by State endeavours. For however spiritually laudable, Ireland's auxiliary State was not an economic success. The extent of the failure was evident by the early 1950s as the nation's young emigrated to Britain in massive numbers, searching for the jobs that could not be obtained at home. Those who remained experienced a declining standard of living relative to that of the United Kingdom. Per capita income in the Free State's first decade stood at about 60 per cent of the UK level. That was to decline thereafter, despite the fact that the national income was being shared out among an ever decreasing population. So independent Ireland was unable to keep pace with the economic progress of Britain after the Second World War.[14] But even that measure of success, had it been achieved, would have proved cold comfort, as UK income had grown at a sluggish rate compared to what was experienced in a war-ravaged continental Europe. De Valera's Ireland was, as he preached, a place for those who were 'satisfied with frugal comfort and devoted their leisure to the things of the spirit'.

The Irish State, as restructured by the 1937 Constitution, remained in its subsidiary role. A considerable range of autonomy had been demonstrated in the 1920s and 1930s and was to be stretched further during the World War II years in the struggle to survive as a neutral. Indeed, on a formal basis, the Constitution of 1937 and the decision to leave the Commonwealth in 1948 vastly expanded the State's autonomy. But the State's capacity had scarcely developed since 1922. Major areas of activity, such as education and health, were controlled by the direct providers of the service under nominal State supervision. Taxes remained low, a consistent policy choice whether governments favoured free trade or protectionism. Low levels of national income in any case provided little opportunity for substantial State revenue. Since State borrowing was a cardinal sin to the main political parties and to Department of Finance officials, governments had, by and large, to react to changing economic circumstances rather than seek to direct them.

THE MOVE TOWARDS STATE ACTIVISM: 1939–58

The turning point of 1958, when the State seized the initiative as the main force in Irish society, was the second part of a two-phased transformation. The first phase began during the 'Emergency' and continued until the late 1950s, setting the foundation for a new State role. Its main components were growing conflict between Church and State, political instability and realignment, change in the composition of the élite, and a profound economic crisis. An overarching theme of the first phase was disillusionment with the fruits of independence. In part this looked back to the egalitarian strain in Irish nationalism; it also, however, looked outward to the far higher standard of living being experienced by the rest of the West.

CHURCH AND STATE CONFLICT

By the 1940s, the Catholic Church had moved away from the anti-materialism it had shared with governments in the two preceding decades. Leading clergymen, including some bishops, were openly advocating material progress, providing that it could be accommodated within a Catholic social order. So the Church's vision for Irish society began to diverge from that of de Valera despite the care with which he had drafted the Constitution, and simultaneously the Church came into conflict with that other power broker in Ireland: the civil service. The conflict surfaced with the Commission on Vocational Organisation's report. Ireland's deficiencies were reviewed by the members of the Commission and traced to their source at the very heart of the State apparatus, the exercise by civil servants of substantial power without accountability. Decisions were being taken, the Commission reported, by bureaucrats who lacked expertise in their areas of responsibility and without consulting the relevant interest groups. Bureaucratic control was to be replaced by an interlocking set of vocationalist bodies bringing together representatives of all those concerned with a field of activity; for example, a proposed Cereals Council would bring together representatives of grain growers, millers and commercial consumers of grain. Such councils would link into one of six assemblies covering all major areas of economic activity, leading to a National Vocational Assembly (Johnson, 1985, p. 26).

This was a frontal assault on the State's autonomy and capacity. The Irish State was and remains based on the principle of ministerial responsibility, in which civil servants are but bearers of their minister's views and decisions and each minister is accountable to the Oireachtas for all actions taken by his or her department. Ministerial responsibility was then and is still a convenient fiction. Whatever its descriptive utility however, it is necessary for the system to function. The response from Ministers and civil servants to the report, and the comments elicited from the 'vocationalists' were acrimonious indeed.[15] But the fundamental issue of the role of the State remained unresolved. Meanwhile, in the late 1940s, the Irish State experienced a period of expansion. Social expenditure in particular grew to meet urgent needs against a background of services that were poorly developed by international standards. Rising expenditure was concentrated in housing and hospital construction, areas particularly depressed during the 'Emergency' years. Fianna Fail provided the institutional scaffolding for the expanding State by undertaking a major consolidation of social welfare schemes under a new government department and allocating responsibility for health care delivery to local authorities. The real expansion was carried out, however, by the coalition government that was formed after Fianna Fail's defeat in the general election of 1948, which had been contested largely on social issues in the context of Britain's massive programme of social reconstruction.

That Coalition and with it State expansionism, foundered on Church opposition to one part of the fledgling welfare state: a proposal to introduce free-to-all health services to mothers and to children under the age of sixteen (the so-called Mother and Child Scheme). The Church's initial intervention, which succeeded in blocking the scheme, was done in private in early 1951. With resignations, and finally the collapse of the Government, the issue moved into the arena of public controversy. The main objection to the scheme was its allocation of responsibilities to the State which, in the hierarchy's interpretation of Catholic social teaching, should instead be undertaken by intermediate institutions with which a family could have direct transactions. During the 1950s some cautious innovations in social policy were undertaken by Fianna Fail, which succeeded in establishing a working relationship with the Catholic Church. But the climate was ideologically hostile to a renewed State expansion: 'There were never so many denunciations of State power as in the year or two after the Mother and Child Scheme crisis' (Whyte, 1980, p. 270).

THE POLITICAL CLIMATE

The Irish political system has come to be seen by political scientists as not so much a deviant case as an extreme one (Garvin, 1981, p. 213). A classic example of peripheral protest became, after secession, a conflict between degrees of nationalism (Sinnott, 1984, p. 303). The intra-nationalist conflict between Fianna Fail and Cumann na nGaedheal in the 1920s and 1930s was complemented by polarisation on economic reformism versus conservatism (Mair, 1987, pp. 17–18). Fianna Fail's subsequent move to the centre enabled it to maintain its dominant position and the stability of its support has encouraged an understanding of the Irish political system in terms of a freezing of those cleavages which were present when the mass of the electorate was incorporated.

The importance of strategic choice however, is illustrated by the decision of the smaller parties who had obtained a combined 30 per cent of the vote in the 1948 election to enter into coalition with Fine Gael (Cumann na nGaedheal's successor), thus blunting their radical appeal (Mair, 1987, pp. 51–5). The 1948 election ended sixteen years of Fianna Fail governments, all headed by de Valera, first as President of the Executive Council (until 1937) and then as Taoiseach. That continuity gave way to a period of political instability, marked by a proliferation of small parties, slim parliamentary majorities and frequent elections. Between 1948 and 1957 coalition governments dominated by Fine Gael alternated power with Fianna Fail, sometimes as a minority government. The resulting intensification of competition for electoral support changed the axis for Irish politics. The search for votes revolved less around the old issues of Treaty and Commonwealth and more around promises of economic and social progress. That shift was particularly evident in the 1951 election, which was fought on much the same issues that dominated post-war politics in Europe generally. Indeed, the election had been forced not by the Mother and Child Scheme crisis but by a true bread and butter issue: the refusal of the Coalition to increase the price of milk, which led to the resignation of two government deputies (Murphy, 1975, p. 135).

The major long-term consequence of this political realignment was to establish two potential sources of parliamentary majorities: Fianna Fail and a coalition. The system of proportional representation with a single transferable vote (PR/STV) requires that, in order to secure a majority in the Dail, a party must achieve the support of close to half of the electorate. As a result, the two largest parties, Fianna Fail and Fine Gael, competed to capture votes across a broad geographical and social class base. In this, Fianna Fail was initially the more astute. Some historians interpret the post-1958 shift in State policy to the desire of Sean Lemass, de Valera's successor as leader of Fianna Fail, to pursue policies that would secure a 'hegemonic relationship' to the urban working class for his party (Bew and Patterson, 1982, p. 195). The dominance of Fianna Fail and the need for the two major parties to seek support across class boundaries has overshadowed differences based on class (Laver, 1986, p. 211). From 1951 the competition for votes ensured that the prize would go to whatever party could put together the election manifesto promising the most to the widest possible range of beneficiaries.

The economy's impoverished situation kept the ante at a low level throughout the 1950s. Once economic expansion was established, however, restraint could be and was rapidly abandoned. The modest social policy reforms of the Fianna Fail minority government of 1951–54 gave way in the 1960s to welfare state policies on the British model. This was made possible both by Church and State *rapprochement* and by the fact that the Irish electorate had never fully shared the Church's aversion to State expansion. In the long run however, the electorate was prepared to vote for policies which the Church did not regard with favour, though politicians preferred to tread warily and to act only after consulting the Catholic hierarchy on the main issues of social policy.

The period of post-war political instability altered the autonomy once enjoyed by the Irish State. Continuity of ministers and policies gave way to a series of rapid changes to which civil servants and State-sponsored bodies had to adapt. Elections, moreover, came increasingly to be fought on the very substance of State decision making: taxation, economic development policies and social expenditure. If the State was less frequently pulled in directions dictated by ideology, it now had to respond to a political system that was increasingly demanding of State performance.

ECONOMIC CRISIS

The real question people asked in the 1950s was not whether the State should expand but whether the nation would survive. Ireland had briefly shared in the economic boom associated with post-war recovery in Europe and even in Marshall Aid, despite having been a neutral during the war. But, as the rest of Western Europe went on to unprecedented levels of economic growth, the Irish economy was stagnant. Balance of payments crises, high inflation, and decline in both industry and agriculture marked the decade. Between 1949 and 1956 the Gross National Products of the European democracies grew by 42 per cent; the rise in Ireland's GNP over those years was a mere eight per cent (*Economic Development,* 1958, p. 11). The true depth of the recession over those years was recorded in the emigration figures however, not in the unemployment statistics. Some 400,000 persons left to seek employment elsewhere, mainly in Great Britain, during the decade. Approximately one person out of every five born since independence and resident in 1951 had emigrated by the end of the decade; for those in the younger age groups, the rate of departure was nearly twice as great (Rottman and O'Connell, 1982, p. 78). In many years, emigrants almost equalled the number of births.

By the late 1950s it was clear that all the policies pursued in search of economic independence were bankrupt. Agriculture, still the dominant form of economic activity, particularly as a source of foreign exchange, depended on the export of dairy products and cattle to Britain. Agricultural production had slightly expanded over the preceding four decades, but the long-standing process by which small farmers and agricultural labourers were forced off the land and into the British labour market continued unabated, even becoming more vigorous in the 1950s. Industry was incapable of expanding to provide the opportunities for employment within Ireland. Insulated by high tariffs from competition with foreign firms, domestic manufacturing was inefficient and geared almost entirely to the small home market. A generally low level of linkages among firms, another consequence of protectionist policies, and a distinct reluctance by private investors to provide capital, offered little potential for industrial expansion without effective and extensive State intervention.

There was a general recognition in the 1950s that exports were the key to economic recovery. As in the 1920s, this essentially meant agricultural exports. The rapidly expanding European continental economies offered a tempting market while the model of the State-sponsored body provided a vehicle for pursuing new policies. During the late 1940s and the 1950s, part of the institutional framework for economic development was indeed erected, most notably the Industrial Development Authority in 1949 (initiated to woo foreign investors) and An Foras Tionscal in 1952 (providing grants to assist in the solicitation). Generally however, politicians, their advisers, and civil servants were concerned with keeping the economy functioning through a series of crises. The need for a policy redirection was recognised, but the circumstances to implement it were still awaited.

THE CIVIL SERVICE

The manifest failure of traditional policies left an open field for innovators. By and large, these individuals came from the ranks of the civil service or from academics who served as government advisers: 'the available evidence suggests that the impetus for economic development in the mid-1950s came as much, if not more, from the civil service as from the politicians' (Fanning, 1983, p. 193). This modernising élite was less constrained by precedents or by ideology. A younger generation of civil servants, drawing upon their experience of economic planning ten years previously during the 'Emergency' and contacts with more recent developments in Europe, were now assuming senior ranks in government departments. The most notable arrival was T. K. Whitaker, appointed Secretary of the Department of Finance in 1956, only the third person to have held that post since 1922. A simultaneous transfer of power took place in the Dail as the old guard of politicians began to retire from public life.

Whitaker and the other civil servants and advisers were very much products of an administrative tradition. Necessity and the stimulus of new influences from abroad in the form of international organisations such as the World Bank and OECD made the difference. The same was true of the politician chosen to chair the Cabinet committee established to oversee the inauguration of economic planning: Sean Lemass. Lemass had been a de Valera stalwart since the early 1920s, a member of every Fianna Fail government, and for most of that period de Valera's likely successor. In 1959 de Valera resigned following his election to the largely ceremonial Presidency, and Lemass, one of the great pragmatists of Irish politics, became Taoiseach.

Lemass's commitment to economic expansion was long-standing and deep.[16] But as in other European countries, the civil service provided the real momentum, comparable to the contribution by public servants which Heclo (1974) has demonstrated in British and Scandinavian responses to major crises. In his work and in Skocpol's a major theme is the extent to which economic and social crises such as the one Ireland experienced in the 1950s did not lead to sustained responses from political parties or interest groups but rather to civil service initiatives to correct State policies that had failed (Skocpol, 1985, pp. 11–14). *Economic Development,* Whitaker's assessment of Ireland's problems and prospects, could serve as an ideal type of such an effort.

The Irish civil service had, by the 1950s, developed its own ethos—meritocratic in recruitment but strongly nationalist in cultural affinities. Attachment to that ethos was reinforced by a policy of recruiting administrators from among secondary school graduates, rather than holders of university degrees, and using that pool as the source for all promotions to senior ranks. The Irish civil service in the 1950s was a small and cohesive body which, despite its recruitment policies, was well integrated with the Universities and increasingly coming into contact with its foreign counterparts.

The civil service and Fianna Fail shared a basic contradiction in their mission: a 'neo-traditionalist ideological stance was combined with a commitment to industrialization and modernization' (Garvin, 1978, p. 346). The re-definition of Irish nationalism that had begun during the 1940s, one that focused on the uses to which independence could be put for the people's benefit, gave the modernising mission pre-eminence.

The mechanism for that mission was already in place. Government departments would outline broad policies to be implemented by State-sponsored bodies. The attraction of such an arrangement was its flexibility and the possibility, not feasible for a government department, of linking those representing the State directly to the interest groups relevant to the area of development activity. The cost was largely exacted from the principle of ministerial responsibility to Parliament. It was a price Lemass was certainly prepared to pay, for 'if it involves some price in the reduction of ministerial responsibility, or of powers of control by the legislature, is that price too high to pay for the more efficient administration of a comprehensive economic programme?' (Morrissey, 1986, pp. 82–3).

THE REVOLUTION OF 1958

The adoption of economic planning in 1958, therefore, was the culmination of forces that had been evolving for some decades. The change was none the less decisive. Henceforth, Irish nationalism proceeded from an assumption that the primary objective was to reap the benefits from full economic participation in the world economy. *Economic Development* was followed in November 1958 by the *Programme for Economic Expansion*. These and subsequent planning documents turned the Irish economy outward with two interrelated strategies. First, agriculture, its pre-eminence as the likely vehicle to prosperity retained, would increase production by integration with the higher priced European food market. But increased agricultural production demanded mechanisation and the consolidation of small farms into larger, commercially viable units; thus success would yield less, not more, employment. So the second strategy was employment intensive. Foreign capital would be attracted through State incentives to invest in export-orientated manufacturing.

This radical departure from earlier policies coincided with a major increase in the internationalisation of trade and investment. External circumstances thus determined that foreign investment in manufacturing would become the linchpin of Irish development strategies. The first Programme's invitation to foreign capital was but one of several options considered at the initial stages of policy formation. Nevertheless, the influx of investment in reply was sufficient to provide 80 per cent of new private investment in the first six years of the planning experiment, contributing much to the first Programme's success (Donaldson, 1965, p. 39).

Along with economic growth, this meant that Ireland became more closely integrated with the international economy and finally began to disengage itself from its heavy reliance on Britain. British-owned companies, which in the period from 1960 to 1970 represented 22 per cent of new industry investment, accounted for less than four per cent of such in 1980 and the proportion of total exports destined for the British market fell from two-thirds of the total in 1956 to one-third in 1981.[17] Emigration from Ireland to Britain declined even more dramatically; the expanding Irish economy was able to provide employment at home.

It was a bold strategy. The growth in new industrial investment had to take place in tandem with integration into the European economy, a move likely to result in a sharp contraction of the traditional domestic industries as protective tariffs were gradually removed. Adaptation grants were provided in order to improve the competitiveness of domestic industries but in the event their decline was compensated for, at least during the 1960s and early 1970s, by firms attracted from abroad. The strategy also incurred certain costs. Industrialisation through foreign capital required the State to provide a wide range of incentives and services to industry: direct aid in the form of investment grants, the provision and upgrading of infrastructural facilities, transport and communications, financing of research and development, as well as subsidising the education and training for an industrial workforce. A range of tax incentives – including export profit tax reliefs, accelerated depreciation allowances and investment allowances for designated areas, enhanced Ireland's attractiveness as a location for both foreign and native investment.[18]

The direct and immediate beneficiaries of the new policies were large farmers and overseas investors. It was assumed that, in time, profits would translate into jobs, jobs into high incomes, and that the chain reaction would ultimately lead to a higher standard of living for all. *Economic Development* advised that 'the aim must be to maintain and, if possible, increase economic activity as a whole, thus ensuring a progressive improvement in real national product and therefore in permanent employment and the general standard of living' (*Economic Development,* 1958, p. 1). This was contrasted with expenditure on social service infrastructure, which created employment in the short term without effecting an economic breakthrough, and indeed inhibiting such a development by requiring high taxes and indebtedness. What the Irish economy required was 'the tonic of significant reduction in taxation, particularly in direct taxation on incomes, profits, and savings' (*Economic Development,* 1958, p. 209). In this, *Economic*

Development echoed Irish economic orthodoxy since 1921. Low taxation could be achieved by 'deferring further improvements in the social
services' until the momentum of economic expansion was sufficiently
established to carry the costs (*Economic Development,* 1958, p. 24). The
State's expanded role would be implemented by adroit and subtle
interventions, not through an enhanced capacity in the form of public
expenditure.

The success of the first planning exercise vindicated the prescription.
In practice however, social spending kept pace from the start with
rising national income. This occurred despite adherence to the dictates
regarding direct taxation – the deleterious effects of which were a
constant theme of Fianna Fail policy.

The first Programme covered the years 1959–63. Its success led to
extensive preparation for a successor, the more methodologically
sophisticated *Second Programme for Economic Expansion, 1964–70.*
Despite continued economic growth, dissatisfaction with progress
towards the specified objectives led to the Programme's formal abandonment in 1967 and its replacement by a Third Programme, this time
for *Economic and Social Development, 1969–72.* The Third Programme
was allowed to run its course but it was the last formal planning
document. Subsequent State initiatives have been shorter-term in
perspective and reflect the growing awareness of the implications of
planning for a small open economy. More emphasis was also placed on
policies and less on targeting desired objectives.[19] None the less, State
interventions continued to be stronger on intentions than on specific
State policies, relying on a role of coaxing and facilitating rather than
directing economic growth.

Our concern is with the consequences of the new State activism, first
for the State itself and second for the class structure. The first issues
focused our attention on the ideology of Irish economic planning, the
altered State administrative apparatus, political ramifications, and the
effects on State capacity. Chapter 3 outlines the consequences for the
social class structure, while Chapter 4 examines the income distributional consequences.

THE PLANNING IDEOLOGY

Irish economic planning was influenced by developments in other
European countries, notably France.[20] With hindsight, critics of the
Irish experience have observed that the programmes failed to allow for

the structural differences between Ireland's economy and society and the countries being emulated. That is particularly evident in the faith in economic progress as the inevitable harbinger of social progress in the form of a universal improvement in the standard of living. Such an assumption is curiously un-European and certainly runs counter to the ideas then current in continental Europe, Scandinavia, and even Britain. The model would instead seem closer to that characterising American policy, which was based on what Maier terms 'the supposedly apolitical politics of productivity' in which the emphasis on productivity serves as 'a substitute for harsh questions of allocation' (Maier, 1978).[21] The affinity is greatest perhaps in the dismissal of the importance and even the existence of social class boundaries. A rising tide in the form of greater productivity would, according to the catchphrase, lift all boats without further State intervention.[22]

STATE STRUCTURES

Irish economic planning proceeded subtly and through intermediaries in the form of the State-sponsored bodies. Some 100 such bodies exist today, the vast majority post–1958 creations. There are two main types: 'those established to administer or regulate some area of social or economic activity or to provide a social service, and those established to engage in producing goods or services for trade, or to carry out developmental activities connected with trade and industry' (Chubb, 1970, p. 249). Each body has a departmental 'sponsor' to which it has some, often statutorily stated, responsibility. However, these bodies are less overshadowed than are government departments by Finance's 'primacy' and generally have greater flexibility and a more direct relationship with interest groups. A State-sponsored body has been the solution, often *ad hoc,* to problems as they arose. Their proliferation in recent decades reflects the difficulty experienced in adapting the central civil service to new situations and the limitations imposed by the principle of ministerial responsibility. Some State-sponsored bodies grew into formidable agencies within the State, becoming instruments of State policy that in practice lay just beyond the State's control.

The commitment to economic development also changed the role of commissions and academic experts in State activities. Governments of all persuasions had sidestepped contentious problems by establishing official committees and commissions. George O'Brien, Professor of National Economics in the National University, served on six such bodies between 1922 and 1940: Commission on Agriculture (1924), Fiscal Inquiry Committee (1926), Select Committee on Wheat Growing (1926), The Agricultural Derating Commission (1930), The Second Banking Commission (1932), and the Second Commission on Agriculture (1938).[23] Vital decisions, such as the continuation of parity with sterling, emerged from the deliberations of such bodies.

In the 1960s a new type of advisory forum became dominant, one with permanent status and comprised of independent experts, civil servants and representatives of the main interest groups. The most important of these was the National Industrial and Economic Council, established in 1963 to discuss and advise on the requirements for economic development and full employment, though it had been preceded by several more specialised forums of interest groups, government and independent experts (Morrisey, 1986, pp. 82–85).

POLITICS AND THE STATE

Economic development and the planning process were not initially items on the political agenda. Neither of the first two programmes was debated in the Dail. There was an obvious change to the rhetoric of political discourse with issues like inflation, unemployment and job creation policies looming larger in speeches and in election manifestos. Such a change may have reflected a growing awareness among the leadership of the major political parties of the increasing importance of instrumental, rather than affective, partisanship among the electorate (Mair 1987, pp. 64–80). But the change was largely superficial:

> The increasing use of terms like 'economic planning' is significant only in that politicians were using different straw from which to make the bricks they hurled at each other, rather than that Irish parties had developed fundamentally different attitudes to subjects around which many west European party systems had traditionally revolved. Irish politics seemed to move straight from a pre-ideological phase to a post-ideological phase. The 'end of ideology' dawned in Ireland before ideology had ever arrived (Gallagher, 1981, p. 273).

Competition was based on an often contradictory set of promises. Throughout the 1960s and 1970s, most Dail deputies remained resolutely preoccupied with local issues and there is scant evidence that general policy issues assumed greater importance. Explanations of such behaviour couched in terms of peasant culture are far from persuasive (Bax, 1976; Sacks, 1976). If anything, the proliferation of State schemes for social welfare and for subsidising firms enhanced the traditional role of the politician as broker, mediating between constituents and the State bureaucracy (Komito, 1984). In the absence of any direct patronage, politicians can operate only as brokers and not as power patrons (Carty, 1981). In fact, what is notable is the extent to which the key bureaucrats in local government operate policy-making which is effectively removed from the clientelistic activities of politicians (Collins, 1985, p. 285).

The cabinet system of government, in which backbench deputies lack a direct role in policy-making or even policy analysis, should serve to allow other actors within the State to be decisive. That occurred in the 1950s and for a time in the 1960s. Civil servants and State-sponsored bodies provided a dynamic that kept the pursuit of economic progress on track, greatly abetted by a favourable international economic environment. The momentum began to falter however, shortly after the international economy began to slide into recession in the mid-1970s. Economic growth and its consequences had by then transformed Irish society. The problems of an industrialised society had replaced those of a predominantly agricultural one. But this industrial society was so complex and so vulnerable to international trends as to preclude effective intervention by an internal group like the modernising élite of the 1950s. The State apparatus had indeed expanded, perhaps exchanging a growing capacity for diminished autonomy. That new capacity did not translate into the necessary institutional arrangements for problem analysis or problem solving, leaving the State active but essentially directionless (Garvin, 1982, p. 35).

CAPACITY: THE ACTIVE STATE

Like the Constitution's Directive Principles, the planning documents assigned to private enterprise the main role in economic development. Economic growth however, was swiftly translated into an apparent enhancement of State capacity. In the first ten years of economic planning, GNP grew by 50 per cent and the size of the civil service administration by 25 per cent. Public expenditure, which had stood at 30.4 per cent of GNP in 1958 had risen by 1968 to 40.4 per cent. The rise in public social expenditure was even more rapid: having stood at 13.3 per cent of 1958 GNP, it was equivalent to 18.0 per cent of the

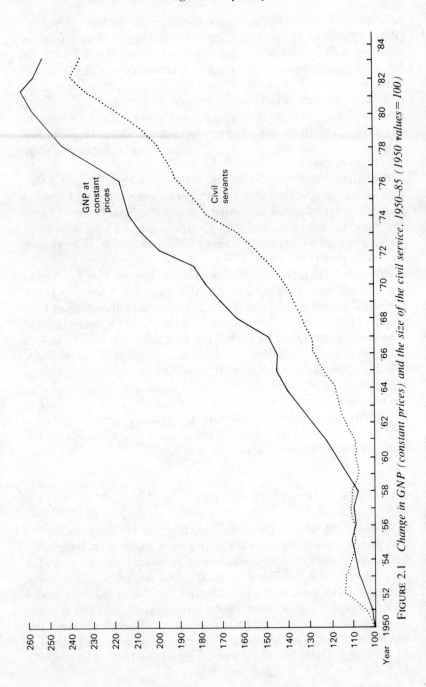

FIGURE 2.1 *Change in GNP (constant prices) and the size of the civil service, 1950–85 (1950 values = 100)*

country's GNP by 1968. Tax revenue increased as well, over those years, from 22 to 28 per cent of GNP. The depressed conditions of the base year–1958–render these changes particularly dramatic. But they are slight when compared to post-1968 trends in the growth of all aspects of State capacity.[24]

Figure 2.1 indicates the expansion over time of Ireland's GNP and its civil service, with 1950 adopted as the base year. The 1958–61 years mark the economy's emergence from a depression, followed by a sustained period of growth which lasted until the 1973 'oil shock', and continued thereafter at a somewhat slower and less even pace until 1980. Growth in the civil service was concentrated in the 1970s, with just under 20 000 civil servants at the start of the decade and just over 30 000 at its end. The total public domain by 1980 accounted for nearly one-third of the total work force. It had expanded from 229 248 employees and office holders in 1971 to an estimated 322 000 in 1983. Some 68 500 of these were employed by the State-sponsored bodies.[25]

Figure 2.2 graphs the progress of three key indices of State capacity, all expressed as percentages of GNP: taxation, public social and total public expenditure. Any upward trend indicates that the State's potential for intervention is growing more rapidly than the economy. In the context of an economic boom, the post–1961 trends in State activity are

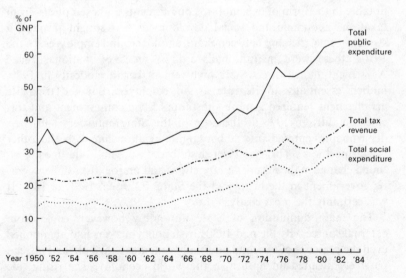

FIGURE 2.2 *Total public expenditure, public social expenditure, and total tax revenue as percentages of GNP: 1950–84*

extraordinary. The underlying dynamic was powerful indeed, sufficiently so that the rate of growth in the State sector was not inhibited by the faltering economic performance of the late 1970s. Borrowing, much of it from abroad, allowed politicians to maintain the momentum to the growth of State capacity through the early 1980s. Public expenditure in 1982 was equivalent to 64 per cent of GNP, nearly half of it devoted to social services, while tax revenue stood at nearly 38 per cent of GNP.

THE LIMITS OF STATE ACTIVISM

Greatly expanded and restructured, the Irish State, after 1960, was potentially the most potent force in the society. It had, by and large, retained substantial autonomy but greatly enhanced its capacity to intervene. The ultimate form of the new State apparatus was obscured in the late 1970s and early 1980s by a period of political instability, interest group conflict and industrial disputes. Now that these have abated, it is evident that the Irish State's autonomy and capacity are considerably more restricted than might have been expected.

The State in the 1980s had lost some of its autonomy to the interest groups that had emerged in the course of economic development. A status quo had evolved that was underwritten by State guarantees, notably in the form of expenditure commitments and exemptions from taxation. Economic and social development was sought through a strategy of partnership between State, employers and employees. In the 1970s, these were institutionalised in a series of National Wage Agreements. Such direct State involvement began modestly in 1970, limited essentially to its role as an employer. But the tripartite arrangement required a more substantial State commitment and this emerged fully in 1976 as the core of the State–ministers and their departments–entered into a bargaining relationship with the other 'social partners'. This has been described as possibly 'the most profound change in the nature and functions and prerogatives of democratic government in the history of the State' (O'Brien, 1981, p. 144). It was certainly the most costly.

The main diminution of State autonomy however, came from external sources. By the mid-1980s Irish policy-makers had abandoned even the pretence of a second internally generated 'take off' and instead passively awaited an upturn in the world economy. The rising tide generated by renewed growth in the economies of North America, Japan and West Germany would eventually lift even the most troubled small open economies from depression. The State, in practice, had ceased to see the goal of economic growth as lying within its purview. Instead, the goals of the State were to meet its spending commitments. Three in particular loomed large. First, with an unemployment rate of over 18 per cent and a population structure dominated by the young and old, much of State expenditure was required for income maintenance programmes. Some 30 per cent of all adults were recipients of social welfare payments. Second, the cost of servicing the public debt, incurred during the 1970s when State spending continued to expand despite the recession, assumed a significant share of public expenditure. Third, industrial development and agricultural modernisation were based on State incentives; if these were withdrawn or even reduced, the entire edifice of existing employment and income generation would be threatened. The State no longer had room for manoeuvre.

Despite a level of public expenditure equivalent to more than 60 per cent of GNP, the capacity of the Irish State is in reality quite limited. Economic planning as practised in Ireland and the semi-peripheral status of the Irish economy, have meant that the State's ability to manage the economy has not increased commensurate with the share of total expenditure that is channelled through the State. In any case, 'size of the public budget is not a measure of the power of the State which possesses many instruments which have either no or negligible impact upon public expenditure totals' (Heald, 1983, pp. 12–22). Those instruments fall within the realm of law: for example, confiscation, coerced private expenditure, and tax expenditures are alternatives to hiring personnel, or direct expenditure, as ways to achieve State objectives. Moreover, in the Irish case much of public expenditure is incurred by State-sponsored bodies, which are not necessarily pursuing the same objectives as the central administration.

So as a tax collector, dispenser of income and consumer, the State has a considerable potential for purposeful intervention. But in practice it does not exercise that potential. It is unlikely, given the structure of the State apparatus, that such intervention would even be feasible. The Irish State today is extraordinarily complex and disjointed. Its foundation of ministerial responsibility exercised through government departments has long since been shown to be inadequate. State-sponsored bodies allowed the deficiencies to be overcome on a case-by-case basis, but only at the cost of devising an administrative system that lacked a core that could provide direction.[26]

The Irish experience therefore, is typical of the semi-peripheral societies, which 'have been impelled by the exigencies of the open economy to expand the role of the State' (Cameron, 1978, p. 253). Cameron argues that the limited autonomy of such nations *vis-à-vis* the world economy leads governments to adopt a defensive strategy which is constituted out of policies that necessarily raise public expenditure to high levels relative to countries in the centre. Ireland is one of the examples that Cameron cites. In the Irish case however, it is clear that increased public expenditure is not to be confused with increased State management. The State in Ireland has undertaken the cost of subsidising private enterprises that otherwise would not be established or continue in existence and subsidising those families who are unable to generate an adequate income from the market economy. Despite this, market forces rather than the State remain decisive in contemporary Ireland.

CONCLUSION

The consistent goal of State policy since independence has been the provision of sufficient employment opportunities in Ireland to avoid emigration or unemployment. That goal was pursued through a variety of strategies. Some strategies restricted the State itself to an auxiliary status, while others, notably those of the 1930s and 1960s, implied state expansion on a considerable scale. Throughout the post-independence period, the State has enjoyed substantial autonomy from internal rivals and, in the early decades, substantial autonomy from external sources. Thus in the 1930s Ireland could pursue, with some success, policies that tended to ignore the harsh realities of the international economic enviroment. Also, the core of the State remained small and cohesive: the ministers of the day and their departments' civil servants. Stimulation from outside the State came mainly from official commissions rather than from organised interests. Until the 1950s the Catholic Church represented the State's most formidable opponent, but conflict was rare, largely perhaps because State officials were prepared to accept the Church's lead in most moral and social matters–though not in the vital question of how Ireland was to be governed.

This combination of an auxiliary State, Church and State partnership, and State autonomy was, by the 1940s, obviously ineffective as a means for achieving the goal of economic viability. Gradually the mechanisms for a new strategy, and consequently a restructured and revitalised State, evolved, culminating in the commitment to economic planning in 1958. The changes that followed in Ireland's economy and society represent a transformation of the social structure. We can identify two brief periods of State activism – the late 1950s and mid-1970s – but despite a still considerable autonomy and vastly increased capacity, the State did not emerge as the prime mover in the direction taken by Irish society. The consequences of State intervention were largely unintended. The main role was left to market mechanisms. In part, this can be attributed to inadequacies in the structure of the State apparatus which, by the 1970s, no longer had an identifiably strong core. The inherited system of ministerial responsibility, even though augmented by the State-sponsored bodies, was recognised as providing a system of government and bureaucracy ill-suited to the demands of policy analysis and policy-making. An impasse had been reached without any prospect for its resolution.

The unique development of the Irish State and its role in Irish society has two main consequences, to be pursued respectively in Chapter 3 and Chapter 4. First, the State's actions significantly affected the distribution of opportunities for market participation but without exercising any real influence over which individuals had access to those opportunities. Thus social immobility accompanied the long-awaited era of prosperity. Second, market criteria continued as the arbiter of income distribution. Economic development and the social progress promised in its train did not reduce income inequalities. This emerged in large measure because of the specific taxation and expenditure policies pursued since 1958, to which we will turn in Chapter 4. The State's imprint is more evident at the top and the bottom of the class structure. At the top, subsidies to proprietors and tax policies that extract revenue from expenditure rather than income shored up a class of entrepreneurs. The bottom of the class structure was formed by a kind of underclass, families dependent on a State income maintenance system that had grown to match that of Britain. The State had assumed responsibility for those families unable to generate an income from the market economy.

NOTES

1. For an overview of such organisations in Ireland, see Basil Chubb, 1970, Chapter 10; the consequences of such a State structure are discussed by Rueschemeyer and Evans (1985).
2. The account of the split over the Treaty draws on the description and interpretation provided by Pynne (1969) and Joseph M. Curran (1980).

3. The quote is from the *Report of the Commission of Enquiry into the Civil Service* 1932–35, cited in Chubb (1970, p. 232).

4. Fanning (1983, p. 61). As Fanning notes, the Department of Finance's primacy was secured in the Civil War by the close working relationship between its staff and the leaders of the provisional Government: 'The bonds of trust were cemented in the worst days of the Civil War when ministers and officials worked closely together under military guard in near-siege conditions in Merrion Street. The passion for order and stability which so characterised the government of the Irish Free State in its early years was a product of that shared experience' (Fanning, 1978, p. 65).

5. The first evaluation is by the historian R. B. McDowell, cited by Chubb (1970, p. 220); the second evaluation is Chubb's (1970, p. 221).

6. Dail Eireann, *Democratic Programme, Minutes and Proceedings,* 21 January 1919, pp. 22–3.

7. The economist, George O'Brien, in his obituary on the first Minister for Agriculture, observed that the first Free State government believed 'that agriculture was and would remain by far the most important industry and that the touchstone by which every economic measure must be judged was its effect on the prosperity of the farmer', (quoted in Johnson, 1985, p. 22).

8. This is the orthodox view of the party's social base. In terms of the social class component, Chubb, (1970, p. 81), is perhaps the most influential statement; Rumpf and Hepburn (1977, Chapter 3), propose the East-West gradient as a stable base for Irish political allegiances. A critique of both orthodoxies and a review of the relevant literature can be found in Carty (1981, pp. 75–6, and Chapter 5). The dismissive quote is from J. J. Walsh, Cumann na nGaedheal's former Chairman, cited in Fanning (1983, p. 101).

9. This is the view of Chubb (1970, pp. 74–5), and remains a convincing portrayal of the electoral foundation of the Party's eleven years in power. See also Gallagher (1976, p. 32) and Sinnott (1978, p. 41).

10. F. S. L. Lyons (1973, p. 479), commends its 'firm and efficient government', Curran (1981, p. 277), offers a similarly favourable assessment. John A. Murphy (1975, p. 64), however, dismisses the same government as having 'lacked any real social and economic policy'. A party which could reduce the old age pension and have a minister who could balance public expenditure restrictions against the fact 'that people may have to die in the country and die through starvation' (see Fanning, 1963, p. 100) is likely to be controversial.

11. Quoted in Whyte (1980, p. 67). For the context, see Whyte's account, especially Chapter III.

12. Most economists, e.g. Cullen (1972); Kennedy, K. A. (1971); O'Malley (1980), agree on the upward trend in both output and employment in industry. Johnson (1985, pp. 29–30) critically summarises the evidence. While the precise magnitudes can be challenged given the quality of the available statistics for the period, it is indisputable that the protectionist era spawned a mini-industrial revolution based on indigenous industry.

13. The framing of the Constitution is described in the Earl of Longford and Thomas P. O'Neill's *Eamon de Valera*, (1970, Chapter 24).

14. The earliest official GNP figure for independent Ireland refers to 1938. The available estimates and (after 1938) official totals in current and constant market prices can be found in Kennedy, F. (1971). Interpretation of change in GNP over the twentieth century is taken from L. M. Cullen (1972, pp. 179–80; 182–4). International comparisons are based on the real GNP per capita estimates for 30 countries between 1830 and 1970, adjusting for boundary changes, given in Paul Bairoch (1981, p. 10). More recent comparisons, based on purchasing power parities, can be found in Chapter 4.

15. The Vocational Organisation Commission's report was followed within two months by the intervention of a Roman Catholic Bishop, Dr Dignan, who published a pamphlet entitled *Social Security: Outlines of a Scheme of National Health Insurance,* which was to be based on vocationalist principles. See Whyte (1980, pp. 101–4).

16. The conventional view is available in Farrell (1982). A more dramatic and radical rendering of his later career is given in Bew and Patterson (1982).

17. Investment statistics are from Industrial Development Authority *Annual Reports;* exports to Britain are derived from *Trade Statistics of Ireland,* Dublin: Stationery Office.

18. These are detailed in O'Malley (1980, pp. 8–13), and The Telesis Consultancy Group (1982).

19. See the critiques by Norton (1974), and Katsiaouni: 'Planning in a small economy: the Republic of Ireland', *Journal of the Statistical and Social Inquiry Society of Ireland,* XXIII, Part V, 1977/78 (the latter source is notable for the replies to Katsiaouni offered by some of the main participants in the planning experiment).

20. See Norton (1974), Katsiaouni (1977/78); O'Malley, (1980, pp. 13–14).

21. Perhaps Marshall Aid provided the medium for the shared outlook; since American economic thought would have been widely aired at the time, however, it is not essential to find a specific connection and instead we leave the link as an example of a Weberian 'elective affinity'.

22. Sean Lemass believed Ireland was a classless society, perhaps associating class with the old Anglo-Irish aristocracy; see Boylan (1985).

23. A unique insight into the role and functioning of such bodies is provided in Meenan (1980, Chapter 9).

24. Public expenditure figures are from Finola Kennedy (1971, p. 303), updated (from 1968) from *National Income and Expenditure,* various years, Central Statistics Office. Post-1960 total tax revenue and GNP (in current and constant prices) are taken from David G. Hurley and Alan McQuaid (1985), pre-1960 GNP series are from Finola Kennedy (1971, p. 3), and tax totals are from *Irish Statistical Survey, 1954,* p. 13 (for 1950–52) and *National Income and Expenditure 1962* (1953–59), p. 46.

25. Ross (1986). 1950–85 trends in the size of the 'core' civil service are from p. 108; the estimated 1983 size of the total 'public domain' is from p. 305. See Ross's Appendix Table A.1.2 for an appreciation of the Byzantine complexity of the Irish State today.

26. Dissatisfaction with the structure of the civil service/ministerial system goes back to the 1940s. The issues and the proposed solutions are outlined

in Barrington, 1982. A classic statement of the system's deficiencies is provided by Charles McCarthy, 1968. Regarding the contradictions posed by the reliance on State-sponsored bodies, see Chubb (1970, pp. 259–68).

3 The Transformation of the Class Structure: Occupations, Opportunities and Occupants

INTRODUCTION

In the span of 25 years, Ireland's class structure shifted from one based on family property to one based on educational credentials. Opportunities for self-employment as labourers – agricultural and non-agricultural – contracted; massive growth occurred in professional and technical employment and in skilled manual labour. The broad outline of the resulting transformation is familiar, experienced by most core and semi-peripheral societies. It is our contention however, that Ireland produced an important variation on that theme and that the deviations are largely attributable to State interventions.

Until the 1950s, the class structure remained one in which a person's life chances depended on the prospect of inheriting a family-owned business. Those who did not inherit were forced to emigrate. There was only a limited number of secure positions that could be obtained through education or training. Economic expansion when it was finally achieved created a new range of opportunities, primarily for wage employment, and by the 1970s the class structure had been transformed to one based on skills and educational qualifications.

Three interrelated change processes underlay the transformation: (1) the availability and viability of various positions for economic participation were altered; (2) the rules governing competition for vacancies in positions became increasingly meritocratic; and (3) State expenditure and taxation reinforced the relative advantage to be derived from controlling various types of resources for economic participation. The first half of this chapter describes the evolving occupational pattern, representing the 'empty positions' available and their relative standing. In the second half, we address the question of how those opportunities were allocated among families. The answer is to be found in the extent of intergenerational social mobility. Chapter 4 continues the theme of class transformation by examining the contribution of the State to the observed changes in employment opportunities and access to those opportunities.

OCCUPATIONAL CHANGE IN IRELAND

Though the core processes that formed the change to Ireland's occupational structure are typical, their sequencing is not. Late and rapid industrialisation meant that the massive decline in opportunities for agricultural employment could not be compensated for by alternative opportunities within Ireland. Emigration filled the gap. Ireland in the 1950s was still very much a sub-region of the UK labour market. The class structure today reflects the selective process of emigration to Britain of young men and women as much as it does the growth in new opportunities (Walsh, 1970; Hughes and Walsh, 1976; Hannan, 1970).

Mass exodus from the land was the main dynamic of class change until the 1960s. The unfolding of that dynamic is traced in Table 3.1. The gainfully occupied male labour force (those at work or seeking work) is disaggregated there into the main distinctions in type and quality of market capacity, indicated separately for the agricultural and non-agricultural sectors.[1] Stability in the class structure before 1961, largely attributable to emigration, contrasts with rapid changes in the 1960s and 1970s. The contrast stems in part from the fact that after 1961 change was occurring within an Ireland that formed a self-contained labour market. In it, the opportunity for self-employment in agriculture diminished rapidly and continuously, as did the possibility for wage labour in low skilled manual employment. Opportunities for middle class employment and for skilled manual work grew with equal rapidity and continuity from 1961. Between 1961 and 1981, the proportion of the male labour force in farming halved, while white collar positions doubled (from 7.4 to 14.9 per cent), a growth rate almost matched by positions in skilled manual employment (from 12 to 21.2 per cent).

The depth of the transformation, and its unevenness, is most starkly represented in the fate of the 'relative assisting' category. Agricultural labourers were often 'relatives assisting', labouring on

TABLE 3.1: *Percentage distribution of gainfully occupied males by social group: 1926–81*

| | Employers and Self-Employed | | | | Employees–Salary/Wage Earners | | | | | Total | |
| | Agricultural | | Non-agricultural | | Non-manual middle class | | Manual (working class) | | | | |
Year	Employers per cent	Self-empl. and rels. assisting per cent	Employers per cent	Self-empl. and rels. assisting per cent	Professional and managerial per cent	Lower non-manual per cent	Skilled non-man. (non-man. farm) per cent	Semi-skilled and unskilled (non-man. farm) per cent	Agricultural: labourers per cent		per cent
1926	4.4	39.1	2.2	5.5	3.7	12.1	6.7	11.7	14.1	950 000	100.0
1936	4.2	36.7	1.9	6.2	4.1	11.7	7.5	13.3	14.0	974 000	100.0
1946	4.1	35.8	2.3	5.0	4.7	12.2	7.7	13.5	14.1	948 000	100.0
1951	3.0	33.9	2.1	5.6	5.2	13.7	10.2	15.3	10.9	931 000	100.0
1961	1.7	32.3	1.5	5.8	7.3	15.4	12.0	14.6	9.3	820 000	100.0
1971	1.2*	24.6*	1.8	6.1	10.3	17.7	16.5	15.6	6.3	828 000	100.0
1981	1.5	15.9	4.0	4.8	14.9	20.0	21.2	13.8	3.8	885 400	100.0

*Estimated

SOURCE: Rottman, Hannan, Hardiman and Wiley, 1982, p. 46.

the family farm in exchange for room and board while, in some cases, awaiting their eventual inheritance. Many also worked as seasonal labourers on other holdings (Fitzpatrick, 1977, p. 55). In 1926 this category represented 22.2 per cent of the male work-force; by 1951 that share had dropped to a still significant 16.4 per cent. But over the next three decades the ranks of relatives assisting dwindled to the inconsequential, a mere two per cent of the 1981 work-force.

The trends over the 1926–1981 period describe a transformation whereby the structuring principle of family property was replaced by that of wage bargaining. The effects of familial inheritance were then expressed indirectly in class specific rates of educational participation and attainment. A contrast between the placement of each new cohort of young men (aged 15–19) in the 1920s and 1970s offers the clearest statement of the transformation. Over one-half of the cohort remaining in Ireland in the 1920s could depend on family employment that would ultimately lead to direct inheritance of the family business, house and household property. By the 1970s, this would be true for less than 15 per cent of a cohort.

THE PERIOD OF CHANGE

The complexity of the changes set in motion by post-1951 State policies is considerable. It includes such strands as selective emigration in the 1950s and 1960s, unemployment, and the changing distribution of opportunities. Such was the devastation sustained through emigration that even in 1985 the male labour force (those at work plus the unemployed, excluding first time job seekers) of 916 000 was still some 17 000 fewer in number than that of 1951.

The fall and rise of various class positions as viable opportunities can be seen in Table 3.2. It is based on a re-categorisation of the Census data into more meaningful class groupings and focuses on the post-1951 trends. It charts the number and percentage share of each major class category of males in employment in 1951, 1961, 1971 and 1981 (all from census data) and in 1985 (estimated from Labour Force Survey results). Slightly less than one-half of the 1950s work-force fell within class categories which derived income from property owner-ship: employers or self-employed proprietors in agriculture made up 38 per cent of the total work-force, with an additional eight per cent engaged in non-agricultural pursuits. Life chances for the children of

TABLE 3.2: *Distribution of males at work by class categories, 1951–85*

	1951 No.	1951 %	1961 No.	1961 %	1971 No.	1971 %	1981 No.	1981 %	1985 No.	1985 %
EMPLOYERS AND SELF-EMPLOYED										
Agriculture										
(i) employers	27 844	3.1	14 001	1.8	212 982[1]	27.5	13,540	1.7	9300	1.3
(ii) self-employed and relatives assisting	314 768	35.1	265 524	34.3			140 841	17.5	119 900	16.2
Non-Agricultural										
(i) employers	19 689	2.2	12 582	1.6	64 624[1]	8.3	35 679	4.4	34 100	4.6
(ii) self-employed and relatives assisting	52 522	5.9	47 897	6.2			42 408	5.3	55 400	7.5
EMPLOYEES										
(i) upper middle class professionals, managers and salaried employees	47 780	5.3	58 959	7.6	84 512	10.9	128 499	16.0	124 900	16.9
(ii) lower middle class (intermediate and other non-manual)	123 011	13.8	121 134	15.6	139 991	18.0	163 012	20.3	162 200	22.0
(iii) skilled manual	90 400	10.1	92 632	12.0	128 056	16.5	163 021	20.3	143 700	19.5
(iv) semi-and unskilled manual										
(a) agricultural	94 957	10.6	64 753	8.4	40 245	5.2	25 780	3.2	21 400	2.9
(b) non-agricultural	124 789	13.9	96 731	12.5	105 384	13.6	89 962	11.2	69 100	9.4
TOTAL AT WORK[2]	896 624	100.0	774 540	100.0	776 507	100.0	808 670	100.0	742 900	100.0
Total unemployed	36 115		46 989		55 157		91 279		172 700	
Total unemployed as per cent of gainfully occupied		3.7		5.7		6.6		10.1		18.9

SOURCES 1951, 1961, 1971, 1981: *Census of Population of Ireland* (various volumes); 1985: derived from unpublished tables provided by the Central Statistics Office from the 1985 Labour Force Survey.

1. Employers and self-employed were not distinguished in the 1971 census.

2. Total numbers at work includes individuals for whom an occupation is not indicated and who are therefore not allocated to a class category. The total also excludes theological students, 'professional students', and 'critical clerks'; in 1981 it excludes personnel in hospital (5905).

those individuals centred on the prospect of inheriting the family business with the accompanying house and household goods.

The growth in employee middle class and skilled manual pursuits compensated for much but not all of the natural increases of the urban middle class and working class; it has not absorbed the results of the decline in agriculture. The increase in non-manual employment over the 1926–71 period could at most have absorbed only 41 per cent of those who left agriculture, had no one else sought those positions. Realistically, education or training could provide a livelihood in Ireland for only the most privileged minority of those aspiring to the work-force from property-owning classes: hence their massive emigration rates.

Overall, of the cohort of males born between 1936 and 1940, only 59 per cent were still resident in Ireland by 1961, and of those remaining, only one-third were at work in some form of family employment. Professionals, managers and senior administrative workers, 48 000 in number, represented by 5 per cent of the 1951 work-force. A further 11 per cent were skilled manual workers. One-fourth of the work-force was involved in semi-skilled or unskilled manual work – typically as labourers; there were 125 000 labourers in 1951, nearly one worker out of seven.

By the 1980s the new class structure was fully in place. Employers and the self-employed represented less than 30 per cent of the 1985 total work-force. The declining size of proprietorial categories however, is attributable to the depletion of the numbers engaged in agricultural production, where a particularly sharp decline occurred in the ranks of self-employed farmers. In contrast, non-agricultural proprietors have increased their numbers and their share of the work-force over the past 35 years, and that growth in numbers was concentrated among employers (20 000 in 1951 and 34 000 in 1985). Ireland has clearly ceased to be characterised as *petit bourgeois*: the predominant categories today are those of large-scale employers and of well qualified employees.

The changing fortunes of categories of employees is evident from Table 3.2. Employed professionals formed some 17 per cent of the 1985 work-force, more than tripling their representation since 1951; skilled manual employees also grew markedly over that period, from 10 to 20 per cent of the work-force, rising in numbers from 90 000 in 1951 to 144 000 in 1985. The number of 'lower' middle-class workers – such as commercial travellers and junior clerks – also increased, but less dramatically, from 14 to 22 per cent. Semi-skilled and unskilled manual workers made up nearly one-quarter of the work-force in 1951 and 12 per cent in 1985. This change includes a particularly massive decline (from 95 000 to 21 000) in the number of agriculture labourers.

So the 1985 employee work-force, 521 000 strong, was over one-half (55 per cent) middle-class (though this covers a diverse range of occupations) and 28 per cent skilled manual; professionals, managers and senior salaried employees also represented nearly one-quarter of all employees, whereas in 1951 they represented one-tenth.

The changes in the class composition of the Irish work-force emerged from industrial development that was more rapid, occurred later, and was more State-inspired than in most Western societies. So intense were the changes that it is easy to overlook their incompleteness. Even in 1983, a substantial share of the work-force was in residual classes stranded in the course of industial development, especially farmers on marginal holdings and labourers without skills. The only European parallels for such a presence are in the south: Greece, Portugal and Spain. People in these marginal categories have little opportunity to transfer to the more favourably placed categories; their children's chances are little better, perpetuating marginality within families. So today's class structure contains a substantial number of positions that are viable only in so far as they are underwritten by State social welfare programmes and from which, especially given present economic circumstances, there appears to be no exit. Today such positions account for more than one quarter of what is ironically termed the 'gainfully occupied labour force'. This reflects the dark side of the progress that class transformation generally brought to Irish society. For those families unable to be upwardly mobile, the cost was severe. Emigration was no longer an attractive alternative and there were no opportunities in the traditional forms of employment in which the last generation of their families had been engaged.

SOCIAL MOBILITY AND THE PROCESS OF CLASS TRANSFORMATION

Periods of sustained expansion have been associated in most countries with higher levels of social mobility. That link is attributable primarily to the shifts within the occupational structure that improve the distribution of the available economic opportunities. In this section we consider the evidence on whether the pattern is applicable to recent Irish experience. That evidence is also vital to another question: the extent to which limitations to social mobility have been such as to mould *economic* class categories, such as the ones we have examined thus far, into indentifiable, cohesive *social* classes. Further, in trying to understand the impact of the Irish State, we are interested in the nature of such mobility as can be observed. So we distinguish between (1) structural mobility, which occurs through the creation of a new range of 'empty positions' within the structure and which may or may not reflect growing equality of opportunity, and (2) relative mobility, in which the degree of observed intergenerational mobility for each category is compared to that found in the other categories.

It is clear from the discussion of occupational change that there is ample scope in Ireland for significant structural mobility. However, we noted that the timing of decline and growth among occupations was not synchronised. We also noted the extent to which new opportunities were concentrated in occupations requiring substantial entrance requirements, in the form of skills and education.

Table 3.3 summarises the evidence from census data on occupational change in three periods: 1951–61, 1961–71 and 1971–81. Some aspects of the 1951–81 change were spread over the full period. The contraction of the agriculture labour force and the expansion of senior white collar work were continuous processes. Most changes were not. For the 1951–61 period, the spectre of emigration overshadowed all trends by reducing the size of the male labour force by one-seventh. The real growth in skilled manual labour and junior

TABLE 3.3 *Changes in employment opportunities by class: 1951–81*

Class Category	1951/61	1961/71	1971/81
1. Small farmers (< 50 acres)	− 55 000	− 51 500	− 47 400
2. Agricultural labourers	− 30 200	− 24 500	− 14 500
3. Unskilled manual labourers	− 16 500	− 67 000	− 18 800
4. Skilled manual labourers	+ 2 200	+ 35 400	+ 35 000
5. Upper non-manual	+ 11 200	+ 25 600	+ 44 000
6. Lower non-manual	− 1 900	+ 18 900	+ 23 000
Total decline (1 + 2 + 3)	− 101 700	− 143 000	− 80 700
Total increase (4 + 5 + 6)	+ 11 500	+ 79 900	+ 102 000

white collar work only commenced in the 1960s and continued unabated through the 1970s. Small farmers, agricultural labourers and unskilled manual workers had a combined decline of 325 400 positions over the full 30-year period. The remaining three categories – 'upper non-manual', 'lower non-manual' and skilled manual workers – ultimately expanded by 193 400, but their pre-1961 increases was virtually nil and the greatest concentration of growth did not occur until the 1970s. So there were no opportunities in Ireland to compensate for the massive losses in traditional forms of work.

SOCIAL MOBILITY IN THE EARLY 1970s

Census data allow us to reconstruct the context within which the structural sources of social mobility in Ireland evolved. However there are limits to the conclusions which can be drawn from such data. An examination of the actual pattern of intergenerational mobility requires that we draw on survey data. The most comprehensive published evidence available to us is derived from samples of Dublin males interviewed in the late 1960s and early 1970s (Whelan and Whelan, 1984; Breen and Whelan, 1985). Though the timing of the survey limits the conclusions we can draw, the loss is mitigated by the very pattern of occupational change we have observed. Emigration removed a substantial proportion of males in the 20–45-year age group from the Irish class structure. Those individuals remaining in Ireland and available to form part of the survey sample represented persons who were able to find positions in the emerging class structure formed out of the opportunities created during the 1960s. As we have seen however, the trends of occupational change continued over the 1970s. This leaves the important question of whether over the 1970s alterations occurred in the method by which individuals were recruited into positions. That will be addressed in Chapter 6, which considers the changing nature of the Irish educational system.

Table 3.4 presents social mobility data using a threefold class scheme in which farmers are allocated to classes on the basis of acreage, the main index of differences in market capacity among farmers. The extent of mobility observed, employing this classification, is summarised in Table 3.5 and compared to that obtaining in England and Wales. Nearly 45 per cent of the Dublin sample had been mobile across a class boundary compared with slightly less than 50

TABLE 3.4: *Class distribution of respondents 21–64: 1968–72**

	Professional and managerial class	Intermediate class	Working class	N	%
Father's class					
Professional and managerial class	58.8 (58.8)	31.7 (26.0)	9.5 (15.2)	648 (1242)	17.1 (13.2)
Intermediate class	24.4 (27.6)	44.0 (36.7)	31.6 (35.7)	1200 (3105)	31.6 (32.9)
Working class	11.0 (15.5)	28.1 (27.2)	60.8 (57.3)	1945 (5085)	51.3 (53.9)
All	24.0 (25.1)	33.8 (30.2)	42.8 (44.7)	3794 (9434)	

Respondent's class / Percentage by row (column header spanning the three class columns)

*Figures in parentheses relate to England and Wales, 1972.

TABLE 3.5 *Absolute mobility: three-class classification, respondents 21–64: 1968–1972**

	% Mobile	44.9	(49.3)
Into the professional and managerial class		13.4	(17.3)
From the working class to the professional managerial class		5.6	(8.3)
From the professional managerial class into the working class		1.6	(2.1)
Into and out of the working class		31.7	(36.8)
Out of the working class		20.1	(23.0)
Into the working class		11.6	(13.8)

*Figures in parentheses relate to England and Wales (1972).

per cent of the English and Welsh respondents. This difference is almost entirely due to the higher probability of upward mobility into the professional and managerial class in England and Wales, where 17 per cent had managed this transition, compared to 13 per cent in Dublin. Upward mobility from the working class to the managerial class provides the greatest contrast between the English and Irish mobility patterns; the respective figures are 5.6 per cent and 8.3 per cent. In both countries, the percentage mobile out of the working class is almost twice that mobile into the working class. There is also little difference in the percentage of those with professional and managerial origins found in the working class – approximately two per cent in each case.

It should be noted that the degree of mobility that we observe will depend on the number, size and character of the class categories that we distinguish. We cannot take a single figure as the rate of social mobility in a society. However, the general picture of an excess of upward over downward mobility, of short-range over long-range mobility and of lower levels of mobility in Dublin, holds true across alternative classifications.

Analysis of the Irish data also indicate that persons born outside of Dublin were the most likely to be mobile. While 43 per cent of Dubliners had been mobile, this was true of 50 per cent of non-Dubliners. Mobility into the professional and managerial class was almost twice as high for those with non-Dublin origins. Two significant factors explain those differences. First, it is clear that those with non-Dublin origins had significantly more privileged class origins than their Dublin peers. However, even allowing for such differences, non-Dubliners were substantially more mobile. The results we observe are a consequence of selective patterns of migration which ensured that while only 21 per cent of the Dublin working class had non-Dublin origins, the corresponding percentage for the professional and managerial category was 39 per cent.

INEQUALITIES OF OPPORTUNITY

We can bring a relative mobility perspective to bear on the data of Table 3.4 by introducing the standard of 'perfect' mobility. 'Perfect' mobility denotes a situation where a son's class is independent of his father's class position. In such circumstances the percentage of men from each origin class to be found in a particular destination class would be indentical. Thus, to take the example of the professional and managerial class, if perfect mobility obtained, 24 per cent of the men from each class background would currently be in this class. The ratio measuring the disparities in opportunities between the classes would therefore have a value of 1:1:1. In fact, as we can see from Table 3.4, the actual percentages observed were 59 per cent for the professional and managerial class, 24 per cent for the intermediate class and 11 per cent for the working class. These percentages can be expressed in the form of a disparity ratio 1:2:6 for the chances of access to the professional and managerial class for men from the three origins distinguished, and may be compared to the equivalent English and Welsh ratio of 1:2:4.[2] Inequality in Table 3.4 can be assessed both by examining the opportunities for access to the professional and managerial class and by calculating the relative risks of the working class as one's destination. Slightly less than 10 per cent of professional and managerial sons are found in the working class while the relevant figures for men of intermediate and working class origins are 32 per cent and 61 per cent. The approximate disparity ratio for these percentages of 1:3:6 compares with the English and Welsh ratio of 1:2:5.5. The inequalities in mobility in Ireland are far more to the disadvantage of men from working class backgrounds than is the case in England and Wales.

In their analysis of mobility in England, Sweden and France, Erikson, et al. (1982) conclude that different patterns of mobility in the three countries are due chiefly to different patterns of structural change rather than to any variation in the degree of inequality of intrgenerational access to class positions. In other words, relative mobility chances are approximately constant across the three countries they examine. If we add the Dublin data to the comparison, though, analyses demonstrate a systematic deviation from the cross-national consistencies in relative mobility opportunities found by Erikson and his colleagues. The deviations in the case of Dublin are exactly the opposite of the less marked deviations present in Sweden. Thus, on a 'scale' of openness, allowing for structural differences, Sweden lies at one extreme and Dublin at the other.[3]

CHANGES IN MOBILITY PATTERNS SINCE THE EARLY 1970s

Consolidation of the occupational structure since the early 1970s has undoubtedly led to upward mobility for many new participants in the labour force. But, the crucial question for our purpose is whether changes have been such as to alter the nature of absolute and relative rates of mobility from that found at the beginning of the seventies. A definite answer would require a recent social mobility survey of the male labour force comparable to the earlier ones. In the absence of such data, we have brought together evidence from a variety of sources which cast light on the extent to which mobility patterns have been transformed. The first source of evidence is the nature of the shift in the occupational structure which has occurred since 1971. A second source is recent survey data on mobility patterns among young people.

From Table 3.2 we can calculate that among employees the size of the upper middle class increased by 43 per cent between 1961 and 1971 and by 48 per cent between 1971 and 1985; the lower middle class increased by 16 per cent in the former period and declined slightly in the latter; skilled manual workers increased by 38 per cent between 1961 and 1971 and by 12 per cent between 1971 and 1985; semi-skilled and unskilled manual workers increased by 9 per cent between 1961 and 1971 and declined by 30 per cent between 1971 and 1985; agricultural employees fell by 38 per cent in the early period and 53 per cent in the later period while the corresponding figures for farmers were 24 per cent and 40 per cent. Finally, the total number at work in 1985 was fractionally lower than in 1971, reflecting the rise of unemployment from 6 to 18 per cent of the 'gainfully occupied' labour force.

The decline in agricultural employment and the increased importance of skilled manual and white collar employment are common to both periods. In the latter period, however, expansion was concentrated in the upper middle class, and the semi-skilled and unskilled manual category displayed a substantial decline in absolute as well as proportionate terms. A comparison of the figures for 1981 with those for 1985 shows that these changes are linked with the substantial increase in the level of unemployment. Thus, with the exception of the upper middle class, all employee categories show a drop in absolute numbers over those years.

On balance, changes in the occupational structure during the 1970s created substantial opportunities for mobility 'at the top', but such a favourable change must be weighed against the increase in the level of unemployment during the 1980s.

In terms of relative mobility, we can examine whether a substantial reduction in inequalities occurred for new entrants to the labour market by utilising a study conducted in 1982 relating to youth unemployment and the transition to working life (Sexton, Whelan and Williams, 1988). For our present purposes we again concentrate on the data for males. Some distortion will be induced by the fact that those in university and other 'third level' education will be under-represented in our sample. However, since information is available from other sources on the social class composition of third level students, it will be possible to make allowance for that source of invalidity in making comparisons. In our analysis of mobility thus far, we have not dealt with the distribution of unemployment across classes. Respondents who were unemployed when interviewed were given a 'present' class position on the basis of their last employment.

However, given both the substantial growth in the levels of unemployment and the increasing proportion of long-term unemployed in recent years, this practice has been questionable. In Table 3.6 we therefore introduce unemployment as a mobility outcome.

TABLE 3.6: *Class distribution of males 18–24 in the 1982 labour force*

Father's class	Professional and managerial	Intermediate non-manual	Manual	Unemployed	Total	N
		Respondent's class percentage by row				
Professional and managerial	28.5	18.6	47.2	5.7	100	495
Intermediate non-manual	12.7	23.3	55.4	8.5	100	480
Manual	6.1	11.1	65.7	17.1	100	1436
N	289	363	1444	315	–	2411
%	12.0	15.1	59.8	13.1	–	–

The age of respondents means that only a relatively low proportion was found in professional and managerial positions. Given the distribution of respondents across occupations, inequalities appear to be most pronounced at the top of the hierarchy. Twenty-nine per cent of those from professional and managerial origins are currently in that class compared with 6 per cent of those from manual backgrounds. Thus, the disparity ratio measuring the degree of inequality of access to professional and managerial positions existing between men with origins at either extreme of the class hierarchy has a magnitude of nearly 5:1. In contrast, the disparity ratio for the same origin groups for the probability of being in manual work is 1:1.4 (65.7 divided by 47.2). With unemployment as a 'destination', though, the underlying inequality emerges starkly. Men from manual backgrounds are three times more likely to be unemployed than are those from professional and managerial backgrounds. That difference can be attributed entirely to class differences in the level of educational attainment. In all, 83 per cent of young males whose fathers were manual workers were either in manual work themselves or unemployed.

We can therefore conclude that the nature of the mobility process does not appear to have altered significantly over the 1970s. The occupational structure shifted towards an increase in professional and managerial positions and a reduction in less skilled forms of manual work and, in consequence, a certain degree of upward mobility took place. The overall picture, however, remains one of a highly structured mobility regime in which opportunities for upward mobility are restricted. Children of middle class parents continue to enjoy a substantial advantage in access to the more privileged occupations. But the corresponding disadvantage of young people from working class origins is increasingly expressed in the risk of becoming unemployed rather than of remaining immobile within the working class. The decline of traditional positions in this class makes immobility a shrinking option. So long-term unemployment has become, in the 1980s, a new category into which those from working class origins may be downwardly mobile. The process of class transformation continues to produce new opportunities in skilled manual and service employment. In the less restrictive mobility regime of England, such trends have led to a situation in which working class males experience a 'heightening of both opportunities and risks' (Goldthorpe and Payne, 1986, p. 18). Their mobility chances polarised over the 1970s into the two main alternatives of upward mobility into newer middle class positions or unemployment. Even this would appear an optimistic scenario in the Irish context, given that class differentials in educational attainment are more pronounced than in England.

CONCLUSION

The swiftness of its class transformation sets Ireland apart from the experience of most other countries, even from those in the European semi-periphery. In Italy for example, employment opportunities in farming and farm labouring halved between 1951 and 1971. But other traditional occupations retained their share of the total labour force over that period and other positions, attainable without extensive preparation, expanded gradually. Thus, changes leading to alternative opportunities coincided with and compensated for those in decline. Such compensation was even more smoothly effected in France, which even in the 1950s retained a significant agricultural labour force (in 1954, 19 per cent of males at work were farmers and 8 per cent were farm labourers). That sector contracted sharply thereafter, but the flow from the land was absorbed through migration to urban areas and to manual work. Recent occupational transition in

England, the first industrial power, was smoother still. In the post-World War II period there was no downward trend in proprietorial positions and for most of the class structure there was a basic stability in their respective shares of a total work-force that remained at a constant 16 million. Change was evident only at the very top and the very bottom of the class structure: professional employment expanded substantially and unskilled manual work declined from 14 per cent to 6 per cent of the work-force. The underlying processes of occupational change were shifting the range of 'empty positions' in the class structure upwards by fostering growth in non-manual and skilled manual employment.

Such an orderly consolidation is the antithesis of the Irish experience over recent decades. We can identify three periods of rapid dislocation. First, over the 1950s many positions in self-employment and in low-skill labouring ceased to be viable. There was no countervailing process creating new opportunities within the class structure in that period. Second, over the 1960s and 1970s the class structure was reconstructed around those positions that were created through industrialisation and economic expansion. That did not synchronise the change process involved in class transformation, as the new positions were largely beyond the reach of occupants of positions whose viability had been undermined. This is reflected in the extent to which relative mobility rates in Ireland are more unequal than in countries like France, England and Sweden. Third, as economic expansion gave way to prolonged recession, the new class structure became firmly implanted. The rate of expansion of new middle-range positions in secure, well-paid occupations slowed considerably and working class categories experienced high rates of unemployment. However, the class position of most families had already been established in the 1960s and 1970s. This depended by and large on the ability to take advantage of the opportunities for education opened up in those decades and consequently to secure access to a favoured niche in the class system.

Within Ireland, there are no evident change processes that threaten the stability of the current system. But the recent resumption of large-scale emigration – there was a net outflow of some 75 000 persons over the 1981–86 period – may provide the dynamic for significant change. The difficulty is that at present we lack information on the composition of the outward movement. It would appear unlikely, however, that the opportunities exist, as they did in the 1950s, for those without skills and qualifications to obtain work outside Ireland. So emigration simply reflects an extension of mobility differentials; those with educational qualifications but unable to find work in Ireland can search elsewhere. Those without such qualifications and who cannot find work remain unemployed in Ireland.

NOTES

1. The restriction of our analysis in this chapter to males reflects both the availability of appropriate date and our understanding that for an analysis of class changes in the period under consideration the family is the appropriate unit of stratification. It does not involve assuming that women's jobs make no difference.
2. In the disparity ratio the first figure is set to unity. The larger the other figures the greater the degree of inequality in access to the destination class under consideration.
3. Results from a national sample of males in 1973 confirm this conclusion. (Erikson and Goldthorpe, 1987); (Hout and Jackson, 1986).

4 The State and the Distribution and Redistribution of Income

INTRODUCTION

The opportunities for white collar and skilled manual work fostered by economic growth were far more secure, well-paid and satisfying than those which change had displaced. Prosperity brought an improved standard of living to the fortunate occupants of positions in the State bureaucracy, manufacturing industry and the services. At the same time, the zeal with which politicians and the public embraced the idea of a Welfare State ensured that those excluded from direct market participation also experienced a substantial rise in their real incomes and thus their standard of living. This chapter scrutinises the distribution of the various forms of income available in Ireland over the 1970s and 1980s, focusing on the role of the State in channelling that distribution throughout the class structure. Giddens (1973, p. 149) argues that 'what appears to be generic to capitalism is a *stable* disparity between the economic returns accruing to the major classes'. We begin our examination of class income differentials by noting some factors that potentially limit the applicability of Giddens's generalisation to the recent Irish experience.

First, processes of class transformation which unfolded over generations in other capitalist societies took place with extraordinary rapidity in Ireland. The upsurge in professional and technical employment created a major new dimension to disparities in economic returns. Second, the State quickly became enmeshed in a set of institutional arrangements, justified in pursuit of economic development, that placed class income disparities on the negotiating table. This marked a decisive break from the 'auxiliary' role previously adopted by the Irish State. The change is manifest in the taxation and social expenditure policies pursued from the mid-1960s onwards. Here too Ireland's experience has not been typical. The Welfare State did not evolve

70

gradually as in other European countries, but emerged as a component of a more general programme of State intervention to promote economic development. This created a vast pool of resources that was more than sufficient to alter, potentially greatly, the relative financial outcomes determined for families in the market.

There are two main policy arenas in which State policy had important consequences for the material well-being of families, unintentional though those outcomes may often be. One is manifest in the extent of inequality in the distribution of market incomes themselves. Here we are concerned with the role of the State as an employer, an agent of job creation, and general facilitator of economic activity. The second role is that of redistribution through taxation and benefits, both cash and non-cash. The combined effects of taxes and benefits will be assessed in terms of the redistribution of income that resulted. In particular, the fund of non-market resources collected through taxation could have been distributed in a manner that served either to abate, in Titmuss's phrase, or to reinforce class differentials based on market income. We do not, however, view taxation and social expenditure policies in the Irish context merely as mechanisms for reallocating income but rather as forces in the process of class formation itself. The Welfare State in Ireland is not merely an alternative to the market as a method for distribution: State policies in taxation and benefits were and are important factors determining the set of positions available in Ireland for individuals to fill and also the degree of openness with which the mechanisms recruiting individuals to positions operated. The net result, in our view, was first to widen the disparities among class categories and then to ensure their continuation.

We begin our analysis with a consideration of the abrupt shift in the State's social welfare role and the nature of the interventions that emerged as a result. The chapter then examines evidence on the income available for distribution through market and other sources, and summarises the results which arise from an application of the standard methodology of redistribution studies to Irish data. The central section of the chapter is a class analysis of income distribution and redistribution in 1980. That material is then placed in comparative context *vis-à-vis* other OECD countries and particularly the United Kingdom. A concluding section evaluates the overall balance that emerged in Ireland between the State's role as an agent in class formation and as a force encouraging class abatement through income redistribution.

CHANGE AND CONTINUITY IN STATE POLICY

After 1958 Ireland enjoyed a rate of growth in its national income that other European countries might well have envied. Its rising per capita income, however, must be seen in the context of the nadir which the 1950s represented in Ireland's economic fortunes. International comparisons suggest that 'income inequality is fairly moderate at extremely low levels of economic development, reaches a maximum at intermediate levels of development, and finally decreases' (Weede, 1980. p. 497; Weede and Kummer, 1985). Ireland in the 1960s and 1970s was at an intermediate level of development, roughly comparable to the other members of the periphery of capitalist Europe.

The novel situation of an expanding income pool brought out a host of claims to share in the good fortune. Hitherto, State policy had been guided by 'tenacious adherence to the classical principle of curbing public expenditure and taxation' (Fanning, 1978, p. 491). That spirit was personified by J. J. McElligott, Secretary of the Department of Finance 1927–53, from whose obituary the above quotation is taken. But in the 1960s, with Keynesian policies as the new 'truth', State policy underwent a sea change in three vital areas: employment creation, social expenditure and taxation. All three represent activities that required and justified a claim by the State to a substantial share of the newly created income. Generally, countries which are at a relative disadvantage in the world economy because of their openness and small size tend to have the largest ratios of public expenditure to GNP (Cameron, 1978). This is certainly applicable to Ireland.

> The biggest single factor responsible for the relatively faster growth of public expenditure relative to GNP in Ireland during the 1960s and 1970s was the need for Ireland to catch up industrially, economically, and in social welfare standards with her neighbours and trading partners, and the subsequent faster growth rate of public outlays that this need simply and directly generated (Gould, 1981, pp. 130–1).

Our central concern is the manner in which this 'catching up' altered the distribution of market incomes, potentially bringing Ireland out of the intermediate phase of high inequality into the greater income equality characteristic of the advanced societies.

STATE DEVELOPMENT POLICY

The State's most direct role was through the creation of numerous places in the more advantaged employee categories within the public sector itself. This accounted for some 110 000 of the new employment opportunities created between 1960 and 1980 (Ross, 1986). State policies also spawned opportunities for industrial employment in new manufacturing industries (see Chapter 7). While virtually all of the white collar opportunities stemming from State expansion were located in Dublin, the State strategy was to disperse, initially among a small number of regional growth centres, the industrial employment that resulted from State incentives to investment in manufacturing. That approach, imposed in the 1958 planning documents, was controversial and it was not until 1972 that a consistent policy evolved. The Industrial Development Authority established Regional Industrial Plans and pursued a policy of distributing new employment so as to moderate the growth rate of the Dublin region, encourage substantial industrial concerns to concentrate in smaller urban centres; and use less populated areas as the nucleus for small industry expansion (Ross, 1978, pp. 306–17).

This policy was greatly to the detriment of the Dublin working class. The industrial employment opportunities available to them and their children were concentrated in the old indigenous Irish industry, which fared poorly in the post-1958 era relative to the new industries attracted through the State's development policies. So the traditional urban working class was effectively marginalised in the course of economic development, without opportunities for manual work and unable to compete for the white collar positions being created on their doorstep.

State subsidies to encourage investment that would create jobs served indirectly to underpin the position of the proprietors who established or enlarged enterprises in response. More generally, entrepreneurial activity since 1958 has relied on a substantial inflow of State 'economic services'. In the mid-1960s, this accounted for some 30 per cent of all public expenditure. Though that share tended to decline subsequently, it frequently stood at about one-half the total sum allocated for social expenditure programmes; in 1984 'economic services' constituted 16 per cent of total central government expenditure. The magnitude of that subsidy can be gauged from the fact that the sum involved was equivalent to 72 per cent of State cash transfer payments to households in the same year. State interventions to the benefit of proprietors in agriculture, industry and services underwrote the viability of a range of positions at the top of the class structure. This tended first to stabilise and then to expand the number of non-agricultural proprietors in Ireland, as shown in the previous chapter. That trend was the opposite of what was occurring in most of Western Europe, where the typical experience was contraction in the share of non-agricultural employers in the work force.

The attraction of foreign investment is the mainspring of State industrial development strategy in Ireland. This too had distinctive consequences. First, the establishment and retention of harmonious industrial relations has been a priority in the efforts to woo overseas investors. This led, particularly in the 1970s, to an ever expanding commitment by the State to apply incomes policies that would suffice to purchase industrial peace. In other countries such efforts have merged into larger strategies of 'corporatist mediation' between the main interest groups. Chapter 8 examines the very limited returns that accrued from the Irish State's efforts in this direction. Second, many of the new industries attracted to Ireland are local branches of multi-national concerns. One-half of the fixed assets of Irish registered industrial and service companies in the mid-1970s were owned by non-Irish interests (Sweeney, 1974, p. 277). Consequently many of the class positions typically associated with the ownership and control of European capitalist development are depleted in numbers within Ireland itself. The class structure therefore does not include the key figures in many of the largest economic concerns in the country, a feature characteristic of semi-peripheral societies. In consequence the State, in such situations, tends to gain autonomy over short range policy decisions due to the absence of a significant resident bourgeoisie. But equally the State is seriously constrained in its ability to redirect fiscal policy specifically and economic policy generally due to contractual commitments to multinational firms and banks.

SOCIAL POLICY

The withdrawal of the Mother and Child Scheme, with which the Coalition Government of 1948–51 sought to implement the preceding Fianna Fail Government's innovations included in the Health Act of 1947, led to an impasse in Irish social policy. All-party agreement on the desirability of the measure was inadequate to overcome the dual onslaught of the Church, concerned in particular by the provision for 'education in respect to motherhood', and medical consultants concerned about their incomes and professional prerogatives. Some minor innovations were undertaken during the 1950s, usually by Fianna Fail governments and often after extensive consultations with the Catholic hierarchy (Hensey, 1982, p. 147). But the impasse continued through the decade of deep economic recession and was only broken shortly after the 1958 commitment to economic planning. The resulting rapid expansion in the value and scope of State social services acted to underwrite the viability, although at a low standard of living, of small farmers and low skilled manual workers. But ironically the most substantial support from that expansion accrued to occupants of advantaged positions in the State bureaucracy and the liberal professions. Providers of services in health care, education and community welfare experienced substantial rises in their real incomes, a windfall that, more than in other European countries, contributed to the growth in public social expenditure (Maguire, 1984, p. 7).

The original planning documents advocated 'deferring further improvements in the social services until a steady growth in real national income is well established' (*Economic Development*, 1958, p. 24). By shifting the emphasis towards productive investment, a long-term universal gain was anticipated – the 'rising tide' whose arrival seemed so imminent to politicians during the 1960s. Despite that stricture social expenditure[1] grew more rapidly than any other area of public expenditure from 1961 until the early 1980s, increasing from the equivalent of 13 per cent of GNP in 1961 to 29 per cent in 1980 (Kennedy, 1981, p. 15).

Kennedy's (1974) study of Irish social expenditure between 1947 and 1974 identified three policy and expenditure phases: 1947–51, an expansionary phase coinciding with the duration of Coalition Government during which total social expenditure increased from 9.6 per cent of GNP to 14.9 per cent; a regressive phase between 1952 and 1962, during which social expenditure contracted as a percentage of GNP, and 1963–74, a period of renewed expansion. The later growth phase in fact extended to 1975, and while social expenditure declined somewhat in proportion to GNP in the two succeeding years, it grew again in 1978, and by 1980 exceeded the 1975 level. That rise, however, and its post-1980 continuation, failed to keep pace with public expenditure generally. Indeed 1974 marked the peak of social expenditure's share in total government spending: 49.4 per cent of the total.

The 1947–51 social expenditure boom was undertaken to meet urgent social needs against a background of services that were poorly developed by international standards. Rising expenditure was particularly concentrated in housing and hospital construction, which had been severely depressed during the war years. Fianna Fail had provided the institutional scaffolding for the expanding State role in 1947 by bringing together social welfare schemes under a new government department and consolidating local authority responsibility for health care delivery. The expansion was implemented, however, by the Coalition government that emerged after Fianna Fail's defeat in the general election of 1948, which was largely contested on social issues in the context of Britain's massive programme of social reconstruction.

Irish welfare provisions prior to the 1960s correspond to what Titmuss termed a 'residual' or 'marginal' model. Korpi (1985, p. 101) succinctly describes this model and its polar opposite, the 'institutional' model:

> The 'residual' or 'marginal' model is based on the assumption that private markets and the family are the natural and central ways of providing for the needs of citizens. Social policy is to come in only in emergency cases and on a temporary basis. The 'institutional' model of social policy, on the contrary, is based on the view that social policy is an integrated part of society, on par with markets, and offers public services and aid on the criteria of need, outside the market . . . social policy thus assumes a major role, potentially of the same scope and significance as the market, in affecting allocative and distributive processes in society.

The post-1961 expansion of social expenditure moved Ireland part way towards the 'institutional' model. It was one component of the general growth in State intervention in pursuit of economic development. In contrast to the 1947–51 growth phase, increased expenditure after 1961 was evenly distributed across programme areas. Health expenditure grew almost continuously after 1961, but housing and education received their greatest injection of State support in the 1960s. Social insurance and social welfare expenditure grew most rapidly during the 1970s, as eligibility was systematically extended through a succession of reforms: social insurance was extended to all categories of employees (1974), a comprehensive 'safety net' of Social Welfare Allowances was put in place to meet needs not explicitly provided for in the various categorical social welfare schemes (1975), and the pension age was lowered to 65 (1970). New schemes introduced over the 1970s include Deserted Wives' Benefit and Assistance, Unmarried Mothers' Allowances, Prisoners' Wives' Allowance, and Pay Related Benefit.

After 1975, other State commitments (notably the cost of servicing the public debt) increasingly competed with social expenditure. And within the social expenditure sphere, the rising level of unemployment after 1980 concentrated an ever growing share of total spending on social insurance and assistance income maintenance programmes. In mid-1984 nearly 30 per cent of all adults were recipients of social welfare payments[2] (Commission on Social Welfare, 1986, p. 94).

The payments they received were determined by a philosophy that broke the link with the Poor Law system. In the decades after independence, income maintenance payments had remained pegged to subsistence levels. From the mid-1960s this was abandoned, and the real value of the average social welfare benefit doubled in the succeeding 15 years (Commission on Social Welfare, 1986, p. 130). The final break of the long-standing link to the Poor Law system of 'Outdoor Relief' came in 1977. Legislation in 1975 had made provision for the abolition of the old 'Home Assistance' scheme, administered by local authorities in a highly variable, often capricious, manner in the form of charity. The new Supplementary Welfare Allowance Scheme, administered by the Department of Health, had a uniform set of payments and a standardised means test. It retained a discretionary element, however, which was seen as suitable for its role as the third, residual, level of the new Welfare State. The top tier in that apparatus is the system of entitlements provided for by workers contributing to the social insurance system. In 1974 social insurance contributions became mandatory for most categories of employees – non-manual employees whose earnings exceeded a set limit had been excluded from its provisions until that year – and benefit payments made pay-related. Five years later, that logic was extended to the level of contributions, which became pay-related. The middle tier was formed from programmes of social assistance, which were available only after a means test and had payment levels less than those for benefits, a difference justified by the fact that benefits are based on a record of insurance contributions while assistance is not. Since the social welfare system had developed in piecemeal fashion, both benefits and assistance were comprised of numerous categorical schemes, each providing for a specific contingency. In the 1970s the criteria for the various contingencies were rationalised and benefits were integrated into a comprehensive social insurance scheme. Supplementary Welfare became the 'safety net' available to cope with all other contingencies and such special and urgent financial hardships as were not anticipated by the framers of the various categorical schemes.

This consolidation was a logical 'catching up' with developments in Britain since the Beveridge Report of 1943. Yet it was more comprehensive and generous than comparable systems in place in other, more prosperous European countries, such as France. It appeared throughout the 1970s that income maintenance payments could expand, in real terms and in their coverage, almost without resistance. Competition for voter loyalty and short-term attempts to 'purchase' electoral support can explain some of this extraordinary willingness to extend the social welfare system's protection. The effect of this in class terms is clearest among small farmers. Their number had indeed declined, but remains large even by the standard of Spain or Portugal. A majority of farmers is in possession of land holdings insufficient to generate an adequate income. State social welfare arrangements made explicit provisions by which many such farmers are treated as if they were unemployed and available for work, implemented through the Smallholders Unemployment Assistance Act of 1965. These supports for farmers, who would otherwise have had to leave the land, were augmented after Ireland's EC membership. Under a 1975 EC Directive, member States are encouraged 'to ensure the continuation of farming, thereby maintaining a minimum population level or conserving the countryside in certain less favoured areas' (*Comprehensive Public Expenditure*, 1985, p. 107). These 'headage' payments for sheep and dairy farmers (funded half by the EC and half by the Irish government) were found, after 10 years in operation, to have failed to halt the decline in the size of the agricultural work-force, but to have 'had a positive impact on the depressed agricultural incomes in the regions' (*Comprehensive Public Expenditure*, 1985, p. 107).

The urban working class analogue to the 'Smallholders' scheme is 'Wet Time' Insurance, introduced in 1942 to provide for construction workers whose terms of employment did not contain provisions for payment during periods of inclement weather. This was extended in 1955 to cover other categories of manual workers, in effect transforming part-time employment into a full-time occupation through a State subsidy. More generally, social welfare payments provided income during the frequent periods of unemployment that punctuated the careers of those in low skilled, insecure forms of employment. Like the top of the class hierarchy, the bottom was formed of positions that were viable only in so far as State support was available. The difference was in the level of aid made available and the status conferred on the recipient.

The 'Wet Time' Scheme was abolished in 1985. By then, the main role of the social welfare system was income replacement for the ever expanding ranks of long-term unemployed. Unemployment compensation was no longer providing for a contingency, but for a way of life characteristic of many urban working class neighbourhoods.

FINANCING THE WELFARE STATE

The class implications of the replacement of a minimalist State by a Welfare State depends on how the expansion was financed. Until the mid-1970s, this was primarily through taxation; more recently, borrowing has paid for a substantial share of current government expenditure. Total tax revenue in 1960 was equivalent to 22 per cent of Ireland's Gross Domestic Product. In 1983, the tax burden stood at 41 per cent of GDP.

That rising tax burden is subordinate in importance to the trend in the relative contribution being made by various forms of taxation. Taxes differ in the sources from which they draw revenues – taxes on wages and salaries versus taxes on capital for example – and in progressivity. Progressive taxes impose a higher rate as income rises, regressive taxes a higher rate as income declines. The design, though not always the effect, of income taxation structures tends to be progressive, while that of taxes on sales tends to be regressive. The long-established welfare states of Scandinavia are characterised by financing through steeply progressive income tax, a substantial tax yield from corporations and capital, and a minimal reliance on taxes on goods and services, especially those which can be regarded as essential.

Table 4.1 compares Ireland's tax structure with those found in other European countries at two time points: 1965 and 1984. Ireland's tax burden in 1965 was low by Northern European standards, but by 1984 it was slightly higher than in the United Kingdom and West Germany. Nearly the identical change had occurred in Italy. Although taxation levels in Greece and Spain were still considerably below the European standard the trend in both countries was very similar to that in Ireland. Even in 1984, however, tax formed a far lower share of Ireland's national product than was the case in countries like Norway or the Netherlands. Ireland's tax burden, though not among the highest in Europe, is at the same level as more economically developed and wealthier countries.

The structure of Irish taxation is far removed from the European

TABLE 4.1 The structure of tax revenue: selected OECD countries, 1965 and 1984*

Tax Category	Ireland		UK		Germany		Holland		Norway		Italy		Greece		Spain	
	1965	1984	1965	1984	1965	1984	1965	1984	1965	1984	1965	1984	1965	1984	1965	1984
Income Tax: Personal	16.7	30.8	29.8	26.7	26.0	27.9	27.7	20.9	39.7	23.8	11.0	24.4	7.3	14.5	14.3	22.8
Income Tax: Corporate	9.1	3.3	7.2	11.5	7.8	5.4	8.1	5.7	3.8	16.5	6.9	9.8	1.9	2.6	9.2	5.0
Employer Social Security	3.3	9.3	7.6	9.1	14.4	19.1	12.6	17.9	10.2	14.9	34.2	24.0	26.9	14.2	21.7	31.1
Employee Social Security	3.2	5.4	7.2	8.5	11.8	15.9	15.3	18.6	—	5.6		6.9		14.9	6.5	7.1
Tax on Inheritance	1.9	0.3	2.6	0.5	0.2	0.2	1.1	0.4	0.3	.01	0.9	0.2	0.9	1.0	1.1	0.4
Tax on Property	15.1	3.8	14.5	12.4	5.8	3.3	4.4	3.4	3.1	1.8	7.2	2.9	10.3	2.7	6.4	3.8
Tax on Goods & Services	52.6	45.1	33.0	30.5	33.0	27.1	28.6	25.5	41.0	36.1	39.5	26.1	52.2	43.0	40.8	25.5
Tax as a % of GDP	26.0	39.5	30.6	38.5	31.6	37.7	33.6	45.5	33.2	46.4	27.3	41.2	20.6	35.2	14.7	28.4

* Totals exclude receipts from payroll taxes and assorted taxes not common to OECD countries.
SOURCE *Revenue Statistics of OECD Member Countries 1965–1983*, Paris: Organisation for Economic Cooperation and Development, 1985.

norm in both 1965 and 1984. Taxes on expenditure provide a remarkably large share of total tax revenue; further, the evidence of the downward trend is somewhat less than in the other developed countries between 1965 and 1984. Instead, in Ireland there was a relatively marked decline in the revenue shares from tax on property. inheritance tax and corporation income tax. Property tax declined through a series of electoral promises that were rewarded with success, notably the removal in 1978 of all taxes on domestic dwellings, which had been the mainstay of local authority revenue.

The career of capital taxation was more dramatic. Until 1973, estate duties were the only form of capital taxation in Ireland. Death duties were imposed on the estate of the deceased, and once the estate had been transferred to the beneficiaries, it was again taxed through succession and legacy duties at rates that varied with kinship or lack thereof to the deceased. The ease with which these taxes could be thwarted had become evident, and after 1973 a series of reforms were attempted as part of the agreement that led to the formation of the Fine Gael/Labour Coalition Government of 1973-77. Capital Acquisition Tax (1974) and an ill-fated Wealth Tax (1975) were introduced to replace the old estate duties, and a Capital Gains Tax (1975) was directed at profits from speculative activities. The central aim of these changes was to introduce greater equity into the tax system. To further that aim, the Coalition also reduced the reliance placed on expenditure taxes. The changes in the abstract managed to address the contradictory interests of the Coalition partners' constituencies. For example large farmers, part of Fine Gael's traditional electoral base, had found estate duties particularly burdensome in a period of rocketing land values (Sandford and Morrissey, 1985, p. 2).

In practice these reforms were so structured that they failed to introduce greater equity into the tax system. Such was the opposition to the proposal for a Wealth Tax that the package finally implemented was ineffectual. Other forms of capital taxation were effectively neutralised by generous exemptions, provisions for indexation with inflation, and tapering relief (decreasing the tax rate with the length of time an asset had been held). The total contribution of capital taxation to government revenue declined precipitously, even before Fianna Fail removed the Wealth Tax in 1978. The old estate duties had been more than three times more effective as a revenue source than the taxes that replaced them were in 1985 (Sandford and Morrissey, 1985, p. 50).

Low corporation income tax, and indeed low direct taxation generally, was consistently advocated by Fianna Fail as a stimulant to economic expansion. With the advent of formal economic planning, corporate income became sacrosanct. Export earnings were largely shielded from taxation after 1958 as part of the package of incentives to investment in industry. In 1978, this was replaced by a policy of a general tax on all profits from manufacturing at the 'negligible' rate of 10 per cent (Telesis Consulting Group, 1982, p. 140). This reluctance to tax the profits from enterprise, whether directly or through share-holders, along with the sacrosanct status of wealth in the form of capital, confers enormous advantages on proprietorial households relative to others with the same income level and facilitates the inheritance of wealth and its concentration among a small number of families.

Ireland's distinctive tax profile is very much a product of State policy. A high rate of expenditure taxation was explicitly sought because, to quote a Fianna Fail Minister for Finance, 'it discourages excessive spending but not earning or saving' (quoted in Sandford and Morrissey, 1985, p. 50). Tax revenue from capital or corporate income was limited in pursuit of the same objectives of economic expansion, and more recently rationalised as a basis for job creation.

The exceptions to this policy stance are the rise in personal income tax revenue and social insurance contributions. In real terms, the yield from personal income tax grew more than fivefold in the fifteen-year period 1965–80. This occurred not so much by policy as by the absence of policy in a period of rapid inflation. Tax allowances and the starting points of tax bands were not indexed to inflation. The result was that the proportion of personal income being taxed increased, as did the proportion being taxed at higher than the standard rate. Given the progressiveness of Ireland's income tax code, revenue from income tax grew far more rapidly than did incomes. with most wage earners crowded into the higher rate tax bands, the actual, as opposed to the nominal, progressivity of the tax system eroded, leaving little differen-tiation between the rates of tax paid by categories of employees despite the substantial variation in levels of income. The effect was dramatic. Over the 1970s, members of the working class received wage increases sufficient to narrow the gap separating them from middle class employees, only to find that taxation offset much of the gains. The 1970s were particularly favourable to members of proprietorial classes, whose ability to pay their taxes on a previous year rather than a current year basis conferred substantial advantages in a period of high inflation (Rottman and Hannan, 1981).

THE FRUITS OF ECONOMIC DEVELOPMENT: A REDISTRIBUTION STUDY

Irish State policy during the 1960s contained an important inconsistency. Administrators remained resolute in their conviction that only economic growth could generate social progress. The Third Programme, published in 1969, reiterated that investment in industry and agriculture would in time finance social expenditure sufficient to provide an 'equitable sharing' out of the nation's resources (quoted in Barrington, 1982, p. 95). At the same time, however, politicians hedged their bets by also committing massive sums to the supposedly non-productive social services like health care and housing and to an extensive network of income replacement programmes. Did these economic and social expenditures by the State in fact generate an 'equitable sharing' of the nation's newfound wealth? A reliable answer requires evidence from a formal redistribution analysis. Before we present the results of such an analysis, we briefly consider the extent of Ireland's economic progress after 1958.

ECONOMIC DEVELOPMENT AND NATIONAL INCOME

Economic development was sufficient to narrow the gap between Irish and British incomes – an important index of independence's benefits. By 1965, per capita income in Ireland reached 58 per cent of that in Britain, and by the mid-1970s had risen futher to two-thirds (64.9 per cent in 1976, using purchasing power parity-adjusted estimates by Summers and Heston, 1984). The extent of what was achieved is, if anything, understated in the per capita income figures, as Ireland's high dependency ratio means that it must draw on a comparatively small proportion of its population to generate income.

Table 4.2 offers a more diverse set of income comparisons in the form of the 1980 per capita incomes of the 12 EC member states and the USA and Japan, with all figures adjusted for differences in costs of living. Per capita income in Ireland is the third lowest in the EC, surpassing only those for Portugal and Greece. The northern European countries all have substantially higher income bases. Since it is the standards of living and social services found in countries like Britain, Holland and Belgium to which Ireland aspires, the income gap is significant. The pool of resources available for redistribution in Ireland

TABLE 4.2   *GNP in the 12 EC countries, Japan and the USA: 1980 purchasing-power adjusted comparisons, dollars*

Country	$
Germany	5516
France	5326
Italy	4253
Netherlands	5108
Belgium	5151
Luxembourg	5761
UK	4500
IRELAND	3027
Denmark	5336
Greece	2719
Spain	3438
Portugal	2344
USA	6656
Japan	4975

SOURCE   Eurostat (1983).

has expanded, but remains modest relative to what it is expected to finance.

MEASURING REDISTRIBUTION

Redistribution refers to the changes that occur in the financial well-being of families because the State imposes taxes and makes services available. Some taxes are collected directly from income earners, as with income tax, while others are collected either from consumers or from holders of property or other forms of capital. State benefits are sometimes received in the form of cash transfer payments, as with unemployment compensation or old age pensions; other benefits take the form of free or subsidised services, notably in the areas of health, education, housing and transportation. A redistribution analysis traces the flow of tax revenue from families to the State and the reverse flow of the benefits from the expenditure of that money, as augmented by borrowing, to families. The totality of the State's interventions may reduce income inequality between families.

Such an outcome is a recognised policy objective in Ireland, with the National Economic and Social Council (1975, p. 5) advising that taxes and benefits are instruments by which the State changes the distibution of income to one that is 'more equitable and fairer'. In this, the NESC adopted the traditional British approach of a 'Strategy of Equality'. In it, the State is the guarantor of the equality of certain vital outcomes for individuals and families rather than of equality of market income. Tax revenue is raised progressively and used to fund a system of social services sufficient that income-based inequalities do not extend to inequalities in the ability to obtain adequate medical care or transportation or to puruse an education (Le Grand, 1982).

The standard methodology of redistribution analyses is based on a comparison of the equality with which four types of income are distributed among families:

Direct income: All market income of a recurring nature earned by members of a household, including wages, salaries, income from self-employment, investments, rental income, pensions from previous employments and the value in cash of any free good or service regularly obtained through employment.

Gross income: Direct income *plus* all subsidies provided by the State through a transfer of money, including social welfare payments, education scholarships and Children's Allowances.

Disposable income: Gross income *minus* income tax and employee's social insurance contributions.

Final income: Disposable income *plus* the value in cash of the cost to the State of providing social services (education, medical care and housing, in particular) and *minus* the taxes on expenditure paid by members of the household when making purchases (customs and excise duties, Value Added Tax, licences and property tax.

The appropriate data for estimating the way in which those four types of income are distributed among Irish families are only available for 1973 and 1980. This chapter focuses on the 1980 data, which provides detailed information on the incomes of 7185 households included in the Household Budget Survey of that year. Where appropriate, comparisons will be made to the distributions found in 1973 (Rottman, Hannan et al., 1982), particularly where differences can be attributed to State policies. The sharing out of the various types of income will be examined first for income groups, then for classes, and finally for different stages of the family cycle.

OVERALL INCOME INEQUALITY

We first examine inequality among income groups in Ireland. By convention, this is done by first ranking households in ascending order of income and then dividing this ranking into ten categories (deciles) of households, each containing one-tenth of the total number of households.[3] Thus, in Table 4.3, we can see that the top decile, which represents ten per cent of all households, receives 29.7 per cent of all market (direct) income.[4] The bottom quintile (i.e. deciles nine and 10), representing 20 per cent of households, controls but one-half of one per cent of all income. That comparison starkly represents the degree of inequality in market income present in Ireland today. Moving from direct to gross income indicates the impact of cash transfers, like unemployment compensation, on the degree of inequality, with the share of the top diminishing somewhat and that of the bottom rising markedly. Overall, the bottom five deciles received 16.7 per cent of all direct income and 22.9 per cent of gross income.

The impact of income tax and social insurance is to continue the flow

TABLE 4.3: *The distribution of direct, gross, disposable income in 1980*

| Decile of population | Share of total income % | | | |
	Direct income 1980	Gross income 1980	Disposable income 1980	Final income 1980
Top 10%	29.7	27.0	25.7	25.2
2	18.3	16.9	16.2	16.1
3	14.3	13.3	13.0	13.0
4	11.5	10.9	11.0	11.0
5	9.5	9.2	9.3	9.3
6	7.7	7.6	7.9	7.9
7	5.7	6.1	6.6	6.6
8	2.8	4.5	5.1	5.3
9	0.5	3.1	3.5	3.9
Bottom 10%		1.6	1.7	1.9
Gini coefficient	47.64	39.26	36.67	35.50

SOURCE   Murphy (1984) and unpublished 1980 Household Budget Survey data.

of income away from the top of the income distribution and towards the bottom. In 1980, the bottom half of the income distribution received one-fourth (24.8 per cent) of disposable income, which is the most certain index of household spending power. Taxes on consumption and non-cash subsidies also are conducive to greater income equality, with the share of the bottom four deciles rising to 25.6 per cent. State interventions, then, clearly reduce the extent of inequalities generated in the markets.

A more 'equitable sharing' of the nation's income was not an empty promise. Economic development fostered greater income equality in Ireland, and State policies can be observed as active participants in furthering that effect (Rottman, Hannan, and O'Connell, 1984). Yet Ireland's 1980 income distribution has a greater degree of income inequality than found in most of Western Europe. The efficacy of the State's contribution to promoting equality is more difficult to evaluate through international comparisons. We can identify Sweden and the United States as representing extreme cases of, respectively, substantial and minimal redistributive effects from taxes and benefits and can locate Australia, Canada and the United Kingdom as occupying the middle ground (Stark, 1977).

The similarity of the Irish and UK patterns of income distribution and redistribution can be assessed comprehensively for 1973 and 1980. Income was more equally distributed in the UK than in Ireland in both years and redistributive effects were far stronger in the United Kingdom. The trends over time, however, are similar. Inequality of direct income actually increased in both countries but was effectively counterbalanced by more determined State interventions, especially in the income tax system to achieve redistribution. The pattern is broadly in line with that envisioned by the 'Strategy of Equality' – accepting substantial inequalities in market incomes and relying on progressive social expenditure funded by progressive taxation to limit the consequences. The evidence for both the UK and Ireland indicates that taxation became a more important source of redistribution over the 1970s. However in Ireland the effect of indirect taxes and benefits shifted from being negative in 1973 to positive in 1980. These trends are shown in Table 4.4 which reports measures of the redistributive effect of cash transfers, direct taxation and indirect subsidies and taxes for both Ireland and the UK. A minus sign indicates that the effect was to increase income inequality.

Redistribution is determined by two components: the progressivity of State interventions and the average level of tax and benefit. In the

TABLE 4.4   *The redistributive effects of transfers and taxes, Ireland and the UK, 1973 and 1980*

Redistribution via:	Ireland		United Kingdom	
	1973 %	1980 %	1973 %	1980 %
Cash transfers	15.0	17.6	19.4	21.8
Direct taxation	2.9	6.6	4.9	7.8
Indirect subsidies and taxes	− 3.0	3.2	3.0	2.4

The measure shown here is the Musgrave–Thin Index, defined as the percentage change in the Gini coefficient between two successive income concepts; i.e.

$$\frac{Gini_1 - Gini_2 \times 100}{Gini_1}$$

Irish case, the enhanced redistributive effect achieved in 1980 is largely attributable to the trends of rising tax rates and social welfare expenditures outlined earlier in the chapter. More money was involved but it was not being raised or distributed more progressively.

A recent study of the advanced capitalist societies concluded that 'when tax, transfer and expenditure programmes are viewed together, it is apparent that public expenditure programmes, particularly the provision of cash transfers, have been almost totally responsible for the changes in income distribution which governments have brought about.' (Saunders, 1984, p. 29). Ireland does not fully conform to this pattern. Rather, the impact of the State is more complex. For one thing, taxation is far from negligible in its redistributive impact. Second, Ireland's high dependency level (in terms of those too young or too old to participate in the labour force) diverts most redistribution to non-income earning households. If we look at redistribution among those households receiving market income, the international evidence draws our attention to the crucial role played by taxation:

> Redistributive processes decrease income inequality between and within active socio-economic groups. Although nearly all such groups are net losers in the redistributive process, the net loss is larger among those groups having higher original (market) incomes ... It is direct progressive taxes which are responsible for the major part of the income equalization, while cash transfers and benefits in kind do not make so significant a difference (Uusitalo, 1985, p. 168).

If that description is applicable to Ireland, then State interventions should contribute to an equalisation of incomes between class categories. In fact, Ireland's low national income and its aspirations to northern European standards of service provision, result in a tax burden which has curious effects on the distribution of income between classes and between households at different stages in the family cycle.

THE STATE AND CLASS INCOME INEQUALITIES

To examine income redistribution between classes, the households participating in the 1980 Household Budget survey are divided into 14 economic class categories, each representing a distinct market capacity. The size of the self-employed work force in Ireland, particularly the agricultural sector, makes a fourteenfold categorisation necessary to capture the important differences present in the resources for economic participation available to families. For example, farm households share a general type of market capacity – agricultural land – but differ in the income potential of their holdings. Such differences lead to class categories based on whether the farm uses paid labour and on the size of the holding. Employees are divided into white collar salaried earners, differentiated according to the educational qualifications their positions require, and manual workers, who bring varying levels of skill to the labour market. Self-employed professionals are treated as occupying the same class position as an employee with identical qualifications; professionals who are employers are treated as part of the proprietorial class. The categories also include a residual class of those who lack any identifiable current or former market capacity. Households in this residual category represent a diversity of situations – including data inadequacies in the survey.

Table 4.5a provides the average amounts earned by households in each class category and the average direct transfers received and taxes paid. Immediately below each comparision, the 1973–80 change is summarised. This summary figure expresses the 1980 average as a ratio of what was received or paid in 1973. The larger the ratio, the greater the amount of increase. Three changes within the table potentially altered the relative standing of class categories: direct income, cash transfer receipts and direct taxation. The net effect of these changes is reflected in each category's disposable income. Each class's experience can be readily evaluated relative to that of other classes or to the change ratio for all households in the sample (shown separately for each type

TABLE 4.5a *Average direct income, direct transfers, direct taxes, and disposable income in 1973 and 1980: class categories (in pounds per week)*

Class Category	Direct income 1973		Direct income 1980	Direct transfers 1973		Direct transfers 1980	Direct tax 1973		Direct tax 1980	Disposable income 1973		Disposable income 1980	N 1973	N 1980
Large proprietors	77.89	(2.53)	197.28	1.56	(2.97)	4.63	4.83	(6.46)	31.19	74.62	(2.29)	170.72	166	177
Small proprietors	38.33	(3.53)	135.41	1.90	(2.97)	5.65	2.50	(5.26)	13.15	37.73	(3.39)	127.91	307	287
Large farmers	65.33	(2.07)	131.25	1.99	(5.38)	10.71	1.16	(5.74)	6.66	64.16	(2.11)	135.30	261	190
Medium farmers	45.23	(2.32)	104.78	2.63	(4.36)	11.47	1.26	(4.83)	6.09	46.61	(2.36)	110.16	392	340
Small farmers	28.70	(2.74)	78.54	3.93	(4.12)	16.18	1.11	(5.83)	6.47	31.52	(2.80)	88.25	461	311
Marginal farmers	18.50	(2.53)	46.83	6.54	(4.10)	26.24	1.12	(2.73)	3.06	23.91	(2.93)	70.01	572	256
Higher professionals	72.67	(2.98)	216.20	1.33	(3.52)	4.68	11.73	(4.28)	50.22	62.27	(2.74)	170.66	353	428
Lower professionals	55.78	(2.74)	153.02	1.58	(3.16)	5.00	8.55	(4.28)	30.31	48.81	(2.74)	127.71	283	310
Intermediate non-manual	45.73	(2.74)	144.25	2.95	(3.16)	8.73	6.53	(3.55)	29.36	42.15	(2.62)	123.63	846	1015
Skilled manual	38.45	(3.15)	119.11	3.72	(2.96)	13.69	5.48	(4.50)	23.29	36.69	(2.93)	109.51	983	1128
Service workers	35.25	(3.10)	104.68	3.80	(3.68)	14.15	4.63	(4.25)	18.35	34.42	(2.98)	100.47	602	632
Semi-skilled manual	33.08	(3.15)	105.12	4.42	(3.72)	16.25	4.34	(3.96)	18.08	33.16	(2.92)	103.29	674	658
Unskilled manual	25.31	(3.18)	62.66	6.70	(3.68)	24.78	3.33	(4.17)	10.00	28.68	(3.11)	77.45	1020	816
Residual	8.71	(3.44)	29.92	6.63	(3.32)	21.98	0.45	(3.00)	3.46	14.90	(2.70)	48.44	699	524
Total	36.00	(3.20)	111.15	4.22	(3.38)	14.26	3.94	(4.81)	18.95	36.28	(2.93)	106.46	7739	7185

Figures in parentheses express the 1980 average as a ratio of that for 1973.

of income) and to the change in the Consumer Price Index over those years, in which any ratio greater than 2.73 represents a real increase.

Direct incomes grew on average by an eighth in real terms in 1973–80, the culmination of the era of economic expansion that began in the late 1950s. The scope for State interventions grew even more substantialy over the 1970s: the average value of cash transfers received by households grew by 24 per cent in real terms and direct tax revenue (the yield from income tax and social insurance contributions) by a massive 76 per cent.

Direct income is the benchmark against which to evaluate those State interventions. Overall, market based income differences between classes (rather than between individual households) tended to decline, as the highest rates of income growth were experienced by lower income categories. This applies both generally and within each of the main subgroups: non-agricultural proprietors, farm households, white collar employees and working class households. Unskilled manual workers represent an exception to those trends, experiencing a decline in their real market incomes.

The allocation of cash transfers reinforced that pattern: while earned income increased by a factor of 3.2, transfers on average grew by 3.38. The bulk of that transfer went to farm households. Farmers recorded the most substantial increase in the size of the average transfer, counterbalancing their relatively poor rate of market income growth. In general though, cash transfers did not tend to have a major equalising impact on class category average incomes.

Direct taxes in 1980 were nearly five times greater on average than in 1973. The rate of increase was such that it exceeded the increase in earnings; and the situation was of course worse for those low income classes which experienced declining real incomes. In consequence, the gains made by many categories through the market were eroded by the structure of the direct tax system. This was true of all working class categories and of intermediate non-manual workers (sometimes referred to as the 'lower' middle class, consisting of employees in junior administrative, sales and technical occupations). The rising tax burden on proprietorial households is partly due to their increased reliance on supplementary wage incomes. Certainly, more farm households were in receipt of such income in 1980 and wage income formed a larger share of such categories' total earnings, a change reflected in their rising tax payments.

When disposable income is examined, we find that all farmer categories were better off after direct State interventions. This is in marked contrast to categories of employees, of which all save unskilled manual workers were worse off once direct transfers and taxes had been allocated. Non-agricultural proprietors were on average worse off in 1980 if they belonged to the 'large proprietor' category and better off, quite significantly so, if they were 'small proprietors'. The tax advantage still conferred by property ownership is most starkly highlighted when the tax rate of large proprietors (who average £197 in weekly income) is compared with that of unskilled manual workers (who averaged a weekly £63 income): in 1980 they shared a common tax rate of 16 per cent. Higher professionals and skilled manual workers paid more of their income as tax, but the difference between their rate and that of low income categories was not substantial (23 and 20 per cent, respectively).

Farmers enjoyed a unique relationship with the cash transfer system. Regardless of their income levels, all farm categories received substantially more in cash transfers than their households paid in taxation. This contrasts sharply with the experience of all employee categories, except unskilled manual workers, where the State emerges as the net beneficiary. Cash transfers were allocated among classes in a progressive manner, but taxes were only weakly progressive. In practice, this had two main effects. First, for employees the State actions left income differences based on the market largely unaltered. Second, State policies generally acted to improve the relative financial situation (*vis-à-vis* categories of employees) of families earning their income mainly through family property.

Income tax and cash transfers represent the visible hand of the State. The tax protests of the early 1980s, drawing tens of thousands to trade union-led demonstrations, were the product of real inequities in the relationship of the Irish State to various classes.However, indirect taxes and non-cash subsidies may exercise as significant an impact on the well-being of families, but their effects are poorly understood and not easily quantified. Table 4.5b extends the examination of class differences to include indirect subsidies and indirect taxes. Here disposable income serves as the benchmark. Expenditure on social services was distributed in both 1973 and 1980 in a manner that did not vary greatly in proportion to income levels. Subsidies to working class households in 1973 tended to be higher than the national average: farmers received an average slightly below the national figure, as did all three categories of middle class employee households. The 1973–80 changes reflect both the growth in and restructuring of the flow of subsidies (as well as some differences in the methodology by which

TABLE 4.5b *Average disposable income, indirect subsidies, indirect taxes and final income in 1973 and 1980: class categories*

Class category	Disposable income		Indirect subsidies		Indirect taxes		Final income	
	1973	1980	1973	1980	1973	1980	1973	1980
Large proprietor	74.62 (2.29)	170.72	5.85 (3.82)	22.36	12.00 (2.37)	28.44	68.47	164.64 (2.40)
Small proprietor	37.73 (3.39)	127.91	5.95 (3.58)	21.29	10.19 (2.11)	21.49	33.48	127.71 (3.81)
Large farmer	64.16 (2.11)	135.30	5.37 (5.01)	26.93	8.72 (2.33)	20.32	60.81	141.90 (2.33)
Medium farmer	46.61 (2.36)	110.16	5.70 (4.23)	24.09	6.96 (2.92)	20.32	45.36	113.92 (2.51)
Small farmer	31.52 (2.80)	88.25	4.96 (4.16)	20.63	5.87 (2.69)	15.81	30.61	93.08 (3.04)
Marginal farmer	23.91 (2.93)	70.01	4.72 (4.59)	21.66	4.48 (2.66)	11.92	24.15	79.76 (3.30)
Higher professional	62.27 (2.74)	170.66	5.21 (3.93)	20.45	12.33 (2.12)	26.09	55.14	165.02 (2.99)
Lower professional	48.81 (2.62)	127.71	5.40 (2.75)	14.87	9.57 (2.34)	22.43	44.64	120.16 (2.69)
Intermediate non-manual	42.15 (2.93)	123.63	4.89 (3.63)	17.77	8.79 (2.35)	20.66	38.25	120.74 (3.16)
Skilled manual	36.69 (2.98)	109.51	7.23 (2.99)	21.59	8.73 (2.30)	20.11	35.18	111.00 (3.16)
Service worker	34.42 (2.92)	100.47	6.09 (3.48)	21.17	7.96 (2.31)	18.35	32.55	103.29 (3.17)
Semi-skilled manual	33.16 (3.11)	103.29	6.68 (3.63)	24.27	7.70 (2.47)	18.99	32.13	108.57 (3.38)
Unskilled manual	28.68 (2.70)	77.45	6.36 (3.57)	22.70	6.57 (2.06)	13.52	28.48	86.63 (3.04)
Residual	14.90 (3.25)	48.44	4.20 (3.96)	16.62	2.73 (2.25)	6.14	16.36	58.92 (3.60)
Total	36.28 (2.93)	106.46	5.69 (3.66)	20.85	7.45 (2.46)	18.31	34.52	107.00 (3.10)

Figures in parentheses express the 1980 average as a ratio of that for 1973.

benefits were estimated and allocated for families). The average indirect subsidy grew more substantially than had cash transfers. Farm households recorded the highest rates of growth in real terms, while working class categories fared slightly less favourably from the change. Generally, there was only a weak relationship between the size of a category's income or its rate of change between 1973 and 1980 and the magnitude in growth in the average indirect subsidy it received. That lack of progressivity of impact was not compensated for by the distribution of the indirect tax burden. For all households, with the exception of one of the farm categories, such taxes decreased on average in real terms over the period.

The net effect of all indirect State intervention is manifest in the difference between disposable and final incomes. Those interventions did provide a cushion for farmers and other groups which experienced relatively poor growth in their market income. Outside these groups, however, indirect State interventions brought about little change as compared with the distribution of disposable income, and over the 1973–80 period all classes experienced an improvement, insofar as their rate of growth of final income exceeded that of disposable income. Such a lack of differentiation had the result that indirect interventions largely reproduced the inequalities evident in disposable income.

The overall effect of State interventions, both direct and indirect, can be gauged by comparing direct with final income. Here some gain by working class households is clear as the growth in final income exceeded that for direct income in all cases. The gain was greater still for farm classes, and the working class would have benefited far more if increases in real incomes and in the value of transfers had not been counterbalanced by trends in taxation, which either 'clawed back' some of the gains (in the case of income tax and Pay Related Social Insurance – PRSI) or were largely income neutral (indirect taxation). The 'residual category', comprised of households without a current or past main source of market income, obviously gained significantly in the course of the redistribution process. However, the gain was formed from a series of relatively small advantages accumulated during the process, rather than a clear preferential treatment at any one stage in particular, and the 1980 impact was no stronger than that in 1973.

In class terms, redistribution over the period was primarily from non-manual employees to farm households and, to a lesser degree, to unskilled manual workers. Non-agricultural proprietors were largely unaffected by changes in State interventions, as were most working class households. In social class terms, State interventions tended to maintain differentials based on the markets.

This leaves some class categories substantially dependent on State support, particularly in the form of cash transfers. In 1980 just over one in every five households (21.8 per cent) received more than half of their gross income from the State in the form of such transfers. Marginal farmers and unskilled manual workers were particularly so dependent: 42 per cent of the former and 45 per cent of the latter derived half of their cash income from the State. But that dependence was general to small farmers and to all working class categories. Even among skilled manual workers, one household of every five got the bulk of its income from State transfers. Despite their very different forms of market capacity, small farmers and low-skilled manual workers shared a common dependence on the State as their main source of income.

In evaluating that income support, its origins in the taxation system cannot be ignored. The only clear redistribution of income across class boundaries is that from non-manual employees to farmers generally and to unskilled manual workers and the residual category. Even there, the contribution made by a class is not rigorously tied to its direct income. A truly massive State effort seems to achieve very little in the nature of that 'class abatement' which was Marshall's (1950) rationale for the Welfare State. The extension of social citizenship rights in capitalist societies was to provide a distributive principle that would contend with those based on the capital and labour markets. It has not been achieved in Ireland.

THE STATE AND HORIZONTAL EQUITY: FAMILY CYCLE REDISTRIBUTION

A particular family income can bring affluence or subsistence depending on the income needs represented by the number and ages of family members that the income must support. Family cycle stages represent the changes in composition and size that most families experience, regardless of their social class or income. We can think of these stages as typical situations of contrasting income 'earning power' and expenditure needs. Welfare State policies can usually be more clearly tied to objectives seeking to equalise incomes, not between income groups but between families at different states in the family cycle. The very concept of social insurance assumes that there is to be a transfer of income from those times at which a participant is in receipt of an income to other times (say, retirement or disability) when income has ceased.

Household Budget Surveys have been used in a series of studies on income inequalities and redistribution of income over the family cycle (Rottman and Hannan, 1981, 1982). The analysis is necessarily cross-sectional (see O'Higgins, 1984, or Uusitalo, 1985, for general discussions of the resulting limitations) but it does indicate the extent to which families with the same income are being treated differently by the State in accordance with the burdens dependency imposes. Direct incomes rose most substantially over the 1970s for households with potential to add 'earning power': young married couples and families with older children in residence. The main trend in the allocation of cash transfers was a shift away from households in which families were being raised, towards the elderly. Families with children of school age or younger received a smaller share of cash transfers in 1980 than in 1973. For example, the average cash transfer received by a family with young children barely kept pace with inflation over the 1970s, while that made available to families with an elderly head of household grew nearly fourfold.

That shift in the flow of cash transfers was exacerbated by taxation policies. The structure of the tax system simply failed to differentiate among families based on their number of dependents. The change has drastic implications. Families in the 'formation' stage experienced an average tax burden of 10.5 per cent in 1973; by 1980, that had risen to 16.6 per cent.

The distribution of disposable incomes across the family cycle stages reflects a general transfer of income to the elderly from all other stages of the cycle. Families with young dependent children experienced the most substantial disimprovement in the situation over the 1970s.

This was not mitigated by the distribution of indirect benefits (through education, health care, housing and transportation subsidies). These too were, in aggregate, directed to the advantage of the elderly. The trend is particularly strong given that one component of such State benefits – that to education – is specifically designated for families raising children. Indirect taxation is not apparently collected in a manner that differentiates on the presence of dependent children, and its impact is essentially neutral with respect to family cycle inequalities.

The overall impact of the State on family cycle inequalities is to the financial disadvantage of households raising families, and this disadvantage was more pronounced in 1980 than in 1973. Redistribution was dominated by the transfer of resources from families at work, irrespective of their burden of dependency, to households in which most or all of their members were past retirement age. Families raising young children were disproportionately used as a source of tax revenue and were relatively neglected as recipients of social services, whether in cash or as benefits in kind. The irony of such outcomes in the Irish context will be pursued in the next chapter. Here, they suggest a failure to use State taxation and social expenditure coherently in pursuit of official social policies of various governments. It would be reasonable to expect that the combination of a progressive income tax code, a declining reliance on regressive indirect tax, and a massive rise in the average real benefit being distributed by the State would be redistributive. Further, that redistribution should serve to dilute the income differences that separate social classes and take into account a range of income needs that families experience. This did not occur. State policies in Ireland blunted the impact of the redistribution mechanisms established in the 1960s and 1970s. We can single out two trends as particularly important. Income tax, impressively progressive on paper, in practice imposed a relatively low burden on proprietors with substantial incomes, and taxed employees with moderate or low incomes at a relatively high rate. At the same time, the value of tax exemptions for child dependents declined in real terms and was then eliminated. The second trend is State subsidies, both in cash and through services, which were concentrated on the elderly, a group traditionally seen as the 'deserving poor'.

CONCLUSION

The expansion of the Irish State is one of the most striking features of the country's recent history. It was justified by the promise that the result would be, first, economic development and, second, social progress in the form of a more 'equitable sharing' of the substantially augmented national wealth. Certainly a massive increase did occur in the State's commitment to income maintenance programmes – both in the range of contingencies covered and the level of support provided – and to social services at the northern European standard. Yet the high levels of expenditure and the taxation needed to finance it did not significantly reduce income inequality and certainly failed to abate the importance of class in determining life chances. Further, some of the by-products of State policy are discordant with the very ethos that legitimises State interventions, as in the treatment of families at the child rearing stages of the family cycle.

The modest returns from the State's redistributive efforts are unremarkable, given the international experience. They are disappointing only relative to the amount of resources assembled by one of Europe's poorer countries for that purpose. We earlier expressed the view that the State's role in class formation is wider in Ireland than in most capitalist societies, though it may have parallels in other countries of the European semi-periphery. This is clearest in the number of positions concentrated at the top and the bottom of the class structure which would not be viable in the absence of massive State subsidies.

The State underpins a class of substantial proprietors. Entrepreneurs are facilitated by a wealth of subsidies to their business concerns and a low rate of corporate income tax. The viability of the class is further assisted by the imposition of low rates of personal taxation relative to employees with comparable incomes and a reluctance to tax either capital gains or the transfers that facilitate the retention of assets within a family. For all but the most modest of entrepreneurs, the State provides a safety net, one that enhances the profitability of the position and the current incumbent's ability to continue to fill it and, later, bequeath it to his or her family.

At the bottom of the class structure, farmers with smallholdings and/or poor quality land benefit from a substructure of State and EC supports. This leaves a self-employed farm sector in Ireland far more substantial than that found even in Spain or Portugal, yet less than a third of Irish farmers operate commercially viable enterprises (see Chapter 9). The low skilled members of the urban working class share this dependency on the State but lack the dignity of an occupation. State policies have focused on generating employment in manufacturing, but have located the resulting opportunities away from those areas in which the old indigenous industry was contracting. The distribution of the tax burden and of the benefits of State expenditure have inhibited the possibility that the children of such families can transfer to the new white collar positions created over the 1960s and 1970s. Their relatively low incomes were diminished, first by the emphasis on expenditure taxation, and later by the interaction of inflation with the income tax code. This restricted their ability to take advantage of the educational system to obtain the qualifications that offer the promise of employment. Most working class families at the middle stages of the family cycle must rely on income earned by children residing within the household to meet their expenditure consumption. This both maximises the family's tax liability and minimises the likelihood that children from such families will participate in second and third level education.

This is connected with a distinctive feature of the Irish Welfare State: the State's extensive commitments to finance services and its lack of control over how the taxpayers' money is spent. Education and health care remain under the firm control of those subsidiary groups which provide the service. The State acts as the financier and paymaster, but private institutions, the most powerful among them being the Catholic Church, make the key decisions on how that money will be used. In fact, in areas like education, the role of the State is often shadowy. Few recipients of the benefit of a State-subsidised university education or their families associate the taxes they pay with the State transfer they are receiving. This too is a theme pursued in later chapters.

For this chapter, the final question is why the Irish State made the transition from minimalist to a welfare state on par with countries that possess far higher national incomes. Some of that growth was justified as investment in human resources. Other expenditure, 'unproductive' like that on housing, was required to ameliorate problems created by the development process.

Economic growth reversed Ireland's historical demographic patterns, causing a sharp rise in the dependency ratio. The resulting demand for social services was exacerbated by rapid urbanisation. Economic development also spawned a set of organised interests. As the State sought to play a mediating role through establishing and ultimately participating in corporatist structures, its commitments and thus its expenditure, rose. Public expectations for enhanced social services were facilitated by the proximity to the British Welfare State. The standard of comparison for the State was thus a country with a far larger national income to draw upon. Finally, the political system was restructured into a competition between two populist, cross-class parties. This led to State expansion, even if only partly implemented. The buoyancy of tax revenues in the 1960s and early 1970s made such promises easy to make and implement; it also pushed back the time at which the consequences of the rapid State expansion would be critically examined.

Ireland's class structure is very much a product of the post-1958 State expansion. It is in many respects a curious product. In particular, cash transfers became essential for many households to retain their position in the class hierarchy. This produces a problem without an apparent solution: State support cannot be withheld, but neither can it be increased to a level sufficient to provide an income above the poverty line. The only option is simply to maintain the most disadvantaged sections of the economically active population in their marginality. And if there are children, that marginality will be perpetuated in the next generation. Since dependence on the State cuts across fundamental distinctions, such as that between property owners and wage earners, there seems to be little prospect for political mobilisation to end the impasse.

NOTES

1. Social expenditure is here taken to include expenditure on health, social welfare, education and housing.
2. Excluding children's allowances.
3. The use of household level data means that this analysis can take no account of variations in household size or composition and how they influence the welfare comparisions.
4. The Gini coefficient shown in Table 4.3 is a standard summary index of income inequality. It is stated as a percentage that can vary from zero, when all incomes are equal, to 100, where all of the nation's income is being received by a single household.

5 State, Class and Family

INTRODUCTION

In word at least, Irish State policy has been least ambiguous in the area of the family. The content of that policy until the 1970s, however, was mainly defined by the Catholic Church, not the State. A series of constitutional and legislative provisions ignored, by and large, the viewpoints of minority religions and meticulously implemented the values of conservative Catholic social thinking, within which the family is the basic unit of society (Whyte, 1980, pp. 26–66). Church and State harmony on the role of the family provided the foundation for the extraordinarily stable and conservative society that prevailed from 1922 until the 1960s. It legitimised and supported both the distinctive kinship and demographic patterns characteristic of a class structure based on the ownership of family property and the substantial class inequalities present in that society.

From the 1960s, the impact of State policy on the family has been as evident but less consistent. The rising tide of economic prosperity and the increased activism of the Irish State left their mark on the Irish family. Irish people today marry at much the same age and form families of much the same size as in other European countries, ending Ireland's demographic uniqueness (Walsh, 1968). Perhaps the clearest indicator of the extent and suddenness of the change in the Irish family is the labour force participation rate of married women: in 1961, one in twenty was in the work force; in 1987, one out of every five married women is a labour force participant.

Such a transformation is the product of a variety of causes, ranging from new opportunities for female employment, through higher aspirations in standards of living, to the EC regulations that forced the removal of legal barriers. Though such changes in the family and in gender roles are linked directly or indirectly to State policies, it is not clear that those policies are today inspired by the ideals of Catholic social thinking. Certainly the evidence from the last chapter on the impact of State expenditure and taxation suggests that such influence is at best weak and inconsistent. Greater State activism in Ireland has been associated with a decline in the financial support given to families raising young children relative to other types of households. Generally, State policy has failed to channel the benefits of economic growth toward the support of families or to reduce the extent of social class differences in demographic practices and financial hardship during child rearing.

The record on social legislation offers further inconsistencies. Legislation by various governments over the past 20 years, at times prodded by an increasingly independent and liberal judiciary (McMahon, 1985; Robinson, 1986), provided for labour market equality, contraception, equal treatment of spouses in property rights, and legal recognition and social welfare provision for categories such as deserted wives and unmarried mothers. Yet relative to the extent of the economic change Ireland experienced, and compared with countries like Spain and Italy, the family has not altered as greatly as might have been anticipated. The decline in fertility, for example, was less pronounced than in Spain and legislative provisions for changing sexual mores and marital arrangements have been less far-reaching. The decisive rejection by the Irish electorate in June 1986 of a constitutional amendment to permit divorce legislation suggests that if the foundations of conservative Ireland have been radically undermined, much of its moral and cultural structure persists.

This chapter considers the continuities and discontinuities in State policies and their impact on the family across six and a half decades of independence. The next section focuses on the period before 1960. It begins with a brief historical account of the emergence in the late nineteenth century of a distinctively orthodox moral and institutional setting within which gender roles and family reationships were, and to some extent still are constructed. The State adapted uncomplainingly to that setting upon independence and acted to uphold the family as defined by Catholic social and moral principles. This took the form of insulating the family from forces of change by a series of prohibitions: of divorces, of contraception, of married women's wage employment. The second section of the chapter looks at the more interventionist period that began around 1960, when the State made legislative and economic provision for changing familial and gender roles. We ask whether this period of State activism has altered basic inequalities in family life chances and demographic patterns. Two main criteria are considered: social class differences in marriage and fertility rates and the allocation of roles by gender within the family and the economy. The chapter concludes with an assessment of the emergent role of the Irish State as a primary agent shaping family structures and relationships. Here a basic concern is the extent to which the State today is acting autonomously from the Church in setting policies for the family.

THE ERA OF ORTHODOXY AND PATRIARCHY

The moral entente between Church and State in independent Ireland consolidated a normative environment in which sexuality was directed into orthodox Christian channels, its active expression being restricted to marriage, and within marriage its enjoyment morally subservient to the procreative function. Marriage was in consequence entered into with an expectation of high fertility. That expectation appears to have had a significant effect on the willingness ('ability' might be a more accurate description) of people to marry and the age at which they chose to marry. Since the late nineteenth century there have been significant social class differentials in marriage rates. Economic and class forces mainly governed the life chance of marrying and forming a family of one's own.

Fertility control therefore operated primarily through constraints on marriage – the 'preventive check' advocated by Malthus – and which had last been characteristic of the rest of Catholic Europe in the eighteenth century (Hajnal, 1965). In Ireland, this method of control became prevalent only at the end of the last century, when about 30 per cent of Irish men and 25 per cent of Irish women never married. The comparable figures for most of Western Europe at that time were about 10 per cent for both sexes (see Walsh 1968; 1984). But even this understates the uniqueness of the Irish marriage pattern. For those who did marry, the event was greatly delayed. The average age at marriage was 33 years for grooms and 29 for brides, nearly six years older than the average for men in most West European countries. Moreover, despite an abnormally low marriage rate and late age at marriage, marital fertility in Ireland up to the 1960s was substantially greater than in other European countries. This is true even if one limits the comparison to countries similar in religion and level of economic development (Spain, Portugal, Austria, for example) and indeed was at least as high as most Latin American countries for which data are available (Walsh, 1968, p. 5).

The historical specificity of this Irish marriage and fertility pattern is quite marked: Table 5.1 summarises information from eight censuses over the 1841–1981 period. High non-marriage rates emerged around the turn of the century and lasted into the 1950s. But by 1981 marriage was as popular as before the Great Famine, approaching normal European levels for the first time in this century.

Although Ireland had a unique level of non-marriage, this propensity to delay or avoid marriage was differentiated by social class. Given no

TABLE 5.1 *Percentage of females never married, in age groups 25–34 and 35–44 years in Ireland 1841 to 1981*

Age Group	1841	1871	1901	1925	1946	1961	1971	1981
25–34	28	38	53	53	48	37	26	22
35–44	15	20	28	30	30	23	18	11

SOURCE *Census of Population of Ireland* 1981, Vol. II, Table G.

effective control on fertility within marriage, expectations of large numbers of children acted as a brake on a decision to marry, particularly in poor economic circumstances. Table 5.2 gives the 1936 marriage rates for a range of occupational groups. Each rate refers to the percentage of males who had never married and who were aged between 45 and 54 at the time of the census.

These marriage rates reflect the economic and social realities of the newly independent Ireland. But so too did the level of emigration. Emigration in the decades at the turn of the century was so prevalent that by the 1926 Census only one-half of the original cohort of Irish people then aged 45–64 still remained in the country. For those remaining, the constraints on marriage were considerable and the life chance of being able to start one's own family was differentiated by social class. This is particularly evident for the agricultural population. Farm inheritors had quite high rates of marriage, non-inheritors negligible rates, and farm labourers low rates. Inequalities within the non-agricultural population were nearly as pronounced.[1] Those born into the lower portions of the class structure had quite rational

TABLE 5.2 *Percentage of males aged 45–54 never married, in selected occupational groups in 1926*

	Farmers	Relatives assisting on farms	Other agricultural occupations (mostly farm labourers)	Other non-agricultural productive occupations	Non-agricultural labourers	Employees & managers (non-agricultural)	Professional occupations	All males 45–54
Percentage never married	20.5	83.9	40.9	22.5	27.8	13.3	19.0	31.4

SOURCE *Census of Population of Ireland, 1926, Vol V. Part II, Table 4A.*

expectations of impoverishment from the high fertility that would result from marriage. Given the dominance of small-scale family property in the economy, marriage decisions were largely determined by the timing and process of inheritance. This set the balance of power within families decisively in the hands of parents and especially the father. Patriarchy was, and in some areas of the economy remains, a potent force. The position of women within these economic arrangements was particularly weak. Their options were either to acquiesce or to leave the system – through emigration – or by refusing to marry if they remained. From the late 1930s onwards such strategies were increasingly adopted (Hannan and Hardiman, 1978).

Given that sexual activity outside marriage was rare in Ireland – as evidenced in a low rate of illegitimate births and the absence up to the 1960s of artificial birth control – what accounts for this extraordinary level of control of sexual activity? Three factors were crucial: the strength of Irish Catholicism; the mainly familial character of the economy up to the 1950s; and finally, an institutional alliance between Church and State which, from the 1920s to the 1960s, supported traditional familial arrangements.

RELIGIOUS ORTHODOXY

The boundaries of the new southern State were carefully drawn in 1922 so as to appropriate the maximum number of Protestant constituents for the six northern counties remaining within the United Kingdom. The result was a Free State which was recorded in the 1926 Census as 90 per cent Roman Catholic. The character of the new State was fixed by more than the overwhelming numerical strength of the largest denomination. Compared to other European Catholics, even in Spain and Italy, Irish Catholics are remarkably orthodox in their religious beliefs and highly attentive to formal religious practice. Today, over 80 per cent of Irish adults attend Mass at least once a week, a rate three to four times higher than in most European countries (Fogarty et al., 1984, p. 8). Orthodoxy is also strongly reinforced by a school system in which virtually all of first level and most of second level education is under direct Church control.

The persistence in this century of such traditional Christian beliefs and practices, when combined with the significance in Ireland of local communal forms of social organisation, promotes equally orthodox beliefs concerning the family and marriage (Fogarty et al., 1984, pp. 39–55). A substantially higher proportion of people in Ireland than in other European countries express a belief in lifelong monogamy, in an orthodox Christian view of a morally directed sexuality, in the importance of children and shared religious/moral beliefs as a prerequisite for a happy marriage, and in the need for parent-child relationships to be based on a stable relationship between spouses. Attitudes to divorce are generally negative. In European comparisons, substantially lower proportions of Irish respondents agree that such 'grounds for divorce' as violence, unfaithfulness, or spouses ceasing to love one another provide 'sufficient reasons' for it to occur.

Today, however, orthodoxy is not monolithic. Irish beliefs and attitudes about sexuality, marriage and divorce are closest to those of southern European Catholic countries like Italy, Spain and Portugal and substantially more 'traditional' than British or North European views. On the other hand, Irish beliefs and attitudes toward gender role equality tend to be much closer to the British viewpoint and thus more liberal than the average European view – particularly the southern European view (Fogarty *et al.*, 1984, pp. 39–55).

The structure and content of interpersonal relationships within the conventional family in Ireland remains closely regulated by orthodoxy. The 'plausibility structures' (Berger, 1967) which define and maintain Catholic beliefs on marriage and family life retain considerable coherence and power. Beliefs, values and expectations regarding sexual access, procreation and parent-child obligations are based on religious tenets which are themselves inculcated within a family and school system which is, by twentieth-century European standards, highly religious. High levels of weekly church attendance and local socio-communal support networks reinforce these beliefs and expectations.

INHERITANCE AND ECONOMIC OPPORTUNITIES

If the religious orthodoxy of the Irish population persists at an extraordinary level, the economic support for traditional family structures is greatly diminished. The family gained coherence first from a trend of 'de-industrialisation' only to lose that underpinning with the post-1958 era of industrialisation. From the 1860s, the Irish economy was being incorporated as a dependent regional segment of the larger British Isles economy. The loss of employment opportunities in industry was a persistent and cumulative trend until the 1930s. This coincided with the rise to dominance of small scale family agriculture.

In 1926, 55 per cent of the male labour force was engaged in family employment. With access to secure economic positions for each new youth cohort taking up employment largely determined by familial inheritance, enormous power was concentrated in the hands of the father. This combination of authoritarian family patterns and an authoritarian Catholic Church, provided the historically active ingredients for what outside observers (Arensberg, 1937; Arensberg and Kimball, 1940; Messenger, 1969) saw as an archaic quality that made Ireland, in the middle of this century, quite distinct from the rest of Europe.

STATE ACQUIESCENCE

A formal separation of Church and State in the regulation of marriage resulted from the disestablishment of the Church of Ireland in 1870. Civil law regulates both marriage and marriage breakdown. With independence, however, that law has institutionalised orthodox Christian – and since 1937, Catholic – principles (Duncan, 1979, p. 26).

The basis for Church and State partnership dates back to the mid-nineteenth century when the Church worked in close co-operation with Catholic political movements that won successive battles with the UK government to gain control over schools for Catholic children and to disestablish the local Episcopalian Church. It also evolved a substantial role in the provision of hospital facilities. So when the new southern State gained independence, the Catholic Church could build on its base as the 'church of the people' and on the shared experience of the long struggle against a foreign oppressive power.

The original 1922 constitution of the Free State, which was agreed in negotiations with the UK government, contained no explicit religious or moral overtones, it was 'an essentially republican constitution on continental lines' emphasising the principle of the sovereignty of the people as the fundamental and the exclusive source of all political authority (Kohn, 1932). Indeed, it provided scope for divorce in a limited range of circumstances (Whyte, 1980, pp. 24–61; Duncan, 1979). The 1937 Constitution, however, was explicitly ethnic and religious in its overtones and in some of its provisions. It formally affirmed the 'special position' of the Catholic Church in Article 44 (removed in 1972) as 'the guardian of the faith of the great majority of the citizens', and in other 'moral' and institutional provisions supported that position. Chief among these was the affirmation of 'the family as the natural primary and fundamental unit group of society, as a moral institution possessing inalienable and imprescribable rights antecedent to and superior to all law' (Article 41.1). In the same article it recognised the special role in the common good that women play in the home and in so doing affirmed that 'the state shall, therefore, endeavour to ensure that mothers shall not be obliged by economic necessity to engage in labour to the neglect of their duties in the home' (Article 41.2.2); and to 'guard with special care the institution of marriage' (41.3.1). It was in pursuit of that same goal that it was affirmed that 'No law shall be enacted providing for the dissolution of marriage' (41.3.2). The 1937 Constitution further strengthened the family by defining it 'as the primary and natural educator', emphasising the freedom of parents to choose their children's schools, and the availability of reasonable aid to bodies engaged in educational provision, 'with particular regard to the right of parents especially in the matter of their children's religious and moral formation' (Article 42.4).

Until the 1960s, this distinctive combination of religious orthodoxy, family based production, and the Church's unrivalled prestige and legitimacy left the family largely outside the sphere of State intervention. The goals of State policy were by and large those of the Catholic Church.

A GRADUAL SECULARISATION

The status of the Irish family has changed in the course of gradual secularisation over the past 20 years. Secularisation was a consequence more of the increasing complexity of Irish society rather than of any direct ideological pressures. Economic expansion and State activism bring a more complex division of labour in which everyday life becomes dominated by an instrumental rationality in which religious values play little direct role. This process of institutional differentiation and 'objective secularisation' (Berger, 1967, pp. 123–5) in Ireland is best illustrated in the areas of education and health care delivery. As second and third level education grew and the health services rapidly expanded since the 1960s, massive changes were recorded in Irish society. Between 1961 and 1983, the proportion of each youth cohort successfully completing second level education rose from 16 to 66 per cent. The expansion in educational provision led to a corresponding decline in the proportion of the teaching force belonging to religious orders –

from over one half of the second level total in 1961 to a mere 16 per cent in 1983. A similar pattern occurred in health care. As hospital services mushroomed, the dominance of religious orders in hospital administration and staffing dwindled. More generally, as the logic of industrial-capitalism overflowed from the industrial and commercial sectors into all aspects of Irish society, non-scientific and religious interpretations and legitimations lost their pre-eminence.

Secularisation meant that the various State functions became removed from the religious domains, while the political system lessened its close alliance with the Catholic Church. This has been viewed as a gradual and initially amicable adjustment, 'not one of conflict but of consensus', in Whyte's view (1980, p. 388). There is certainly evidence for such a characterisation in the removal by referendum of the Constitution's recognition of the 'special position' of the Catholic Church (1972), the move to a more restricted church role in the control over second level education, changes in the legal status of children, and the 1979 amendments to laws governing the sale and distribution of contraceptives. In its language and its action, the Catholic Church throughout the 1970s drew clear and explicit distinctions between the religious and the civil role of citizens. Moreover, a number of prominent bishops, sensitive to the nuances of the Northern Ireland problem, argued for a greater separation of Church and State, articulating the view that legislators are free to form their own opinions about the balance of social advantage on most moral issues; and, if they came to the conclusion that the law need no longer prohibit what was condemned by the Church, they were entitled to act accordingly (Whyte, 1980, pp. 407–8). This episcopal policy, however, did not outlast the 1970s.

In many respects, however, the judiciary rather than the politicians or parliament provided the important State agents of change (McMahon, 1985, pp. 34–46). The Supreme Court has been particularly active in expanding individual citizenship rights through 'judicial review' of legislation: striking down the law prohibiting the sale of contraceptives (1973), expanding the right to marital privacy and the rights of dependent spouses, generally expanding women's rights, and prohibiting discriminatory employment and taxation provisions against married women (McMahon, 1985). The McGee case of 1973 is a particularly significant example. The Supreme Court held that a 1935 Act which forbade the importation of contraceptives was unconstitutional, violating the basic personal rights guaranteed in the Constitution. The

Supreme Court in a number of related judgments affirmed a wide arena of personal rights, following precedents set in other jurisdictions with written constitutions – particularly the United States.

Legislation providing for a new law on the sale of contraceptives took six years of unsuccessful attempts and considerable political controversy, before it was passed. It limited the sale of contraceptives to chemists' shops and then only under prescription to married couples for 'legitimate family planning practices'. The Catholic bishops did not actively oppose the provision – in marked contrast to the position the Church took in regard to less revolutionary legislation earlier in the decade.

The 1970s brought a flurry of legislative initiatives. The most important changes were those introduced to bring Irish law into conformity with EC law. The 1974 Equal Pay Act and the 1977 Employment Equality Act – both implementing the First and Second EC equality directives – established a legal framework to fight discrimination and established institutional arrangements to ensure effective access to legal remedies. They also provided an enforcement agency: the Employment Equality Agency. Subsequent legislation on maternity leave and entitlement to equal treatment under the social welfare code was also introduced to conform with EC law.

Although there are limitations to the efficacy of these legislative provisions, they create a dramatically different legal and institutional environment than that which had been characteristic of pre-EC Ireland (Robinson, 1986). The initiatives of the women's movement and the trade union movement[2] pre-dated entry to the EC in 1973 (Mahon 1987). There is no doubt, however that the EC-inspired legal developments place women's equality issues in a new environment insofar as entitlements to equal treatment now fall within the ambit of European 'fundamental human rights' legislation, enforceable by law – with eventual recourse, if necessary, to the European Court.

In the 1980s, the period of amicable mutual adjustment of political and church leaders ended with disagreements over contraception, divorce and abortion. The restrictive 1979 Act was updated and considerably liberalised in May 1985 after open conflict, although the conflict was less with the Catholic hierarchy than with ultra-conservative lay-Catholic organisations. And it was these highly organised lay-Catholic groups which succeeded in stampeding a majority of politicians in 1983 to propose a new constitutional amendment to prohibit abortion. Finally, in June 1986 a government constitutional amendment to allow divorce was lost in a referendum, again after bitter conflict, mainly with lay-Catholic organisations, but this time with the support of a more militant Catholic hierarchy. The battle lines are drawn for decades of future conflict as economic and institutional developments lead to increasing 'objective secularisation' and the process of cultural and ideological change makes increasing inroads. Paradoxically, these moral battle lines often seem to ignore class boundaries, despite the fact that the impact of religious norms on family life has clear class differences.

What was the fate of class differences in Irish family and demographic patterns during the period of partial secularisation? The question is important because marriage is a basic life chance, one that economic development might have equalised. Moreover, the growing activism of the Irish State might be expected to have evened out some of the factors underlying previous class inequalities. Differences in the source, amount and security of income might have become less closely associated with class differences in fertility levels and gender roles, as well as in marriage chances. The remainder of this chapter considers and then interprets the available evidence.

CLASS DIFFERENCES IN MARRIAGE AND FERTILITY AFTER 1960

Despite the massive economic and social change that Ireland experienced in recent decades, State activism in family policy, and a quiescent Catholic Church, class differences in the ability to marry are widening. Today, marriage rates are more class-specific than had been the case in the 1920s.

The magnitude and pattern of recent (post-1951) changes in marriage rates can be traced through the data in Table 5.3. Four census years are compared, using 11 socio-economic categories. An overall measure of the extent to which one's social category predicts the likelihood of marriage is provided at the bottom of each column. That overall measure of inequality grew by 65 per cent between 1951 and 1981. This occurred through a persistent improvement in the marriage chances of those occupying middle class positions; that has reached a saturation point of 95 per cent for employers, managers, and salaried employers. Over the same period, the situation of lower middle class categories and of the working class 'élite' (skilled manual workers) also improved, while the marital fortunes of semi-skilled manual workers remained stable. The rising inequality is attributable to the deteriorat-

TABLE 5.3   *Percentage of males aged 45–54 who were single, in each socio-economic group, 1951–81*

Socio-economic groups	1951	1961	1971	1981
Farmers, farmers' relatives and farm managers	39.9	39.9	40.9	37.8
Other agricultural occupations	44.9	43.1	47.1	42.4
Higher professional	9.7	10.4	9.2E	7.4E
Lower professional	20.9	13.3	11.7	9.4
Employers and managers	12.1	8.7	5.8	5.0
Salaried employees	11.4	10.5	7.4	4.4
Intermediate non-manual workers	19.0	18.5	17.7	14.6
Other non-manual workers	19.5	17.1	16.0	14.4
Skilled manual workers	17.5	16.5	14.5	12.8
Semi-skilled manual workers	18.9	18.6	18.1	.16.8
Unskilled manual workers	23.6	24.9	27.6	32.5
Coefficient of 'between group' variation	.42	.55	.66	.69

E = Estimated for 1971 and 1981 as the Census volume does not exclude celibate clergymen from the denominator.
SOURCES   *Census of Population of Ireland*, 1981, Vol. 7; 1961 and 1971, Vol. 5; and 1951, Vol. 2, Part 2.

ing marriage chances of those who are at the bottom of the class structure: small farmers and unskilled manual workers. The rate of non-marriage of the latter rose from 25 per cent in 1951 to 33 per cent in 1981, reflecting their declining labour market position. The pattern for farmers remained stable, perpetuating the long-standing low marriage rates in that group.

So the actual application of Catholic moral principles to marriage and to fertility control closely followed class differences. These class differentials were evident earlier in the century but agricultural modernisation and industrial transformation have exacerbated their impact. This is particularly evident when our comparisons make distinctions among farmers based on their employment status and the size of their landholdings. Table 5.4 provides the necessary information. The 1951–61 contrast reflects ten years of disastrous economic policies, which forced nearly half of each cohort of young jobseekers to emigrate. The celibacy rate among the poorer agricultural population, especially

TABLE 5.4   *Percentage of male farmers aged 45–54, who were single in 1961 and 1981, by size of farm*

| Year | Total | Acreage | | | | | Coefficient of variation |
		1–15	15–30	30–50	50–100	100+	
1961	30.2	37.3	35.0	30.6	25.3	20.5	.21
1981	34.5	65.4	47.0	41.6	34.0	18.8	.37

SOURCE   *Census of Population of Ireland* 1961, Vol. V; 1981, Vol. VII.

farmers' relatives and farm labourers, stood at about 40 per cent – more than four times higher than the rate experienced by professional workers. Even unskilled manual workers had a 1961 rate more than double that found in agriculture. The position for almost all class categories, but especially the urban middle classes, had improved substantially by 1981. That improvement bypassed the unskilled urban working class and the less advantaged agricultural categories. Even in this most basic of life chances – that of marrying – the rising tide of economic prosperity failed to benefit those in the most disadvantaged class categories. Table 5.4 provides clear evidence of the class-specific nature of the impact of economic and social change. Over the 1961–81 period, the position of the larger farmers (over 100 acres) improved, that of the small farmers steadily deteriorated. For those who were unable to supplement their incomes by off-farm employment, life chances declined drastically. Two out of three farmers with farms of under 15 acres were single at around 50, with nearly half of the next farm size group being equally disadvantaged. In fact, today only those who have no alternatives choose to enter or stay in small scale farming.

Such low levels of marriage are not due to the unwillingness of the 'favoured' inheriting son to marry, but rather to the almost universal propensity of their sisters to escape as early as possible from such economically deprived backgrounds. Even by the mid-1960s there were more than three single younger male farmers for every single farm woman in rural communities.

FERTILITY AND CLASS, 1961–81

Historically, marital fertility is inversely related to the marriage rate of social classes in Ireland. In 1961, the correlation between the percentage of males in a social class who were single at age 45–54 and the standardised marital fertility rate of the class was 0.78 (Walsh 1968, p. 13). This reflects the realities of a cultural context in which high levels of fertility were expected within marriage. The decision to marry, therefore, was necessarily constrained by economic circumstances. We first examine the historical pattern of fertility control in Ireland and then turn to the question of whether social change has diminished social class differences in marital fertility.

High marital fertility was a stable feature of Irish demography over the 1841–1911 period (Geary, 1935/36), but declined sharply thereafter. Average completed family size (for marriage of 25–29 years duration) declined from 6.5 to 4.8 between 1911 and 1946 but then remained steady, declining only to 4.4 by 1961 (Walsh, 1968, p. 6). Between 1961 and 1981 there was a further marginal decline to 4.3. This coincided, however, with a decline of almost 2 years in the median age of first marriage for brides. When this is taken into account – say, by looking at fertility rates for women married between 1951 and 1956 – marital fertility levels in Ireland were still remarkably high in the 1980s, with no significant change between the fertility levels of that cohort and of its predecessors who had completed their families 20 years earlier. Later cohorts of married women, however, provide clear evidence of a demographic transformation. They marry earlier, have lower fertility of marriage and the modal age of completion of child-bearing declined by almost seven years in the 1960–75 period (Walsh, 1980; Rottman, Hannan et al., 1982, p. 107). The effect is evident in the moderate decline of less than 10 per cent in overall fertility over the 1970s and more evident still in the 1980s when marital fertility is expected to decline by around 40 per cent (CSO, 1985, p. 8).

So the 1970s ended a half-century long period of remarkable stability in fertility levels. There has been a dramatic decline in fertility from the mid-1960s onwards for young married couples and this decline is accelerating in the 1980s: the decline in the 1970s took place at 2 per cent annually; in the 1980s fertility is declining at a rate of 5 per cent per annum (Blackwell, 1986, p. 11). Completed families of four or more children have become consistently less common from the mid-1960s and third order births have been declining from the mid-1970s. For all marriages, if we control for the marriage rate and age structure, fertility declined by 40 per cent between 1961 and 1981. The widespread use of artificial contraception means that voluntary fertility control allows families to adjust to the realities of the current economic recession.

The overall fertility change is summarised in Table 5.5. Between 1961

TABLE 5.5 *Average number of children born to women married for 5–9 years, and of various ages at marriage, for 1961, 1971, 1981*

| Census year | Age of wife at marriage | | |
	20–24	25–29	30–34
1961	3.03	2.81	2.42
1971	2.82	2.75	2.46
1981	2.35	2.36	2.19
1981 figure as proportion of 1961 figure	.78	.84	.91

SOURCE *Census of Population of Ireland*, 1961, Vol. VIII; 1971, Vol. X; and pre-publication tables from Fertility Volume 1981.

and 1981, fertility of younger brides (aged less than 25 at marriage) declined by 22 per cent. For those aged 25–29 at marriage it declined by 16 per cent, and for those 30–34 at marriage, by 9 per cent. Despite this decline, Irish fertility is still substantially higher than in most other EC countries.

Such a portrayal of fertility trends in Ireland conceals the substantial class differences that are present. Fertility levels have traditionally been highest for the urban working class, farm labourers and farmers. The lowest levels were found in the urban middle classes. Moreover, age at marriage and duration of marriage had substantially less influence on fertility in the middle classes than in working class or farm families (Walsh 1968, pp. 8–9). Voluntary fertility control within marriage has been a consistent characteristic of middle class families in Ireland since the beginning of the century, while celibacy and postponed marriage were of substantial importance to working class and farming families.

In recent times, class differences in fertility have widened. Effectively the urban middle classes experienced the greatest decline, while small farm holders and the lower working class families have changed the least. Table 5.6 provides a more complete overview of 1961–81 fertility trends by class.

The more conservative and marginal catagories – farmers and labourers – manifest the least decline in fertility between 1961 and 1981 (14 and 18 per cent respectively), compared to the decline of 27 per cent for the upper middle class. The greatest decline, however, occurred in the lower middle class. On this basis, we can identify a general trend among young couples between 1961 and 1981 towards contraception

TABLE 5.6   *Average number of children born to women married at ages 20–24 and who were 5–9 years married in 1961, 1971, 1981*

Social Group	1961	1971	1981
Farmers and farmers' relatives	3.4	3.3	2.9
Other agricultural workers	3.3	3.0	2.7
Professional	3.0	2.8	2.2
Semi-professional	3.0	2.8	2.1
Employers and managers	3.0	2.8	2.3
Salaried employees	2.8	2.6	2.3
Intermediate non-manual workers	2.9	2.7	2.0
Other non-manual workers (lower service)	3.0	2.8	2.3
Skilled manual workers	3.0	2.8	2.4
Semi-skilled manual workers	3.0	2.7	2.3
Unskilled manual workers	3.2	3.1	2.7
Coefficient of variation (between groups)	.054	.067	.110

SOURCE   *Census of Population of Ireland.* Fertility Volumes (1961, Vol. X; 1971, Vol. VIII; pre-publication tables from 1981 Fertility Volume).

and fertility control. Alongside this are class-specific influences in which the change is most marked among those placed at the start of the career ladder in lower white collar positions, and least evident among the lower working class.

It is no surprise that one finds 'a reluctance to assume the married state', as Geary (1935/36) puts it, among those whose economic prospects are very poor. The more optimistic marriage decisions of the better educated and more liberal middle classes assume an ability to control fertility – a case where increasing education and a morality that is less legalistic in context reinforces economic class advantages. More than mere income differences separate social classes in Ireland. The post-1958 class structure divides the nation's families according to life chances to a degree far in excess of that attributable to the older structure.

ECONOMIC CHANGE, WOMEN'S ROLES AND HOUSEHOLD FORMATION

The process of economic change in Ireland served to differentiate adult gender roles. As the predominance of farming and family economies declined so did the active productive role of married women in the commercial economy. Within farm families mechanisation meant that married women withdrew – indeed most insisted on withdrawing – from active farm role tasks (Hannan and Katsiaouni, 1977).

The labour force participation rate of married women in the non-farm population had been extremely low by European standards; the overall female labour force participation rate stood at 5 per cent in 1961 and at 8 per cent in 1971, a mere fraction of the British figure. The evidence suggests that up to the mid-1970s the main priority of the majority of married women was their child care and housekeeping responsibilities. A national survey carried out in the early 1970s found that only 15 per cent of married women were in any form of paid employment, and another 25 per cent wished to, or intended to, return to paid work at a future date (Walsh and O'Toole, 1973, p. 33). A similar study carried out a decade later indicated little growth of interest in returning to the labour force – with just over a third of married women interviewed wishing to return to work – with the dominant priorities influencing such decisions again being household and child-rearing roles (Fine–Davis, 1983, p. 131).

While attitudes and expectations among older married women have changed but little, the behaviour of their younger counterparts has greatly changed. Legislation guaranteeing equality of treatment in the labour market and improved maternity leave arrangements, combined with substantially increasing costs of child-rearing and new household formation, resulted in rapid growth in the proportion of younger married women continuing to work after marriage and the birth of children.

The female labour force participation rate, which was relatively stable over the 1960s, increased rapidly in the 1970s from 1 in 13 in 1971 to 1 in 6 in 1981; by 1984 it reached 1 in 5. The increase among younger married women was particularly dramatic: the 1971–84 change was from 15 to 41 per cent for 20–24 year olds and from 9 to 27 per cent for 25–34 year olds. The marital status composition of the female labour force has been vastly altered as a result. Over one third of the female labour force is now married, compared to one fifth in 1961.

THE IMPACT OF THE STATE

State policy regarding the family has been aggressive in its prohibitions but not in mediating the impact of the economic markets on the family. This is true generally, with a failure to compensate families for the costs necessarily incurred at the main child-rearing stages of the family cycle. The more glaring failure, however, is the widening of class inequalities in those family decisions that are strongly affected by financial considerations.

In terms of legislation, the main features have been prohibitions that conform with Catholic social teaching and, more recently, statutes that often reflect the concerns and values of the urban middle class. Examples of the latter legislation include The Succession Act of 1965, which guarantees a surviving spouse and children a share in an estate,[3] The Family Home Protection Act of 1976, which requires the permission of both spouses before a family home can be sold, and the Family Planning Act of 1985, which finally made the purchase of contraceptives available to all adults. Legislative and social welfare provision for deserted wives has been expanded, but remains rather weak. In particular, the relevant statute (The Social Welfare Act, 1970) sets eligibility requirements that place a substantial burden on the deserted wife to prove both the fact of desertion and the unavailability of other income support (Commission on Social Welfare, 1986, p. 43).

The State mechanism for channelling financial support to families is the Children's Allowance Scheme, which is universally available. It was introduced in 1944 to be redistributive in favour of families raising large numbers of children (Commission on Social Welfare, 1986, p. 35) and had an element of selectivity to further that objective. In practice, the real value of Children's Allowance payments declined by 8 per cent between 1973 and 1985 for a family with two children. The decline in value for families with four and six dependent children over those years was 26 and 19 per cent respectively.

The other universal scheme for child support operated through the tax system in the form of child dependant allowances. The real value of those allowances was allowed to dwindle and then disappear: when it was abolished in 1986, the allowance stood at one tenth of its 1971 purchasing power. Inflation in the 1970s virtually rewrote the Irish tax code, substantially altering the distribution of fiscal welfare among types of families. Many forms of allowance or relief were not indexed against inflation. The effect of this, when combined with changes in earned income and tax policy, was that the main contribution to the rise in tax revenues came from families in which children were being raised.

That rising tax burden was not reflected in the system of cash transfer payments to families through the social welfare system. Over the 1970s, the increased State expenditure on social welfare was channelled towards those categories of households in which few young children would be present, particularly households with old age pensioners. On balance, 'households in which a young family was being raised ended the decade less well off, relatively, than other households. This was the case despite the very considerable increase that occurred during the decade in the overall flow of State transfers' (Rottman and Hannan, 1981, p. 104). For families whose main income is social welfare, the value of payments for dependent children was maintained at a constant value; about one quarter of all children under age 19 were receiving such a payment in 1984. In sum, the growth of the Irish Welfare State has not served to lessen the burden of raising dependent children or to diminish class inequalities in the resources families can devote to their children. An economist has noted that 'from the viewpoint of those liable to income taxation, the late 1960s were the halcyon days for the family' (Kennedy, 1986, p. 95).

Households with children constitute about two-thirds of all Irish households compared to less than half (46 per cent) of all households in England. Economic recession and State policies in taxation and social welfare have made household formation increasingly difficult for young people from working class backgrounds. That may be extending into the middle class. The costs of purchasing a new house and meeting mortgage payments has risen sharply in real terms. The average mortgage payment in 1976 was equivalent to 42 per cent of the average earnings from non-agricultural employment; by 1982, the average payment was equal to 53 per cent of the average earnings (National Economic and Social Council, 1983, p. 23). State housing policies have not provided a set of counterbalancing forces to facilitate the purchase of a family home for new families or to ease the cost of housing for those renting or purchasing local authorities' houses.

The verdict on the State role in shaping the contemporary Irish family is mixed. That role has for the most part supported the stability of the conventional family, while making concessions to demands for greater equality of treatment for women and has also facilitated urban middle class families. However, the State's generosity has not extended to financially compensating women for the child rearing responsibilities so cherished in the Constitution or to equalising the costs of child rearing through redistribution of income. Indeed, the trend over the past 10 or so years has been to lower the support available to families with young children. This exacerbates the implications of the substantial inequalities between families in their market incomes. At the same time, new family problems are emerging or being officially recognised. Some 5.6 per cent of all households are headed by a woman receiving social welfare payments due to marital desertion or to unmarried motherhood (Commission on Social Welfare, 1986, p. 59). The challenge this represents is not merely financial. It brings to the fore concerns about the appropriate role of the State in family matters similar to those involved in the ill-fated 'Mother and Child' scheme of thirty years ago.

CONCLUSIONS

The Irish State, almost from its inception, adopted a strongly conservative approach to gender roles and family relationships, being mainly concerned with reinforcing an orthodox Catholic morality. This, perhaps, is not an astonishing outcome in an economy dominated by family enterprises and in which religious practice was and is extraordinarily high. Given the petit bourgeois nature of the economic system for much of the post-independence period, and a Church role that emphasises moral regulation rather than the provision of material support, class factors operate sharply in differentiating marriage chances and fertility rates. The exercise of the permitted 'moral restraint' on sexuality was strongly influenced by economic selectivities which acted to reduce substantially the marriage chances of the class categories experiencing economic marginalisation.

The rapid differentiation in the economic and social structure over the past 20 years provided a gradual 'objective secularisation' of economic and social life. The new role of the State, through direct legislative and judicial initiatives, can be viewed as an adjustment to this reality and to the reality of familial problems associated with the process of industrial development. However, the redirection also reflects the State's new-found autonomy in this policy area. It has moved away from the close alliance of earlier decades.

The State's role is largely indirect, its impact deriving from the often unintended consequences of economic, industrial and fiscal policy. These indirect influences tend to increase class inequalities in family formation processes. Such inequalities, combined with a gradual weakening of the religious plausibility structures and growing unemployment rates, almost necessarily imply increasing strains on conventional institutional arrangements. Such strains are manifest in, for example, the recent substantial declines in marital fertility. As unemployment increased and economic conditions have worsened, increases occurred in the level of sexual activity outside marriage and in the rate of marital breakdown and, most noticeably, in the increasing illegitimacy rate. While continuing to be extremely low by Northern European standards, it nevertheless trebled between 1960 and 1980 (from 16 to 80 per thousand live births) and the number in receipt of unmarried mothers' allowances increased from 7400 in 1976 to almost 26 000 in 1985.

It is within the urban working class that these institutionalised arrangements are coming under the greatest pressure. The likelihood of marriage within those groups who have traditionally experienced the most difficulty in forming conventional marital and familial arrangements has declined further due to high levels of long-term unemployment. However, a diminished attachment to religious beliefs, together with growing financial provision for unmarried mothers and their children, has freed at least a proportion of the urban working class young from the constraints of lifelong celibacy which would have been their lot in 'traditional Ireland'.

Until the 1960s, Church and State acted with a remarkable harmony of purpose to legitimate and support a distinctive family pattern which was generally consistent with the dominant economic system. Today, the State possesses rather more autonomy in determining its policies relating to the family, though the decisive rejection by the electorate of a referendum permitting divorce provides dramatic evidence of limits to State action in Ireland that have disappeared in the rest of Catholic Europe.

Overall, however, the Irish State's policies combine today to perpetuate and even exacerbate class inequalities in family formation and functioning. The life chance of marriage is now more strongly related to one's class of origin as are fertility differentials. The burden of dependency is heaviest for working class families. State policies are also reinforcing generational divisions within Irish society. The marriage and fertility patterns of young people contrast sharply with those of their parents. This rapid change in behaviour is taking place within a cultural milieu which remains strongly conservative. It is, however, a milieu that is proving to be more flexible in accommodating change than sociological theories of secularisation would predict. That flexibility, at least, is in part a contribution by the Irish State to changing family patterns.

NOTES

1. The celibacy rate amongst employers and managers was around 13 per cent, among non-farm labourers 28 per cent, with rate of about 20 per cent for categories of skilled manual workers.
2. Particularly in the work of the Commission on the Status of Women and the Equal Pay Committee of the Irish Congress of Trade Unions.
3. This particular piece of legislation was possibly of even greater significance for the owners of agricultural land.

6 Education: the Promise of Reform and the Growth of Credentialism

Two related concerns – equality of educational opportunity and the link between education and the labour demands of a modern capitalist economy – lay at the root of many of the major changes brought about in public education by Western governments during the post-war period. These changes have led to a rapid expansion of both the provision and the utilisation of public education, with a concomitant growth in educational expenditure.[1]

Ireland was a late starter in the process of post-war educational reform – a lateness mirroring her situation in regard to economic and industrial development. However, in the 1960s a series of changes was set in train which greatly increased State involvement in education. The best known change is the introduction, in 1967, of free post-primary education and free school transport, but there were other important innovations: the opening of the first comprehensive school in 1966; the extension of the main national public examinations to pupils in all types of post-primary schools in 1967; the establishing of a Higher Education Authority in 1968; the raising of the school leaving age from 14 to 15 in 1972, among others (Tussing, 1978, pp. 66–7). Hardly surprisingly, public expenditure on education grew very rapidly, from just over three per cent of GNP in 1961/2, to 6.3 per cent in 1973/4 (Sheehan, 1982, p. 64).

It is our contention that, despite the shift of the financial burden of education on to the State, the degree of control possessed by the State over the system remains limited – much more so than in centrally or locally administered systems of education such as those of, respectively, France or England and Wales. In the terminology of Chapter 1, the capacity of the Irish State to carry through educational policy is restricted by the nature of the system. The reforms of the 1960s – particularly the advent of free secondary education – have entered Irish popular mythology as the work of the then recently appointed Minister of Education, Mr O'Malley. O'Malley is perceived as having brought

123

about – almost at a stroke – the most thoroughgoing reform of the educational system since the founding of the State. This perception is mistaken: the impetus towards change was already under way before O'Malley came to office, and we begin this chapter with an examination of the reasons behind the educational reforms of the period: what goals was it hoped to achieve via these changes? We then look at their effects: how comprehensively in fact have these goals been attained and what unanticipated consequences have resulted? In particular we look at how, if at all, these changes have influenced the inter-generational reproduction of class inequalities. And lastly we review the role of the State in Irish education during this period. We argue that the State's lack of control over the system which it funds has been crucial in determining the consequences to which the reforms gave rise. Before embarking on these tasks, we begin with a description of the Irish education system and of its position until the mid 1960s.

THE IRISH EDUCATIONAL SYSTEM

The Irish educational system has a tripartite structure, in which pupils transfer from primary to second level education around the age of twelve, and some students subsequently enter universities and other third level institutions, generally at age eighteen. Post-primary education takes place in either secondary, vocational, comprehensive or community schools, and is conventionally divided into two cycles – the junior cycle, usually lasting three years, culminating in the national Intermediate Certificate examination and the senior cycle, usually lasting two years, leading to the Leaving Certificate exam. On average, pupils are examined in eight subjects for the Intermediate Certificate; six or seven for the Leaving Certificate. The Group Certificate, a set of exams, many of which are practical or technical in nature, is taken by some junior cycle students, mainly in the post-primary vocational, community and comprehensive schools. Third-level institutions can broadly be divided into the university sector; the technical or technological sector (the National Institutes of Higher Education, Regional Technical Colleges and the colleges of the Dublin Institute of Technology); and the teacher training colleges.

Before the reforms of the 1960s, the great majority of the Irish population experienced only primary education, which was provided free at the point of use through the National School system established in the nineteenth century.[2] Conflict between the Catholic Church and the United Kingdom government over the denominational character of primary education led to the overwhelming majority of national schools falling under the effective control of the former. Until 1975 the patron of the school (usually the local Catholic bishop) appointed the school manager (usually the local parish priest); subsequently managers were replaced by Committees of Management, the majority of whose incumbents are nominees of the patron (Tussing, 1978, p. 23).

Likewise, secondary schools in Ireland are overwhelmingly denominational in character, with about 88 per cent of existing secondary schools owned and controlled by Catholic orders and a further 6 per cent belonging to other religious denominations, mainly the Church of Ireland (Hannan et al., 1983, p. 82). Until the 1960s secondary schools charged tuition fees (though the Exchequer paid the bulk of teachers' salaries): in 1967 the majority of them agreed to participate in the Free Education scheme, under which an annual per-pupil grant from the State was paid in exchange for the abolition of tuition fees. Approximately sixty out of a total of 500 secondary schools remain outside the scheme and continue to charge fees. In the case of the majority of secondary schools and national schools, although the Department of Education meets the bulk of their current and capital costs, the school buildings themselves are not State owned: they remain the property of Church bodies and religious orders.

Following the 1930 Vocational Education Act a parallel system of post-primary education in the form of vocational schools, was established by the State.[3] These schools have never charged fees and are publicly owned, being administered by local Vocational Educational Committees (VECs), made up of appointees of the local government authority. The curriculum of the vocational schools was distinctive from that of the secondary schools. Whereas the latter provided a grammar school type education concentrating on non-technical subjects, vocational schools were specifically orientated to providing 'general and practical training in preparation for employment in trades, manufacturing, agriculture, commerce and other industrial pursuits' (Vocational Education Act, 1930). Thus the curriculum of the vocational schools was explicitly linked to the perceived labour demands of the local economy and as a result, until the mid-sixties, vocational schools did not provide the more academic courses leading to the Intermediate and Leaving Certificate exams. Instead, they provided a two- or three-year course, culminating in the Group Certificate. Secondary schools, on the other hand, orientated themselves less directly to perceived labour demands: as Tussing (1978, p. 12) puts it, 'the major function of secondary education was religious, moral and intellectual construction', and the products of this form of education were (if male) destined for jobs in professional and other white collar occupations, achieved in some cases via third-level education. Until the late 1960s, however, the provision of third-level education was limited: the major institutions were the universities and teacher training colleges, and the only two technological colleges of any size were both run by Dublin VEC (Tussing, 1978, p. 40).[4]

The system, then, was one in which the State provided the bulk of the finance while owning and exercising a managerial function (via, for example, locally elected representatives or their appointees) over but a small proportion of educational institutions. With the exception of the vocational sector and third level the Exchequer funded individuals and orders to provide the educational service on its behalf. Religious interests in particular were able through their ownership of, and control over, primary and secondary schools, to pursue not simply the State's goals in respect of education but their own goals of what is often termed 'religious formation'.

EDUCATIONAL REFORM – PROCESSES AND AIMS

The immediate impetus for change came from the publication in 1965 of the OECD/Irish Government funded report, *Investment in Education*, which itself was the product of concern about the articulation of the existing school system with the needs of a newly industrialising economy.[5] Two issues raised by that report were particularly important in accounting for subsequent policy developments. The first of these was the finding that there existed large social class and regional disparities in educational participation rates. The reforms of the second half of the 1960s were intended to reduce these disparities through the abolition of fees for post-primary education, the introduction of free school transport, and so on. In other words, a central aim was to move towards greater equality of educational opportunity than had previously existed.

The second issue related to the needs of the economy. Here the concern of the *Investment in Education* Report appears to have been that the level of trained manpower, given the current rate of Irish economic growth, would be insufficient to meet the needs in the 1970s without reform of the educational system. Most of the expansion in educational participation that the reforms of the late 1960s were intended to encourage was meant, so far as one can now judge, to be an expansion in a particular direction. This was bluntly put by Dr Patrick Hillery during his term as Minister for Education:

> Secondary education ... is only one stream. What we really need in this country is the other stream, technical and scientific. We need to develop these ... if you were to give secondary grammar academic type of education to everybody, you would be wasting your money ... you would be getting too many people taking a course which is no use to most of them – we haven't jobs for them, we haven't need for them. (Interview in *Hibernia*, February 1964, p. 8, quoted in Mulcahy, 1981, p. 21).

In other words, the expansion of enrolment at the post-primary level was meant to take place in broadly defined 'vocational' subject areas. To this end, plans were set in motion to introduce more vocational subjects into the curriculum (for example, Business Organisation, Accountancy, Economics, Building Construction and Engineering were all introduced in the late 1960s); comprehensive and, later, community schools with very broad curricula were set up; and the Regional Technical Colleges (RTCs) and the National Institutes of Higher Education (NIHE) were developed. There was also an attempt to reduce the curricular distinctions between the Vocational and Secondary sectors, by the introduction of academic subjects into the former (and the extension of the Intermediate and Leaving Certificate examinations to their pupils)[6] and of practical subjects into the latter.

These two aims of reform – ideological and economic, as Craft (1970) labels them – were closely related, as *Investment in Education* made clear. Increased participation would not only be egalitarian in itself but would prevent the loss of talent that the pre-existing obstacles to participation at second and third level had brought about. This increased participation, however, was to be largely vocational: educational outputs would be matched in a broad sense to the needs of the economy for scientifically and technically trained manpower.

Such a view of the link between the manpower and equality issues was common in educational thought and policy at the time: an educational system which was non-meritocratic entailed a wastage of talent and resources and to this extent was ineffective or inefficient in its function of providing trained manpower for the economy (Karabel and Halsey, 1977, pp. 9–11). Perhaps the most widespread influence on educational thinking at the time, however, was the newly established theory of human capital, which came to prominence in the early 1960s (Blaug, 1968), and provided a clear justification for extensive State funding of education. According to the theory, investment in training (in 'human capital') was the principal factor accounting for the rapid growth in the national output of post-war western economies (Schultz 1961, p. 1). This was a point of view which, as Karabel and Halsey (1977, p. 13) point out, was taken up enthusiastically and promoted by international agencies such as the World Bank, the IMF and OECD. Its influence on Irish educational thought is evident in the title of the 1965 OECD report, and the approach to education which prevailed in that document (as well as in the attitudes which both led to and followed from it) was widely held in the western industrial nations and beyond: Craft (1970), for example, points to the clear parallels between contemporary Irish and British educational thinking.

However, there were also important cross-national differences in the considerations that led to educational reform. In particular, whereas 'all over Europe social democratic notions of equality of opportunity conceptualized the existing unequal access to education in terms of social class and proposed remedies supposedly attuned to working class demands' (Wickham, 1980, p. 34), in Ireland these deveopments were presented rather differently. Equality of opportunity and increased access to education, together with the proposed move towards a more vocationally orientated system, were presented as being of benefit to the nation as a whole, rather than any one class: they were part of the policy of economic development and of the 'rising tide' which would raise all boats. This difference in conceptualisation, Wickham suggests, relates to the absence in Ireland of any social democratic political party: the reforms of the 1960s were, instead, presented in a 'populist' fashion by the broadly based Fianna Fail government.

BEFORE AND AFTER – THE EFFECTS OF REFORM

The most obvious effect of the Free Education Scheme was the growth in post-compulsory educational enrolments, as shown in Table 6.1. Although participation rates had been increasing during the pre-1960 period (and thus we must assume that some of the post-1967 participation rate growth would have occurred even in the absence of the Free Scheme), only half of all 15-year-olds were remaining at school during the period of the *Investment in Education* team's researches. However, by 1970 this had risen to 70 per cent, increasing to over 94 per cent by

TABLE 6.1   *Participation rates and numbers in full-time education 1963–4 and 1984–5.*

A. Age	14	15	16	17	18	19
Percentage participation rate						
1963/4	66.4	51.5	36.8	24.8	14.5	8.8
1984/5	99.4	94.4	80.3	63.3	39.7	23.6

B. Educational level	Primary	Second-level	Third-level	Total
Number in full-time education				
1963/4	496 068	129 365	16 819	642 252
1984/5	576 846	332 565	52 164	961 575

SOURCE   *Investment in Education*, (1965, Table 1.2, p. 4). Department of Education, *Statistical Report* 1984/5. Table 2, p. 3.

1984/85 and indeed Irish post-compulsory participation rates, as Tussing (1978, p. 90) and Murphy (1983, p. 3) note, now compare very favourably with those of the other EC and OECD countries. Virtually all pupils now experience some post-primary education, and only about eight per cent of each year's outflow from post-primary education has not sat for at least one of the national certificate examinations, while roughly one in four post-primary leavers enters third-level education.

Growth in the absolute numbers in full-time education at ages 14 and upwards has, of course, two components: demographic change and participation rate change. However, the latter is by far the more important source of increase in the numbers in education at these ages, accounting for five-sixths of the total growth. If we look at the lower part of Table 6.1, we see the least increase in the numbers in the primary sector, where participation rate changes have had little or no influence, and the greatest growth at second and third levels.

Overall, the numbers of pupils and students have grown by roughly half over the period 1963/64 to 1984/85 and over a quarter of the population is now classed as being in full-time education. Likewise, the number of teachers (full-time or equivalent) employed in the primary, secondary and tertiary sectors has risen, over the same period, from 24 000 to around 50 000, equal to just over four per cent of the employed labour force. Total annual government expenditure on education is approximately £1000 million; this figure is exceeded only by expenditure on social welfare and on health. However, following the rapid growth in educational expenditure in the· 1960s, government expenditure on education, as a share of GDP, remained roughly constant over the 1970s and 1980s, at around 6 per cent (6.1 per cent in 1985).

EQUALITY OF OPPORTUNITY

There is no doubt that up to the end of second level all pupils can now reasonably be supposed to enjoy the opportunity of educational participation, insofar as education is substantially free and access to schools is provided to all pupils. On the other hand, this does not mean that all pupils receive the same quality of education. The fact that the State spends roughly the same amount on each child at each stage of its education means that those who can draw on additional non-State resources will probably receive a better quality of education. Tussing (1978, Ch. 5) has shown that even within the free scheme there is significant regional variation in per-pupil expenditure at the post-primary level. For example, within Dublin expenditure is greater in the higher income areas. Such differences in per-pupil expenditure 'account for differences in educational opportunity which seem contrary to egalitarian standards' (Tussing, 1978, p. 168). The additional funds from parents and the community, available to schools serving a middle class clientèle, and the disadvantages suffered by schools in run-down deprived areas – vandalism, theft, a high turnover of teachers – mean that the quality of education available to working class and middle class pupils is far from uniform.

A further source of inequality of educational opportunity lies in the existence of fee-charging, private secondary schools outside the Free Scheme. Tussing's (1978, p. 169) analysis indicate that per-school and per-pupil expenditures in these schools are considerably greater than in comparable schools in the Free Scheme. It is perhaps ironic, therefore, that these private schools continue to receive the bulk of their funding from the State.[7]

Notwithstanding these caveats, there can be no doubt that the reforms of the late 1960s led to a much greater degree of equality of provision (in the sense that the quality of education formally available to all is the same). But because the provision of education has been made largely without regard to pre-existing differences between pupils and their families, in terms of not only their financial but also their cultural resources, inequalities in educational opportunity have not been eliminated. Furthermore, *Investment in Education* identified a problem of class and regional disparities in educational *participation* and it is by now well known that greater equality of provision (in the sense referred to above) is unlikely to be sufficient to tackle inequalities in educational outcomes. Of course, even given equality of opportunity, one would not necessarily wish for equality of educational outcomes between individuals, but what is disturbing in the Irish context is the degree to which differences in educational outcomes are related to class origins, and the magnitude of these differences.

Some indicators of these differences are presented in Table 6.2, which compares data on class differences in age participation rates taken from *Investment in Education* with some recent comparable estimates. In the earlier data, class differences in participation rates are more pronounced in the 15–19 age group than at 14, as we might expect, and the most marked disparity lies between the rates for students of professional, employer or managerial backgrounds and those of semi-skilled or unskilled manual origins. The estimates for 1981 show a near doubling of overall participation rates among this age group, together with the continuation of marked class differences. At worst, overall class disparities in participation rates have remained unchanged; at best they may have been reduced by up to one fifth. However, the gap between the highest and lowest rates is, in absolute terms, wider in the later than in the earlier data. This arises because the group with the highest participation rates in 1961 – professional, employers and managers – has shown a much greater increase in its rate than has the semi-skilled/unskilled manual group. The skilled manual group and the two non-manual groups have benefited to the greatest degree from educational reform, while the lower working class seems to have fallen further behind.[8]

Table 6.2 also shows some recent estimates of class differences in participation at various levels of the post-primary system and at third level which reveal the extent of social class and gender related disparities in educational attainment. In particular, we note that, among a cohort entering second-level education in 1976–7, those male pupils from an upper non-manual background (that is, whose father is an executive, manager or professional) were at least six times more likely to sit for the Leaving Certificate than boys from an unskilled or semi-skilled labouring family, and almost thirteen times more likely to enter third level. Such differential participation rates have important conse-

TABLE 6.2   *Social class differences in educational participation, 1960–1 and 1980–1*

A: Social group participation rates in full-time education, by age

Year	1960/61		1980/81*
	14 yrs	15–19 yrs	15–19 yrs
Farmers	69.4	27.7	45.7
Professional, employers, managers	73.6	46.5	76.4
Other non-manual†	63.4	28.0	50.1
Skilled manual	52.6	17.3	47.7
Semi/Unskilled manual	43.4	9.8	30.5
All	64.0	29.8	55.9

B: 1980/81 estimates. Percentage of entrants to second level reaching:

	Leaving Certificate		Third level	
	Boys	Girls	Boys	Girls
Upper non-manual	97	100	50	35
Lower non-manual	59	71	26	16
Skilled manual	32	74	10	11
Semi/Unskilled manual	16	41	4	7
All	50	69	21	16
Both sexes	59		19	

SOURCES   *Investment in Education* 1965, Tables 6.27, 6.28, pp. 150–1, Breen 1984b, Table 2, p. 105.
* Authors' estimates based on unpublished data from the 1971 and 1981 Censuses.
† These figures combine groups C and D of the *Investment in Education* tables. The class categories in panel A are derived from the Census; in panel B they are based on the Hall Jones scale with farmers allocated according to Breen (1984c, p. 24).

quences when pupils leave education and enter the labour market (Breen, 1984c; 1985), as we show in Chapter 7.

As well as class differences, there are also substantial gender differences in participation rates. As Table 6.2 shows, class differences in participation rates are less marked among girls than among boys, and this occurs within a context in which a greater percentage of females than males sit for both the Intermediate and Leaving Certificate examinations. However, the female transition rate to third level is much lower than the male, leading to a reversal of the gender difference, with

21 per cent of males who entered second level in 1976–77 going on to third level, against 16 per cent of girls.[9]

Recent debate has focused on the degree to which the Irish educational system can be said to be 'meritocratic'. Using data from a sample of the cohort which entered post-primary education in 1967/68, Greaney and Kellaghan (1984, p. 263) conclude that 'the fact that ability played such a dominant role in the educational progress of students in our study suggests that the meritocratic ideal is at least being approached if not quite attained'. If this were so, it would imply that the class differences in participation rates shown in Table 6.2 could largely be accounted for by class differences in ability. However, (and notwithstanding issues such as the age of these data and the problematic status of the measure of ability used), this conclusion has been challenged (Whelan and Whelan 1984, 1985; Hout and Raftery 1985). Re-analyses of these data have shown that, even allowing for differences in ability, class origins exert a significant influence in determining how far a pupil progresses within post-primary education. Additionally, using more recent data, Breen (1984c, pp. 45–6) found that access to third-level education could not be considered wholly meritocratic, insofar as, even allowing for performance differences at the Leaving Certificate (which acts as the qualifying criterion for entry to third level), both class origins and gender exert a substantial influence on a pupil's likelihood of entering third level.

We can draw three main conclusions regarding the effects of the 1960s changes on educational participation. First, it is clear that little headway has been made in terms of the lessening of class disparities in educational outcomes: the expansion of the educational system and the growth of credentialism have acted as intervening factors between class origins and class destinations but do not appear to have changed the relationship between them to any marked degree. Second, it is clear that public educational expenditure, at any rate at the senior cycle of the post-primary level and at third level, is regressive. Per-pupil or per-student costs rise as one moves from primary through to tertiary education.[10] At the same time, the divergence between class participation rates (in favour of pupils of middle class backgrounds) also increases as pupils move into post-primary education and beyond. Thus, the benefits of public educational expenditures at the higher levels tend to accrue to pupils of better off families. Third, the blanket introduction of free secondary education in 1967 can now be seen to have been a blunt instrument – if the purpose of the change was intended to tackle undesirable differences in participation rates. Indeed, one immediate result of the changes was the transfer of a sizeable ongoing 'windfall' benefit to those parents of pupils who would have paid fees to send their children to secondary schools but who, under the scheme, receive this education free of charge (Tussing 1978, pp. 34–7).

EDUCATION AND MANPOWER POLICY

The second aim of the 1960s reforms was to reorientate the educational system away from the predominance of academic subjects and towards a technical and scientific – a more avowedly vocational – bias. To what degree can this be said to have occurred?

In terms of the kinds of post-primary school entered by pupils, virtually all the growth in enrolments brought about since 1967 has taken place in the secondary schools and, to a lesser extent, community and comprehensive schools (which were established during this period). The relative position of the vocational sector has worsened since the 1960s. The percentage of boys leaving primary schools and entering vocational schools has remained largely unchanged over the period, but among girls the percentage entering this sector declined by 9 per cent. On the basis of these figures then, the academic, rather than the vocational side of Irish education appears to have benefited from increases in pupil enrolments.

Turning to the takeup of individual subjects, the pattern becomes less clear. For example, while vocational schools adopted many of the pre-existing academic subjects, secondary schools were slow to adopt the technical subjects, particularly at senior cycle level, so the new technical Leaving Certificate subjects were largely limited to the vocational and community/comprehensive sectors.

Nevertheless, the takeup of the technical, scientific and commercial subjects did increase over the 1970s, although in the technical subjects and some of the sciences this was mainly confined to male pupils. Also, the shift towards vocational subjects was more obvious at the junior cycle (Breen, 1984b, p. 110). At the senior cycle the position was less favourable. While there has been a very rapid growth in the popularity of biology, and substantial increases in some of the commerce subjects, the increased takeup of other sciences and of technical subjects has been more modest and confined largely to boys. So today a large percentage of senior cycle school leavers lack what we might term vocational subject qualifications. Even in the case of pupils who do take vocational subjects, the majority only take one or two rather than specialising in depth in, say, science or commerce; this is particularly true among girls. It appears that the predominant bias, at least at Leaving Certificate level, is still for pupils to study a broad range of subjects rather than to specialise.

Movement towards a more scientific/technical form of education has been in greater evidence at third level, where the growth in the numbers of students at RTCs, Technical Colleges and the NIHEs has been pronounced (Breen 1984b, p. 114). Well over half the additional enrolments in third level over the period between the early sixties and early eighties have gone to the technological institutions, which now have almost two-fifths of all students.[11]

There has also been some movement within third level institutions towards greater enrolment in science/technical and commerce courses, and taken together with the growth of RTCs, NIHEs and so on, this has led to a marked increase in the share of all students entering faculties of Science, Engineering and Commerce. However, such trends at third level are of no direct relevance to the majority of school pupils, given that, as Table 6.2 shows, currently about four out of five entrants to second level do not reach third level.

Why do the vocational subjects appear to have made so little mark at the senior cycle level? One important consideration relates to the nature of the labour market and the kinds of jobs available to those leaving schools after the senior cycle. During the 1970s far from manufacturing industry demanding large inflows of vocationally trained young people, employment in white collar work expanded dramatically while in manufacturing it grew more slowly in the 1970s than it had in the 1960s. While over the 1970s total employment increased by almost 15 000 per annum, the increase in employment in services accounted for 80 per cent of this (Sexton, 1982, p. 36). Within the services sector the two areas that showed the most rapid growth were the public sector (which increased employment by 43 per cent between 1971 and 1979) and the insurance and finance area of private services in which employment grew by about 55 per cent. In other words, 'labour market demand and . . . educational supply remained roughly in equilibrium up to the 1980s recession' (Hannan and Breen, 1987b, p. 101). No radical changes in educational goals or curriculum were required to meet the nature of the jobs becoming available to most school leavers.

The position of the Irish language in the educational system declined from the 1960s, reflecting a more general change in emphasis from a nationalism based on 'Irish identity' to an economically grounded nationalism. In practice, if not explicitly, the revival of the Irish language ceased to be central to the educational system. In the 1960s Irish-speaking teacher training colleges were phased out, and in the 1970s the necessity of gaining a pass in Irish in order to obtain the Leaving Certificate was abandoned, as was the requirement of Irish in the Leaving Certificate for entry into the Civil Service. Although Irish remains a compulsory subject for most pupils, failure rates at the national examinations have increased dramatically. In 1975, 15 per cent of Inter Cert Irish candidates failed the exam; by 1983 this had risen to 26 per cent. At the Leaving Certificate the increase has been equally sharp – from 7 to 17 per cent.

THE ROLE OF THE STATE IN EDUCATION

In seeking explanations of why the effects of the educational changes undertaken in the 1960s were, in many respects, quite unlike what seems to have been envisaged, we must return to the structure of the Irish educational system and, crucially, to the degree of control over that system exercised by the State.

At the primary level, there is a common curriculum, and national schools have always relied on the State for the bulk of their finances, each school having a direct relationship with the Department of Education largely unmediated by the existence of intervening layers of organisation. Thus, although these schools are privately owned, they are subject to a higher degree of central control over their activities. This is not generally true of post-primary education, which has been the scene of the bulk of the 1960s reforms. Here, despite completely centralised syllabuses, examinations, and funding for both capital and current costs, the Department of Education exercises relatively little control over major areas of post-primary education. For example, while all post-primary schools are obliged to provide courses of study in a small number of prescribed subjects, beyond this they have total freedom in determining which other of the 26 approved Intermediate and 32 Leaving Certificate subjects they will teach, and the manner in which they will make those subjects available to pupils. Hannan et al. (1983, p. 196) note that 'school management decisions are . . . crucial in shaping schools' curricula, particularly in the secondary sector'. The net effect is wide variation in curricula between post-primary schools.

Another area in which the State has relatively little control is in the physical structure of the system, secondary schools being the property, in the main, of private individuals, boards of management or trustees, or religious orders. So, for example, the Mercy order of nuns runs and controls about one fifth of all secondary schools; a further 15 per cent are held by the Christian Brothers and 10 per cent by the Presentation nuns. These and other orders are able to exercise specific educational policies in schools under their control. Furthermore, despite their reliance on the State for funding, the State's reliance on them as the owners of educational 'capital equipment' imposes major restrictions on State educational policy in terms of structural change.

These difficulties were exacerbated by the nature of the move to free education. When this policy was announced, in 1966, it effectively negated much of the groundwork that had been carried out to provide for curricular development along the desired lines, and ensured that progress towards a vocationally orientated curriculum would be less than it might have been.

The Government's proposals for equality of educational opportunity were bound up with the idea of a common or comprehensive curriculum. The latter would involve the amalgamation of schools, the sharing of facilities between schools and the setting up of educational centres serving specific catchment areas. The move to free post-primary education had been targeted for 1970: the period to that date was to have been used for increasing the capacity of the system to cope with greater numbers. As the idea of the comprehensive curriculum made clear, this new provision was to be made in the areas of technical/vocational education, rather than within the existing framework. The introduction of free education in 1967, however, led to the virtual abandonment of these intentions, and the consequent rapid growth in participation rates invalidated the projections of enrolments, costs, facility requirements, and so on, that had been made (Mulcahy, 1981, p. 29).

Once free post-primary education was in place, it became impossible for the Department of Education either to direct enrolments into specific kinds of schools or to effect curricular changes that would ensure a substantial move to a more vocationally orientated form of education. Although some changes were made in this direction (e.g. the introduction of new subjects) a good deal of effort appears to have been expended, post-1967, in coping with the effects of free education. In other words, because of the State's lack of control over the system, combined in this instance with the precipitate action of the Minister for Education, the introduction of one set of changes – free education – made the success of the other – the move to a more vocationally orientated system – less likely.

Of course, the proposals for curricular reform and the restructuring of the system met with opposition from other sources, particularly from religious interests. The Catholic Church was the principal opponent of proposals for a 'uniform system of post-primary education' whether this was to be achieved via the notion of 'educational centres' or through community schools. The proposals for rationalisation, amalgamation and co-operation which these notions incorporated would clearly have diminished the control exercised by religious denominations over education: such proposals seemed to envisage the replacement of the largely denominational post-primary sector by a 'general system of State-schools' which would be non-denominational (Randles, 1975, p. 303). The Church was largely successful in opposing these policies: it engaged in an active campaign against the proposals made in 1970 by the Department of Education for the amalgamation of existing secondary and vocational schools into community schools and it succeeded, after many years, in making such community schools as were established, denominational, rather than having them non-denominational as the Department had originally proposed.

Had the State, directly or otherwise, owned the schools themselves then the prospects for the rationalisation of facilities and a comprehensive curriculum would have been much brighter. As it was, faced with the failure of its attempts at reorganisation, the State introduced community schools in which the comprehensive curriculum could be established.[12] Even today, however, these account for no more than about 5 per cent of all post-primary schools. At third level the university sector initially refused to recognise the new vocational/technological subjects for the purpose of gaining admission and it was in the new forms of institution, namely the nine RTCs and the two NIHEs that technological education developed. It is in these new institutions, at both second and third level, that the State's intentions have been most clearly mirrored in reality.

CONCLUSION: TWENTY YEARS A-GROWING

The most evident change in the educational system over the past twenty years has been the marked increase in participation rates which, taken together with the growth of the relevant age sector of the population, has brought about a large expansion of the system. The major impact of the reforms of the 1960s has been neither a more technologically nor vocationally orientated system (though some progress has been made in this direction) nor a considerable reduction in class disparities in attainment. Educational change has not taken Ireland very far towards equality of labour market or occupational opportunity: the educational qualifications that school leavers bring into the job market continue to be strongly related to their social class origins – a state of affairs which has obvious and considerable implications for the degree of social mobility possible in Irish society. By and large, those who appear to have gained most from educational reform have been middle class – both the old middle class, who might otherwise have had to pay for their children's education, and the new middle class of families which have experienced mobility as a consequence of the massive structural shifts in the economy of the post-1958 era.

When we compare the present situation with that prevailing twenty-five years ago, we see a rapid growth in credentialism and in the formalisation of the labour market. The increase in the employee labour force and its growing specialisation and differentiation have been accompanied by an increased use of impersonal, objective criteria in the selection of individuals for jobs. The expansion of the educational system and the pervasive use of educational credentials in governing access to jobs have developed in tandem; the system's chief role has evolved as neither the more equitable redistribution of life changes nor the training of labour skilled in specific job-related areas but, rather, as one of discrimination and selection.

In this sense, then, a crucially important relationship between education and the labour market developed over the 1970s. This has been threatened in more recent years by large scale youth unemployment: there is insufficient demand to accommodate the outflow from the system and accordingly educational credentials have been devalued in absolute, if not relative, terms (Breen, 1984c, pp. 80–3). To a great extent, the problems that have arisen as a result of labour market changes – the overall recession and, in the case of the youth labour market, the decline in recruitment by bodies such as the Civil Service and large corporate employers – have been presented as being due to deficiencies in the supply of labour, which can best be addressed, so it is argued, by curricular change. Second level education is seen by many as 'inflexible' and as having an 'over-academic bias', and may be 'directing young people to forms of employment which are declining' (Conniffe and Kennedy, 1984, pp. 236–7). Most obvious is the perception that the educational system is not preparing young people for work: apparently lacking suitable skills and experience of work, school leavers must, if they are to be employable, be given these via a plethora of training schemes. This situation – in which such training intervenes between the educational system and the labour market – obviously represents an important change in the view of the labour market/education relationship held twenty years ago.

The relatively minor changes in class differentials in participation rates brought about by free post-primary education were, in retrospect, only to be expected, given the evidence from Britain and elsewhere that had begun to accumulate after the late 1950s regarding the effects of similar measures (for example, the 1944 Education Act). However, the failure of rationalisation and reorganisation may also have been important in the Irish case in blunting the impact of free education. Sharp differences continue to exist between the intake of secondary and vocational schools. Middle class children and girls are over-represented in the former, working class children and boys in the latter. In addition, the intake to vocational schools contains substantially greater proportions of children with numeracy and literacy problems (see Hannan et al., 1983, pp. 90–2). This not only places a greater burden on vocational schools, but leads to the post-primary system itself coming to reflect, to some extent, class divisions within society at large. At the local level this is manifested in competition among post-primary schools for pupils and among parents for places for their children in those schools which have a better reputation. The net result of this is that low-achieving working class boys, in particular, are placed together in a pupil environment which does little to encourage educational attainment.

Ironically, then, the present weaknesses of the educational system are much the same as those identified by the *Investment in Education* team. In retrospect, however, this constancy can be seen to derive not only from the failure of educational reform to bring about 'solutions' to these difficulties (a failure related, in turn, both to the structure of the system and to specific events which occurred in the late 1960s), but also from the development, in the 1980s, of a set of economic circumstances that could never have been envisaged, either by the authors of *Investment in Education* or by the policy makers who sought to respond to its findings.

NOTES

1. Of course not all the increase in educational expenditure has been due to increased utilisation of the service. In Ireland, for example, per-pupil costs have themselves grown considerably over the recent past (see Maguire, 1984).

2. Although local contributions to current costs are required, these are raised by the Committee of Management of the individual national schools.
3. In fact, the 1930 Act consolidated, rather than instituted, the existing provision of post-primary technical education.
4. A full description of the post-primary system is given by Hannan et al. (1983, pp. 82–92). A useful overview of the structure of Irish education will be found in Elvin (1981, pp. 135–52).
5. *Investment in Education* can now be seen to have been as important a watershed for Irish education as the 1958 Whitaker Report was for the Irish economy. Lyons (1973, p. 652) noting the apt symbolism of the fact that *Investment in Education* was partially financed by the OECD, calls the report 'epoch making', while Brown (1985, p. 250) suggests that the report reflected 'a radical ideological departure in Irish educational thinking'.
6. There were also important changes at the primary level, notably the abolition of the Primary Certificate examination (in 1971) and the introduction of a new curriculum and syllabuses.
7. Both fee-charging and Free Scheme secondary schools receive the bulk of their teachers' salaries from the State: until 1986 both types of school also received a capitation grant of £31 per pupil, though this was withdrawn from private schools under the provisions of the 1986 budget. In addition, Free Scheme secondary schools also receive a per-pupil grant 'in lieu of fees'. However, the extent of additional State support to free secondary schools is considerably less than the level of tuition fees paid in private schools. Thus the income of private schools is much greater than that of Free Scheme schools. At the time of the introduction of the Free Scheme, the grant in lieu of fees was £25 – roughly equal to annual tuition fees in Catholic Secondary schools (Tussing, 1978, p. 33). Since then, however, the divergence between the grant and the typical level of fees has widened considerably.
8. It is important to note that certain inaccuracies may arise in these estimates because of the limitations of the available data. The method of estimation for both the 1960s and the 1980s figures involves expressing the number of 15–19-year-olds in full-time education in each class (obtained from the Census) as a percentage of the number of 5–9-year-olds in the same class at the Census of ten years previously (see *Investment in Education*, p. 149). Thus there is some scope for inaccuracy here, particularly insofar as the class composition of the parents of the relevant age cohort has changed markedly (via migration or shifts in the occupational structure) over the ten-year period. The *Investment in Education* team made no attempt to allow for this: they write (p. 149) that their figures 'may, therefore, be regarded as giving the relative probabilities that a child in a particular social group in 1951 would be participating in full-time education in Ireland in 1961. This is subject to the qualification that we do not know how a particular parent's social grouping may have altered between 1951 and 1961'. A similar interpretation may be applied to the 1981 figures. However, some attempt was made to take account of changes in the occupational structure over the 1970s, notably by looking at the changing occupations of males in the age group likely to contain the parents of these young people. In general these estimates yield much the

same picture: the most favourable of them indicates a reduction in class disparities in participation rates of up to 16 per cent over the 1961–81 period.

9. See Hannan et al. (1983) for a comprehensive treatment of gender differences in Irish second-level education.

10. Annual costs per pupil in post-primary education are twice those for primary education while third-level costs are six times greater than at the primary level.

11. Social class imbalances in the intake to third level technological institutions are somewhat less pronounced than in the University sector (Clancy, 1982, p. 21), though gender imbalances are rather more marked.

12. The development of new community schools was partly financed through two loans from the World Bank in 1972 and 1974 (Wickham, 1980, p. 331).

7 Employment, Unemployment and Industrial Policy

Since the founding of the State, Ireland has been unable to create jobs on a scale sufficient to meet the requirements of its potential growth in population. The consequences of such failure have been high levels of unemployment among the employee labour force and high rates of emigration. In this chapter our purpose is to examine the way in which the Irish State has sought to address the employment problem, particularly in the post-1958 period – through industrial, public sector and manpower policy – and the resulting consequences. Of particular concern to us, of course, are the questions of how these policies have influenced the class structure of Irish society, and the degree to which the particular strategies pursued reflect the autonomy and capacity possessed by the State in this area. We begin, however, with a discussion of the current unemployment situation and an attempt to outline the dynamics of the Irish employment problem.

UNEMPLOYMENT: THE CURRENT POSITION

Despite the creation of many thousands of jobs since 1958, unemployment levels in Ireland have remained high by international standards. Unemployment in Ireland has been characterised by a high overall rate and a high level of long-term unemployment, which is reflected in a relatively long average duration of unemployment. As economic conditions have worsened, not only has the Irish unemployment rate increased, but so has the proportion of long-term unemployed, as Table 7.1 shows. Currently, over one in six workers is unemployed and nearly half of all registered unemployed males have been out of work for a year or more.

For much of the post-independence period, however, overall unemployment rates in Ireland have not been as high as might have been expected, fluctuating between 5 and 8 per cent over the 1926–51 period. This was largely an illusion, due both to high levels of emigration and

TABLE 7.1   *Irish unemployment rate 1972–88 and percentage of unemployed males, Live Register for more than one year*

Year	Unemployment rate (%)	Percentages of males unemployed more than 1 year
1972	5.2	15.8
1973	4.7	20.9
1974	4.6	24.0
1975	6.4	18.6
1976	7.8	20.4
1977	7.6	26.6
1978	7.1	29.0
1979	6.1	32.6
1980	6.0	38.8
1981	8.6	33.5
1982	10.7	35.3
1983	14.1	34.4
1984	16.1	43.5
1985	17.0	45.0
1986	17.4	48.8
1987	17.7	49.3
1988	16.6	49.4

SOURCES   Unemployment Rate:
1972–81 Bacon, Durkan and O'Leary (1982, p. 33, Table 22)
1982–88 *Quarterly Economic Commentary* The Economic and Social Research Institute, Dublin (various issues).
Percentage unemployed more than 1 year:
1972–79 O'Mahony (1983, p. 126, Table 2: first quarter figure for each.
1980–87 CSO, Age by duration analysis of Live Register (April figure for each year).

to the simple fact that such a large share of the work-force was made up of the self-employed (in agricultural and non-agricultural sectors) who could not, as a result, become 'unemployed' – at least in official terms. As this group has declined as a proportion of the labour force so the overall rate of unemployment has come to reflect more fully the position of employees. Table 7.2 shows the employee unemployment rate at censuses since 1926. Such rates are much higher than the overall unemployment rate, especially in the early years, where the level of unemployment among employees was nothing short of appalling. Also striking is the degree to which unemployment has been concentrated in the working classes: the level of unemployment among non-agricultural

TABLE 7.2   *Percentage of male employees in each employee class unemployed or out of work 1926–81 (total employees in parentheses)*

				Year			
	1926	1936	1946	1951	1961	1971	1981
Upper middle (service) class	2.6 (34 285)	3.2 (38 390)	3.0 (46 804)	1.2 (47 780)	0.9 (58 959)	1.2 (84 512)	3.0 (128 499)
Lower middle class	8.3 (103 954)	10.2 (101 414)	6.1 (106 800)	4.0 (121 418)	4.2 (120 241)	4.8 (139 041)	8.8 (161 942)
Skilled manual	19.1 (54 745)	14.8 (63 438)	9.1 (66 807)	5.0 (90 400)	5.9 (92 632)	6.9 (128 056)	15.0 (163 021)
Semi-skilled manual	21.8 (30 664)	22.1 (32 296)	14.9 (30 301)	7.4 (41 375)	8.6 (29 776)	9.8 (37 870)	20.0 (41 267)
Unskilled manual non-agricultural	45.6 (50 884)	47.4 (61 489)	28.9 (72 475)	17.2 (82 414)	31.2 (66 955)	29.4 (67 514)	49.4 (48 695)
Unskilled manual agricultural	12.6 (118 711)	22.8 (111 236)	9.9 (121 382)	7.0 (94 957)	18.1 (64 753)	30.1 (40 245)	29.5 (25 780)
All	16.7 (393 243)	20.3 (408 263)	10.2 (444 569)	7.5 (479 344)	10.7 (433 316)	11.1 (497 238)	15.9 (569 204)

SOURCE   *Census of Population of Ireland* (various).

unskilled workers fell below 25 per cent at only one census, while that for the service class only once exceeded three per cent.

In the twenties and thirties it was precisely the most disadvantaged categories – the semi-skilled and unskilled among both urban and rural populations, as well as the smaller farmers – whose support gave power to Fianna Fail (Chubb, 1970, p. 77). However, the persistence of high levels of unemployment within certain of these categories points to an absence not only of social, but also of geographical mobility. Such people could neither advance in the occupational structure nor, apparently, could they migrate in search of greater opportunities, and it is these groups which today comprise the 'underclass', to which we have earlier referred, heavily dependent on social welfare provision, but with little or no prospect of improving their own or their children's situation.

DYNAMICS OF EMPLOYMENT

The imbalance between the size of the labour force and the availability of jobs arises for two chief reasons. First, the rate of inflow into the labour force exceeds the outflow; and second, there are within the labour force substantial flows out of employment into unemployment, which in recent years have exceeded flows from unemployment into work.

The largest and most consistent source of labour force growth comes from young people leaving full-time education: between 1983 and 1984, there was an inflow into the youth labour force of about 40 000 from this source.[1] A second source of increase, which was particularly significant in the 1970s and continues to affect labour force growth, was inward migration. High levels of net emigration from Ireland prevailed for over a century until, in the 1970s, the outflow ceased and subsequently became a net inflow. Ireland's increasing prosperity was doubtless a prime factor in encouraging immigration, and many who came to Ireland in the 1970s were returning former emigrants. This immigration directly and immediately increased the size of the labour force, but continues to have an indirect effect in so far as the children of these immigrants are now entering the labour force.

These sources of growth are not offset to any appreciable extent by sources of decline through death or retirement – a situation which reflects the relatively youthful age structure of the Irish labour force.

Furthermore, women are becoming increasingly less likely to leave the labour force when they get married (as had been the traditional pattern) and as a result the labour force participation rate of married women doubled over the 1970s, reaching 20 per cent in 1984. Despite such rapid growth, married women's labour force participation is low in Ireland by OECD standards, and seems likely to increase further (though the magnitude of any increase will depend upon the condition of the labour market). Official estimates are for a rate of 21 per cent in 1991 (Central Statistics Office, 1985).

Traditionally, emigration was the route chosen by many of those who could not find work in Ireland and, as Table 7.3 shows, after the brief turn around of the 1970s, net emigration is again increasing.

Within the labour force, there are trends of long-term decline in the numbers at work in agriculture (where the male labour force more than halved between 1961 and 1985 from 360 000 to 151 000), and in indigenous Irish industry, particularly in sectors such as textiles, clothing and footwear. Job losses in manufacturing industry were substantial throughout the 1970s, and have increased in the 1980s. The number of newly created manufacturing jobs has been impressive. However, gains in manufacturing jobs tend to be inversely related to losses, fluctuating according to economic conditions (low gains and high losses in the early/mid-1970s and 1980s, high gains and lower losses in the late 1970s), and, in recent years, the gains have been more than outweighed by substantial losses.

By far the largest area of employment growth in the 1970s was in

TABLE 7.3   *Net emigration in inter-censal periods, 1926–86*

Period	Net emigration	Net migration per annum
1926–36	166 751	16 675
1936–46	187 111	18 711
1946–51	119 568	23 914
1951–56	196 763	39 353
1956–61	212 003	42 401
1961–66	80 605	16 121
1966–71	53 906	10 781
1971–79	− 108 934	− 13 617
1979–81	5 045	2 523
1981–86	75 300	15 060

* A minus sign indicates net immigration.
SOURCES   Meenan, 1970, p. 209; *Census of Population of Ireland* (various).

services: employment here grew by 136 000 between 1971 and 1981. However, the bulk of this (85 000 jobs) was in the public sector, whose expansion proved to be the major source of job creation (Sexton, 1982, p. 36). Ireland's large public debt now effectively precludes the public sector from this role, at least in the short to medium term. In 1981, the Government imposed an embargo on new recruitment to the public service and stringent limitations on the filling of vacancies. Since 1987 cutbacks in expenditure have led to job losses among non-permanent employees in the public services, while a voluntary redundancy/early retirement scheme has been introduced for permanent employees. Employment in the public service has declined since 1982 (Walsh, 1985, p. 163) and government policy is to reduce further the number of State employees. Without employment growth in this area, the private services, construction and manufacturing are left to provide the necessary jobs. However, not only is employment in indigenous manufacturing in decline but the employment levels in manufacturing as a whole have shown a steady fall between 1980 and 1985. Between 1985 and 1986 the numbers were constant. Furthermore, employment in building and construction has reduced from 102 000 in 1981 to 72 000 in 1986. Thus in two of the three conventionally defined sectors of the economy (agriculture, industry and services) the absolute numbers at work are falling. This fall has not been offset by growth in the level of non-public sector services, so there has been an overall reduction in the numbers at work since 1981.

This decline has been substantial: between 1981 and 1986 the numbers at work fell by 168 000 or 13 and a half per cent of the 1981 figure. Over the same period, the labour force grew by 43 000 overall. Depending on the level of net emigration, the labour force is officially expected to grow by between 11 000 and 17 000 per annum to the end of the decade.

EMPLOYMENT, UNEMPLOYMENT AND EMIGRATION

The relationship between agricultural and non-agricultural (particularly industrial) employment has been crucial in determining Irish employment prospects during this century. As we show in more detail in Chapter 9, the agricultural labour force – and especially the non-proprietorial occupations such as farm labourer and assisting relative – have been in a process of accelerating decline during this century. Furthermore, since partition had removed virtually the whole of the

Irish industrial base the new Irish State faced a situation in which over half its labour force was located in a declining sector while at the same time it possessed only a very small industrial sector in which jobs might be created to compensate for this decline.

Despite this unpromising position, the first inter-censal period, 1926–36, recorded growth in both the size of the labour force and the numbers at work – two trends, neither of which were to recur until the 1960s. Although the Cumann na nGaedhael government pinned most of its hopes for economic growth on the agricultural sector, it did, nevertheless, introduce limited measures designed to protect Irish industry. The succeeding Fianna Fail administration espoused a much more thoroughgoing protectionism. This derived in part from a change in the world economic climate following the Great Depression. Tariff barriers were being erected by all countries and Ireland had little option but to do likewise. However, as Johnson points out (1985, p. 26), had Fianna Fail not come to power, it is unlikely that protectionism in the Republic would have proceeded so fast or so far. The move to protectionism also sprang from values of self-sufficiency and self-reliance that had a long history in nationalist philosophy. In particular the new government was concerned to develop industry within Ireland and thus to create jobs.[2] This policy met with a degree of success: industrial employment increased and the overall numbers at work changed little between 1926 and 1951, despite huge declines in the agricultural labour force. However, the policy was not sufficiently successful to provide work for all. The unemployment rate of the employee work force remained high, and despite temporary abatements in emigration due the the Depression and the Second World War, there was substantial net emigration, as Table 7.3 shows.

The post-war period opened with a short-lived economic boom, one effect of which was to encourage the Government, with assistance from Marshall Aid, to institute a Public Capital Programme for the building of roads, hospitals, houses, schools and so forth. This boom, however, led to a perceived balance of payments crisis, which the Government attempted to tackle by means of severely deflationary budgets. Industrial employment stagnated, agricultural jobs continued to disappear, and the results were increasing unemployment and dramatically rising emigration. Emigrants were attracted to Britain, where jobs were readily available, and as Table 7.3 shows, in the latter half of the 1950s annual average net emigration exceeded 40 000, and in 1957 exceeded 50 000.

Although Walsh (1979) has suggested that the crises of the 1950s arose largely through mistaken policy responses to the perceived balance of payments difficulties, there was a widespread feeling among policymakers at the time that protectionism had failed.

Before the scene was changed in the late 1950s, a general mood of despondency prevailed. Economic growth had been so slow and erratic, so many vicissitudes had been encountered, so much population lost by emigration, so few new jobs created in relation to need, that the community was experiencing a dark night of the soul in which doubts were prevalent as to whether the achievement of political independence had not been a failure. But at least some lessons had been learned, in particular, the lesson that the pursuit of self-sufficiency, through policies which fostered inefficiency, offered no prospect of employment in Ireland at an acceptable income for those who sought it. (Whitaker, 1986, p. 11).

The scene was changed by the appearance of the *Programme for Economic Expansion* in 1958, which followed on the heels of the report, *Economic Development*, published in the same year. The nature of these changes in industrial policy has been referred to briefly in Chapter 1: basically, they were twofold. First was the attempt to encourage export-orientated foreign-owned manufacturing to locate in Ireland. The *Programme for Economic Expansion* explicitly proclaims the State's willingness to facilitate foreign-based investment, and the Industrial Development (Encouragement of External Investment) Act of 1958 set this in motion by easing many of the restrictions which had been imposed by the Control of Manufactures Acts.[3] Second was the commitment to free trade. While this was probably an indispensable element of the strategy to encourage foreign investment in Ireland, it nevertheless represented a major break with the policy of protectionism which had prevailed since the 1930s. In the first Programme, the Government indicated its willingness to join any Western European free trade areas, foreshadowing Ireland's attempts to join the EC in the early 1960s. Despite the failure of this attempt, there were moves towards freer trade in the 1960s, in particular the Anglo-Irish Free Trade Area Agreement of 1965: however, the most important move in this direction was accession to the EC in 1973.

Before addressing the question of the effects of this shift in policy, four points can highlight the nature of the shift in State policy in the late 1950s. First, as originally conceived, the *Programme for Economic Expansion* envisaged agriculture as the primary engine of economic growth, and indeed, the bulk of the Programme is devoted to the prospects for increasing net output and exports of agriculture. In as much as the agricultural sector failed to live up to these expectations, so manufacturing industry (or at least, that sector of it attracted to Ireland from overseas) exceeded them.

Second, the employment strategy of economic development was one of indirect job creation. Despite the subsequent high levels of government expenditure on industrial development, primacy was accorded to free, rather than State-owned or controlled, enterprises. The *Programme for Economic Expansion* (p. 34) stated that 'there is no substitute for private enterprise, and the main objective of government policy in this field is to create the conditions in which it will be stimulated'. Although job creation was the ultimate objective of industrial policy, the immediate aim was 'higher productivity and greater competitiveness' (*Second Programme*, 1963, p. 17): if these were secured, then jobs would follow. In other late industrialising economies, whose position is, or recently was, similar to that of Ireland, such as South Korea, Taiwan and post-war Japan, a strategy of industrial growth was based upon some measure of *de facto* protectionism coupled with direct State involvement (in terms of directing the operation of markets or setting up a large share of State-owned enterprises). Paradoxically, Ireland's reliance on the free play of market force is a strategy more usually favoured by larger and stronger economies – Britain in the nineteenth century, the USA in the twentieth (O'Malley, 1986).

The absence of direct intervention by the State is related to our third point, which is that while there has been substantial public expenditure to promote industrialisation, the State possesses relatively little control over manufacturing development in the sense of, for example, having little or no control over the disbursement of profits or over matters like the location of new industry. Such control as has been exercised over those issues has been achieved indirectly through, for example, differential grant rates for different regions or the provision of actual premises. Policy has centred on seeking to provide a climate – of grants and tax incentives; of free trade and access to EC markets; of trained manpower and quiescent labour – which will be attractive to foreign industry and allow free enterprise to flourish. Such a policy has necessarily been expensive and according to prevailing international standards, possibly unnecessarily generous (Telesis Consultancy Group, 1982, p. 198).

Fourth, the long period of protectionism had led to the growth of a native Irish industrial bourgeoisie, whose attitude to the new policy might have been expected to be hostile. For all intents and purposes, however, the transformation met with relatively little opposition, and there were a number of factors which helped secure this. Thus the dismantling of protectionism was a policy which commanded the support of all major political parties (Bew and Patterson, 1981, p. 130) and indeed it can be argued that it was set in motion under the Coalition Government of 1954–57 rather than by the Fianna Fail administration under Sean Lemass (from 1959 onwards), who subsequently gained many of the plaudits (Fanning, 1983, p. 194). Furthermore, the policy was one which had been formulated by members of the Civil Service and was not, therefore, identified with the programme of any one party. Indeed, *Economic Development* was published not as a government White Paper but as a report by the Department of Finance, thus freeing it from party political overtones.

As well as the absence of any political party around which their opposition could coalesce, the Irish industrial bourgeoisie were themselves divided in their interests and thus in their attitudes to free trade (Bew and Patterson, 1982, pp. 129; 144). So, for example, they were differently positioned with regard to the likely fate of businesses under free trade – many envisaged difficulties, but some hoped at least to maintain their position. Likewise, some members of the Irish industrial bourgeoisie had close links with foreign-owned concerns. As a result, Irish industrialists were by no means united in opposing the new developments. Finally, Lemass's government adopted a policy in which the stick was heavily counterbalanced by the carrot. Although certain industries could indeed expect to lose their market share, the Government promised financial and technical assistance to help firms adapt to new conditions.

EMPLOYMENT GROWTH AND THE PUBLIC SECTOR

In the period since 1958, industrial policy has been one of the two major ways in which the State has sought to provide for employment growth: the other has been through the direct creation of jobs by the State itself, in the Civil Service, local government, and the so-called semi-State and State-sponsored bodies. In the 1960s there was a small net change in employment, the decline in agriculture being offset by growth, particularly in manufacturing and the public sector. However, in the 1970s, growth in manufacturing and in building slackened and the Government responded through two measures: (1) it sought to give extra impetus to economic growth (which, it was hoped, would create jobs) through direct involvement in the labour market, and (2) in the late 1970s, the policy of making employment creation contingent upon economic growth gave way to the use of the public sector as a vehicle for the creation of jobs. Clearly, of course, a proportion of the large employment growth in the public sector over the 1970s would have been anticipated because of, for example, the demand for increased provision of social services or the requirements arising out of economic growth and social development. However, in this period, the

> organic growth of public service employment, as a consequence of the general economic and social development of the country, was being deliberately accelerated, by government policy, in order to ameliorate the adverse employment effects of diminished labour demand in other sectors of the economy. (Humphreys, 1983, p. 119).

So, for example, under the terms of the National Understanding for Economic and Social Development 1979, the Government, as part of its agreement with the trade unions and employers' organisations, accepted a job creation target of 25 000 jobs per year and committed itself to meeting any shortfall in this number up to a maximum of 5000 jobs via a joint public/private sector employment programme.

The low rate of growth in industrial employment in the 1970s, and the decline in employment in manufacturing in the 1980s, were related not only to the recessionary conditions following the increase in energy costs at the start and the end of the decade, but also to the growing vulnerability of indigenous industry, caused by the removal of protectionism. While it might have been hoped that a free trade regime would introduce greater efficiency in indigenous Irish manufacturing (much of which had developed behind barriers to overseas competition), in fact in the period between 1973 and 1980, employment in this area fell by 3 per cent, a decline concentrated in the internationally traded sectors, such as chemicals, textiles, clothing and footwear, in which Irish firms are most fully exposed to competition (O'Malley, 1985, p. 147). As a result, most of the employment growth in industry has been generated by foreign-owned concerns. Beyond that, however, long established foreign companies have also recorded a decline in employment. For example, in the 1973–80 period, employment in foreign firms established before 1973 fell by 2 per cent and, in those established before 1969, by 10 per cent.

The declining trend in the longer established foreign firms means that Ireland had depended on new first-time foreign investors for manufacturing employment growth. If the newcomers themselves tend eventually to go into decline, there will be a gradually increasing proportion of relatively old declining plants, necessitating continuous increases in new first-time investment to attain net employment increases of any given amount (O'Malley, 1985, p. 151).

MANPOWER POLICY

In addition to industrial and public service policy, a third area has developed in response to the perceived need to create jobs: manpower policy. Broadly speaking, Irish manpower policy has tended to follow closely international trends. In 1966, the Department of Labour was established[4] with overall responsibility for manpower policy and in 1967, AnCO, the Industrial Training Authority, was set up to organise and promote all forms of industrial and vocational training. 1971 saw the establishing of the State's employment exchange or placement system, the National Manpower Service, within the Department of Labour.

In the period of the 1960s and early 1970s the role of manpower policy was seen to lie in training the labour force (and re-training those sections of it leaving declining traditional industries), and generally facilitating the efficient matching of the supply of, and demand, for, labour. These aims were consistent with the then current notions of an 'active manpower policy' as advanced by the OECD in the mid-1960s (see Danaher et al, 1985, pp. 48–51) which, in turn, arose out of a European climate of full employment and economic growth. In Ireland's case, however, the emphasis on training was also in accord with the view of the education/labour market link advanced in *Investment in Education*. The development of AnCO, for example (with responsibility for apprenticeship training and to extend the availability of training to Irish industry), the encouragement of technical education, and the opening of institutions such as regional technical colleges, can all be seen as part of a strategy to develop a well trained labour force which would enhance Ireland's attractiveness to overseas manufacturing concerns.

In the mid-1970s, the role of manpower policy was widened – as it was in most other Western European countries. Poorer economic conditions and increasing unemployment led to an emphasis on stimulating the demand for labour. The State increased its provision of training, a development facilitated by entry to the EC and the availability of European Social Fund (ESF) finance. Employment subsidies were introduced as were training and temporary employment schemes to combat unemployment.

In the 1980s, manpower policy has, for all intents and purposes, become employment policy. In 1988 the variety of agencies – AnCO, the National Manpower Service and the Youth Employment Agency (YEA) – organising intervention schemes within the labour market were amalgamated into one body, FAS (Foras Aiseanna Saothair). The range of job creation and training programmes which FAS administers, together with the Department of Education's Vocational Preparation and Training Programme (a one-year course for school leavers) and some smaller programmes, provide about 60 000 places at any one time, a figure equal to about 4.5 per cent of the registered labour force.

THE CONSEQUENCES OF DEVELOPMENT – SKILLS AND THE CLASS STRUCTURE

Thus far, we have been concerned with describing the employment problem in Ireland and the State's response to it. We now turn to an assessment of the effects of such policies and ask how they influenced the class structure, and how, if at all, they altered the process of class reproduction.

Although it is clear that government policies of job creation failed to overcome the obstacles to full employment, it is equally evident that they helped to re-shape the occupational structure. These changes were discussed in Chapter 3: a dwindling in the viability of self-employment, counterbalanced by growth in wage employment and, among the employed workforce, a shift away from semi-skilled and unskilled labour towards white collar and skilled manual work. This has occurred within the context of a rapid alteration in the sectoral pattern of employment. In 1921, 36 per cent of the employed labour force were engaged in agriculture, 24 per cent in manufacturing and 41 per cent in services. Sixty years later there has been a dramatic shift: only 16 per cent are now located in agriculture, with 29 per cent in manufacturing and 55 per cent in services. This decline in the importance of agriculture as a direct employer of labour is mirrored by changes in Ireland's trading position with the rest of the world. Ireland has moved from a reliance on primary produce for exports (so, in 1958, live animals made up 37 per cent of Irish exports, with manufactured goods accounting for 17 per cent) to a reliance on manufacturing (in 1980, live animals made up 5 per cent of Irish exports, manufactured goods 55 per cent).

Analysis of the services sector (by O'Leary, 1986) shows a shift in employment patterns between 1971 and 1981 both towards more skilled areas of service sector work and to more skilled occupations within these areas. Inspection of tables such as 3.1 and 3.2 also suggests a comparable increase of skill in industry. Male skilled manual workers increased by over 50 per cent between 1961 and 1985. More detailed analysis of the change in the occupational composition of industry between 1971 and 1981 (O'Leary, 1986) shows a move away from less skilled areas such as labourers and operatives (declining from 54 to 42 per cent of the industrial workforce) and a move towards more skilled jobs. So the percentage of the industrial workforce in craft, professional, technical, administrative and managerial occupations grew from 33 to 41 per cent over the period.

Such an up-grading in skills in the industrial workforce, however, commenced from a base of relatively low skill levels. This can be seen in the light of the fact that, although the electronics industry in Ireland is more heavily biased towards unskilled production work than in the UK or USA, its overall skill profile is actually better than that of most Irish industries (O'Malley, 1985, p. 149; Danaher et al., 1985, p. 321).

Despite such up-skilling there are, within the non-agricultural sector, substantial numbers in the marginalised working classes, dependent on welfare provisions. These groups – particularly the unskilled among both the agricultural and non-agricultural labour force – are not only declining numerically but as Table 7.2 shows, since 1961 their rates of unemployment have increased dramatically. Their position was exacerbated by the logic of Irish industrial development policy through imbalances or disjunctures between the forms of employment created and the kinds of jobs which have been lost. In broad terms, the jobs which have been lost have been in traditional, indigenous industries, which failed to survive once protectionism was dismantled, and have been of relatively low skill levels, predominantly located in urban areas, notably Dublin. The jobs which have been created have often required greater levels of skills and have been more widely dispersed throughout the country.

The degree of dispersal of industry in recent times is reflected in the fact that, although an ever increasing share of the total labour force has come to be located in Dublin over the past twenty-five years, the share of the industrial labour force there has diminished. In 1961, 37 per cent of males engaged in industry were in Dublin; by 1981 this had fallen to 29 per cent. Among females the decline is even more marked – from 55 per cent in 1961 to 36 per cent in 1981. This is because female employment in Dublin has declined over the period (probably with the decline of traditionally 'female' industries such as clothing and textiles) whereas it has increased everywhere else.

The dispersal of industrial location into rural areas in the 1960s and 1970s had long roots in Fianna Fail policy. However, during the recent past its purpose has been not simply to provide an alternative to agricultural employment for those who could no longer acquire it, but also to yield a second occupation for those farmers whose acreage is too small or too poor to ensure their viability. This was explicitly stated in the *Third Programme for Economic and Social Development*, and is a policy whose details and results we deal with in Chapter 9. It can be argued, however, that the costs of the policy of locating industry in 'new' areas were carried by the urban working class – particularly the lower working class, whose jobs in indigenous firms were fast disappearing.

From the point of view of the new firms themselves, rural location carried with it both advantages and disadvantages. The disadvantages – experienced particularly by those firms locating in Ireland earliest – related to the absence of a tradition among employees of the discipline required for regulated work in manufacturing. Offsetting this, however, are what many companies viewed as the advantages inherent in employing a work-force with little or no history of trade unionism, with little previous experience of management/labour relations and possibly lacking the negative attitudes towards management that workers in longer established industrial areas display (Whelan, 1982).

Because much new industry require a more skilled work-force, younger rather than older workers are favoured. The educational reforms of the 1960s and the subsequent development of training policy mean that younger sections of the labour force are, on average, better educated and trained. The consequences of this can be seen in, for example, the results of a 1979 Industrial Development Authority (IDA) survey which showed that 55 per cent of jobs created in new grant-aided industries were held by people less than 25 years of age (OECD, 1984, p. 26).

Labour market position and educational attainment have a close relationship within the youth labour force. However, as we showed earlier, the benefits of education accrue disproportionately to children of the middle classes (Breen, 1984b and c; Clancy, 1982; Greaney and

Kellaghan, 1984; Hannan et al., 1983; Whelan and Whelan, 1984). Thus, insofar as educational credentials provide access to jobs, the educational advantages of middle class children are subsequently transformed into labour market advantage. Unemployment rates among young people are strongly related to levels of educational qualification: the higher the level of qualifications, the lower the likelihood of unemployment (Breen, 1984c; 1985). This relationship arises through two factors: educational credentials influence the chances of a young person finding a first job and thus making an initial entry into work, and they influence the kind of occupations entered, which carry different risks of unemployment.[5] As a result, the risk of unemployment among those in the youth labour force is much higher among working class than among middle class children, and unemployed young people overwhelmingly originate from working class origins, largely because of the class differentials in the benefits obtained from education. More generally the close relationship between class origins and educational attainment, between the latter and the labour market position, accounts for the continuation of a highly structured social mobility regime (with limited opportunities for upward mobility).

Although the opportunities in unskilled or poorly skilled work are continually diminishing, there is at the same time little provision for either intra- or inter-generational mobility out of the marginalised semi-skilled and unskilled working classes. The absence of large scale adult training and retraining means that unskilled adults cannot acquire skills, while the Irish educational system does not afford the children of lower working class families the means by which to acquire qualifications and skills. There remains, therefore, a large proportion of each cohort of school leavers – about 15 per cent – who come in to the labour market each year wholly lacking in formal qualifications. So a marginalised underclass is being reproduced through the educational and training systems while being sustained by social welfare provisions. The creation of employment for the members of this underclass was an option which was never seriously implemented and which now appears to lie beyond the capability of the Irish State.[6]

CONCLUSION

The policies of job creation pursued over the recent past have not been sufficiently successful to reduce Irish unemployment to a level comparable with that of its neighbours, and of course in the 1980s the unemployment rate has climbed seemingly inexorably. Furthermore, it now seems most unlikely that a continuation of previous policies will be feasible, regardless of its desirability. Any increase in the numbers employed in the public sector is out of the question, given the state of the public finances: indeed, a continued and probably accelerating decline in employment in this area seems inevitable. It is unlikely that the employment growth in manufacturing during the 1960s can be replicated. That increase was largely due to the establishment of new foreign-based firms in Ireland. Past trends suggest, therefore, that further growth depends upon the ability of the IDA to continue attracting such firms; however, the international climate in the mid-1980s looks less favourable in this respect than previously. There is now increased competition both within and outside the EC for mobile investment: in recent years Ireland's share of new investment in Europe by US companies, for example, has declined, while countries like Italy, Holland and the UK have increased their share (Fitzpatrick and Kelly, 1985, p. xxiii). But beyond this, even if sufficient jobs could be created to increase the numbers at work (thus reversing the post-1981 trend), this will not necessarily lead to a commensurate reduction in the level of unemployment, since the size of the labour force is itself responsive to the perceived availability of jobs. The creation of new jobs tends to draw into the labour force those who have not previously been seeking work – notably married women and, in the 1970s, returned migrants. As a result, in attempting to lower the level of unemployment, Ireland is 'chasing its own tail' (OECD, 1984).

The recent history of Irish industrial policy reveals the extent to which external forces limit the State's autonomy. Reliance on the attraction of overseas capital necessitates considerable expenditure, not only directly through the IDA and others, but also indirectly. Indirect costs include expenditure on the provision of a trained work-force, and expenditures incurred in a variety of other areas as a result of the national wage agreements which were, ostensibly, the price to be paid for industrial peace (Stanton, 1979). To this must be added the substantial potential tax revenues foregone from manufacturing enterprises through the existence of tax breaks and low rates of corporation tax. A less readily quantified loss came from the State's willingness to allow the full repatriation of profits by foreign owned firms, an increasingly severe drain on Ireland's balance of payments. For example, the total outflow of profits, dividends and royalties in 1986 was over £1346 million, equal to almost 7.5 per cent of GDP.

Reliance on foreign owned manufacturing has other consequences. Since a chief source of Ireland's attractiveness to overseas firms is that it affords access to EC markets,[7] it tends to mean that only the final production or assembly processes are located in Ireland. As a result, 'Foreign owned industrial operations in Ireland . . . do not embody the key competitive activities of the industries in which they participate. (Telesis Consultancy Group, 1982, p. 151).

High skill areas such as research and development are generally absent.[8] Furthermore, foreign owned manufacturing has developed few links with Irish firms. For example, foreign firms purchase very few of their inputs from native enterprises and thus the former have done little to stimulate indigenous industrial growth. As a result, the multiplier effects of the investment in attracting foreign industry have proved disappointing. To compound the problem, those indigenous Irish companies which have been successful over the recent past have concentrated their expansion outside Ireland, so they themselves are Irish-owned multinationals. This expansion has mainly taken the form of overseas acquisitions, chiefly in Britain and the United States on the part of companies such as Jefferson Smurfit, CRH and others. While these strategies have conferred benefits on the shareholders of these companies they have been irrelevant in addressing the unemployment problem.

More broadly speaking, the limits of the State's action in regard to the employment crisis is evident through the fatalism that now seems to inform job creation policy – at least at the macro economic level. It is now widely accepted by policymakers and their advisers, that any large scale improvement in the situation is outside the hands of an Irish administration. Hopes – such as there are – focus on the prospects for reflation in the larger economies which would generate a tide of growth on which the Irish economy might expect to rise.

NOTES

1. Based on unpublished figures from the 1984 Labour Force Survey.
2. However, industrialisation was to be by native Irish enterprises, and in the 1930s the Government passed the Control of Manufactures Acts which specified that control of companies must be in Irish hands. Foreign businesses could operate in Ireland only under licence and usually under restrictive conditions (Johnson, 1985, p. 29).
3. As O'Malley (1980, pp. 6–7) and others have noted, some of the foundations for this policy had already been laid: the Public Capital Programme

had begun to develop the necessary infrastructure; the Industrial Development Authority (IDA) had been established in 1949, and the Export Board (Coras Tractala) in 1952, while Export Profit Tax Relief (EPTR) had been introduced in the 1956 budget. This measure allowed for 50 per cent tax remission on profits earned on increases (over the previous year) in export sales. The rate was doubled to 100 per cent in 1956. In seeking to encourage industrial development and multinational location in Ireland, the Government, operating largely via the IDA, offered not only EPTR but also grants covering percentages of the costs to new export-orientated industry, of buildings, land, plant and machinery. Later, in the 1960s, these incentives were expanded: the repeal of the Control of Manufactures Acts removed all restrictions on foreign ownership and on the repatriation of profits. Advance factories on industrial estates were established after 1966, and grants were further made available for re-equipment, housing and training of workers, and research and development. In 1978, EPTR was replaced by a flat rate of corporation tax, set at a very low level of ten per cent. In addition favourable tax treatment is allowed in respect of other costs (Telesis Consultancy Group, 1982, p. 191).

4. Or strictly speaking, re-established, since a Department of Labour had existed in the 1920s.

5. This argument is developed at greater length in Breen (1985).

6. This situation is unaffected by the wide range of programmes of intervention (training, work experience, temporary employment, etc.) in the youth labour market that is now in place. Although the level of provision is such schemes has been increasing, the relationship between participation and educational credentials has been relatively constant. Those young people who are likely to experience the greatest labour market difficulties are the least likely to participate in training programmes, while those with the most valuable post-primary educational qualifications are the most likely to participate.

7. The significance of location, as a source of Ireland's attractiveness, thus distinguishes the Irish experience of industrial development via multinational investment, from that of many Third World, less developed countries, whose attractiveness resides chiefly in the availability of cheap labour.

8. Paradoxically, Ireland's low rate of corporation income tax may discourage multinationals from establishing activities like R and D in the country. Given a company which operates in a number of countries under a variety of tax regimes, it is likely to site operations like R and D, some of whose expenses can be written off against tax, in those countries where its tax liability is greatest.

8 Industrial Relations and the State

THE CHANGING ROLE OF THE STATE IN INDUSTRIAL RELATIONS

The shift away from a residual State role in industrial relations was a direct response to the problems created by the industrialisation strategy pursued in Ireland. Free trade and the heavy reliance on attracting foreign investment made it imperative to maintain stable industrial relations and wage competitiveness (Hardiman, 1986; Roche 1982; Stanton, 1979) and in these respects, the traditional role of the State in industrial relations could no longer suffice. The new State role in the 1960s brought the Government, trade union and employer representatives together in a variety of bodies established to facilitate the programme of economic development. The next decade brought another role for the State; as a 'partner' to a series of National Wage Agreements. It was that extension of the State's role that ultimately blurred the boundary between the economic and the political in Ireland. Industrial policy, industrial relations, wages and taxes all entered the political arena – and remained there, despite the gradual dissolution of tripartite arrangements.

These changes in Ireland should be viewed against the background of a variety of efforts in post World War II Western European countries to restructure industrial relations. Such efforts were initially associated with the displacement of neo-classical liberalism by Keynesianism (Bornstein, 1984, pp. 55–6). Subsequently, with the increasing power of trade unions and the perceived damage which interest-group activity caused to the operation of market mechanisms, the indirect controls associated with Keynesianism could no longer suffice:

> Government became increasingly aware that macroeconomic parameters are influenced by large organisations and might therefore be more effectively manipulated with their support (Lehmbruch, 1984, pp. 63–4)

The main objective of such institutional developments was to find *political* substitutes for the declining efficiency of the market mechanism.[1] Incomes policy has been central to this attempt to re-direct the increased power of trade unions away from the labour market and into the political arena.[2] Institutional arrangements of this type are generally termed 'neo-corporatist'. They involve developing and strengthening trade union and employer interest associations to the point where they have a representational monopoly, granting them privileged access to Government, and creating a social partnership between business, labour and Government.[3] In this scheme, trade unions and employer associations will simultaneously represent their members' interests while constraining and disciplining their members in the pursuit of the 'general' interest.

The alternative strategy of strengthening market control by reducing the power of organised labour was never feasible in Ireland.[4] The non-ideological character of party politics made such a 'right wing' approach unmarketable and in fact governments derived no electoral benefits from those occasions on which they did attempt to stand up to trade unions. Consequently, all of the political parties pursued a policy of seeking to involve trade union and employer organisations as partners in economic development (Hardiman, 1986, pp. 245–6).

Given the small size of the country, its ethnic and religious homogeneity, the importance of informal networks of communication, and the weakness of class politics, such a strategy had, it seemed to many observers, much to recommend it. In fact, the conditions were not present for the development of tripartite arrangements sufficient to mediate distributive conflict through a shared policy understanding. The stumbling blocks included the structure of trade union and employer representation, the basis of political partisanship and the nature of electoral competition. They contributed to a situation in which distributive conflict was accommodated rather than resolved and at a cost that could be sustained only for the short term (Hardiman, 1986, pp. 240–7).

THE STRUCTURE OF THE IRISH TRADE UNION MOVEMENT: CAPACITY FOR STRATEGY

By the early 1980s trade union membership in Ireland stood at over half a million workers and union density (members as a proportion of potential members) had reached 55 per cent (Roche and Larraghy, 1987). There were more than 80 separate unions, although five general unions held nearly half of the membership. Still, divisions within the trade union movement are accentuated by the duplication of function by Irish and British unions and by the existence of a significant minority of unions not affiliated to the Irish Congress of Trade Unions (ICTU) (McCarthy, 1979).

Other factors have limited the impact of the trade unions in Ireland. Their small size makes it difficult for them to provide an adequate level of service to members, while competitive recruitment policies inhibit unions from raising their membership fees and thus their ability to deliver services (Cardiff, 1982; Schregle, 1975). With other unions organising the same categories of workers, a union's control over its members is weakened sufficiently that 'Irish trade union leadership must be very circumspect so as to make sure that it is followed by the rank and file membership' (Schregle, 1975: 11). Despite official reports, numerous recommendations, and legal provisions to facilitate union amalgamation and inter-union transfers, progress towards a more coherent structure has been modest. The most direct attempt by the State to promote rationalisation came in the Trade Union Act 1941, which attempted to introduce the concept of 'one industry, one union' into Irish industrial relations. That part of the Act was found to be unconstitutional in a Supreme Court decision of 1947.[5] Subsequent legislation, such as the Trade Union Act 1975, was specifically introduced to facilitate and encourage the amalgamation of trade unions. The act made possible the provision of grants towards certain expenses of a union upon amalgamation. By 1983, only four unions had amalgamated in accordance with the Act's provision. Although the most recent proposal from the Department of Labour contains a number of suggestions for legislative changes to encourage rationalisation, it is now clear that the responsibility for initiating such change largely rests with the trade union movement itself (Department of Labour, 1983).[6] In recent years the pace of amalgamation has accelerated. The number of unions has been reduced to 70 and current discussions regarding amalgamation include those between the two largest general unions, the Irish Transport and General Workers' Union and the Federated Workers Union of Ireland.

CLASS CONSCIOUSNESS AND COMPARABILITIES

The Irish trade union movement has been dominated by short-term relativistic and sectionalist concerns. As a result, it lacks a class-based identity and the capacity to define interests in terms of a class-based analysis of inequalities.

There is general agreement on the importance that short range comparabilities have had in Irish industrial relations. A detailed study of wage bargaining in Ireland in the 1960s concluded that the most important non-economic factor influencing the process of wage determination was feelings of 'relative deprivation', which manifest themselves in a widespread use of comparability arguments (McCarthy, O'Brien and Dowd, 1975). However, the kinds of comparison that Irish workers take seriously are complex, based on their understanding and evaluation of the distribution of rewards across class groups.

Also, there are substantial differences between class groups in the level of pay they deem appropriate for particular class groups; over 30 per cent of manual workers, for example, regard managers as overpaid (Whelan, 1980, pp. 39–49, 59–76).[7] However, there appears to be an absence of class consciousness in the sense of both worker identification with one class group and with a perception of opposition of interest to other class groups. The gains of one class are not seen to be at the expense of another. Such evaluations can be explained on the basis of an underlying consensus regarding the manner in which work rewards are distributed between classes. On the other hand, employees are extremely unwilling to legitimate situations where they perceive themselves to be under-rewarded in comparison with their own occupational group or where they consider this group to be under-rewarded in comparison with their own class (Whelan, 1980, pp. 77–85). Such restricted frames of reference were both reflected in, and reinforced by, the prevalance of comparability arguments in wage bargaining in Ireland, thus exacerbating the consequences of a fragmented trade union structure.

In committing their members to the political bargaining that is the essence of neo-corporatism, trade unions have to resolve the distributional dissent arising from sectionalist interests within their membership. Writers on neo-corporatism identify unity and centralisation of the trade union movement as essential facilitating conditions.[8] In their view, however, it is not centralisation *per se* that is crucial, but the capacity for centralised strategic action (Lehmbruch, 1984, p. 69). Thus, industrial unionism in Sweden has been seen as providing favourable conditions for class-based strategies which centre on equal pay for equal work and a reduction of differentials for different kinds of work (Korpi, 1978, 1983; Korpi and Shalev, 1979, 1980). Such a transcendence of sectional interests requires a degree of cohesion and discipline which must ultimately be based on class solidarity (Goldthorpe, 1984, p. 327). The absence of such solidarity in Ireland was the major factor denying the ICTU the capacity to transform the centralised collective agreements of the 1970s into meaningful political exchange.

THE ROLE OF THE IRISH CONGRESS OF TRADE UNIONS

The ICTU attempted to strengthen its role in the National Wage Agreements (NWAs) of the 1970s by insisting that its Executive Council should be the sole representative of organised labour. Throughout that decade the endeavour was reinforced by both Government and employers. For example, the Government introduced legislation on several occasions to block agreements in breach of the NWAs negotiated between the commercial banks and the Irish Bank Officials' Association, which is not affiliated to the ICTU; and employer federations encouraged recruitment practices on the part of new and existing member organisation that discriminated in favour of affiliated unions.

The authority of Congress was potentially constrained by the existence of 13 non-affiliated unions. Given that those unions represented only 7 per cent of total trade union membership, their non-affiliation did not create appreciable direct wage costs and conflict. However, the indirect consequences were substantial. The wage policies of some non-affiliated unions seemed to have the objective of not only increasing their current members' wages, but also enticing members away from affiliated unions. The threat of desertion to non-Congress unions by disaffected members in affiliated unions produced pressure to breach NWAs or to demand higher norms and greater 'flexibility' in NWA terms than would otherwise have been judged appropriate. The only countervailing penalties which Congress could impose were either negligible and ineffective or substantial and counter-productive. Congress therefore chose to avoid policies such as restrictive NWAs, which might lead to breaches by affiliated unions (O'Brien, 1981, pp. 161–2). The ICTU is a consensual, not an authoritative, federation – a significant factor in shaping corporatism, Irish style.

THE STRUCTURE AND ROLE OF EMPLOYER ORGANISATIONS

Generally, students of corporatism have given little attention to the 'strategic capacity' of employers.[9] However, the Irish case illustrates how the structure of employer organisations substantially influences the stability of neo-corporatist arrangements (Hardiman, 1986). Stability requires employers as well as trade unions to possess the authority to commit their members to an agreed common strategy.

In Ireland, inter-organisational and intra-organisational tensions diminished this authority. Throughout the 1970s there were differences between the three major employer federations: the Federated Union of Employers (FUE), the Construction Industry Federation (CIF), and the Society of the Irish Motor Industry (SIMI). SIMI never joined the employers' umbrella organisation, the Irish Employers' Conference, and when the 1972 NWA was about to be ratified, indicated that it did not wish to be bound by the agreement. Such decisions reflected the preference of its multinational manufacturing members to conduct their own wage and labour negotiations (O'Brien, 1981, pp. 165–6). The collective interests of the FUE and CIF were also at odds on more than one occasion (Hardiman, 1986, pp. 214–5).

It was, however, the limited authority of the FUE over its members that was crucial to the fate of centralised collective bargaining in the 1970s. The FUE was the major employer organisation: it had a total membership of 3000 firms, which employed in excess of 50 per cent of the non-agricultural labour force and its membership was drawn nationally from a broad range of activities in industry and services. The FUE was solely concerned with industrial relations and it had exclusive responsibility for nominating employer representatives to the body which administers the NWAs.

The pattern of industrialisation in Ireland meant that the FUE had the task of formulating a pay policy for a diverse membership. Thus, a report by Fogarty et al. (1981, p. 20), which was published by the FUE, conceded that because of the variability in the impact of wage settlements on their members, 'the FUE as a voluntary organisation was no more able than the ICTU to impose a maximum increase on its members' pay bill, even if the majority of its members voted for it'.

PARTY POLICIES AND THE EXPANSIONIST IDEOLOGY

While institutional factors (such as the capacity of Irish trade union and employer organisations to pursue a course of action based on systematic, long-term, political exchange) serve as constraints, a strategy's institutional feasibility is not a guarantee of success in forming neo-corporatist arrangements. More general societal factors relating to the social bases of political partisanship play a vital role. In two groups of countries the trade union movement has gained access to political power through the party system. The first consists of those countries where social democratic parties have dominated government. The second group includes those countries, such as The Netherlands and Austria, where a number of parties each command a major part of the electorate which is not accessible to competing parties (because, for example, of religious definitions of political preferences) but where there is still a commitment to negotiation of political differences (Lijphart, 1968). Such an electoral system and the presence of proportional representation both encourage the sharing of power. In both sets of countries the consequence is to remove the goal of a 'fight to the finish' from the agenda of labour and capital (Katzenstein, 1985, pp. 135–50). The party political arrangements associated with successful neo-corporatism allow for mechanisms to achieve class compromise.

In Ireland, the absence of class cleavages in the political system and the form of electoral competition implicit in a Proportional Representation/Single Transferable Vote (PR/STV) system, encourage the development and persistence of political ideologies which deny the importance of class conflict. The result is to limit severely the scope for the political exchange that underlies successful neo-corporatist arrangements.

THE INSTITUTIONALISATION OF CONSULTATION

The shift away from a residual role for the State in Irish industrial relations rested on what has been described as an 'expansionist ideology':

> The ideology ... involved the central premise that the unions, employers and the State could co-operate on a range of crucial problems bound by economic expansion without the issue of *distribution* arising with its inevitably divisive consequences. (Roche, 1982, pp. 53–4)

The first major offshoot of that ideology was the National Employer–Labour Conference (ELC) established in 1962. At the end of that year the economic sub-committee of the ELC expressed its mandate in the following broad terms.

> ... a rational approach to the problems arising in the field of industrial relations necessitated consideration of all matters related

to the national economy, the competitive position of industry generally and the impact of external development.

In 1963, the Government published a White Paper on incomes and productivity. *Closing the Gap* first raised the idea of Government representation in the Employer Labour Conference. The ICTU's reaction was hostile. It argued that in the absence of price and profit controls it would not accept either compulsory wage restraint or official interference. It rejected the suggestion that the ELC become an instrument of Government policy and suspended its participation. In mid-1963 the Government proposed an alternative tripartite arrangement, the National Industrial and Economic Council (NIEC) with a wide brief, but particular responsibility for consultation in the area of wage and income policy.

Consultation in the early phase did not lead to confrontation on the distribution issue. However, the NIEC increasingly stressed the significance of incomes policy for the success of economic growth strategy. For example, a 1965 report concluded that above-the-norm income pay increases would have to be balanced by below-the-norm increases, and that this required a consensus on pay differentials. Distributive conflict, in this view, was the primary source of economic instability.

THE EMERGENCE OF INCOMES POLICY

Competitive wage bargaining intensified during the 1960s within a number of key groups setting the trend. The Government's response alternated between attempts at moral persuasion and threats to introduce legislation in an attempt to curtail the autonomy of bargaining groups and centralise collective bargaining (Hardiman, 1986, pp. 260–2). The decade ended with a maintenance craftsmen's dispute, which arose out of an unsuccessful attempt by the FUE to break the relationship between contract craft and maintenance craft wages (McCarthy et al., 1975, pp. 121–48). The dispute caused widespread disruption of industry and seriously threatened the solidarity of the trade union movement. The shortcomings of the collective bargaining system, made transparent by the maintenance dispute, increased the pressure to centralise negotiations (McCarthy, 1973).

One consequence was the Government's request to the NIEC in 1970 to prepare a *Report on Incomes and Prices Policy*. The report placed particular emphasis on establishing a tripartite Income and Prices Committee, which would take a leading role in monitoring pay developments. The terms of reference for a reactivated ELC, which included 'developments and problems in money incomes, prices and industrial relations', were approved by both the ICTU and the IEC. However, debate on that move in the Annual Delegate Conference of the ICTU highlighted the lack of commitment to a clear strategy. Motions calling for 'implacable opposition' to prices and incomes policy and 'commitment to a voluntary incomes policy' were both rejected. The rejection of the idea of 'guidelines' as enunciated by the NIEC was decisive, however, and led to that body's demise: 'The ELC ... was left alone at the centre of the stage to salvage whatever it could from this totally unanticipated setback' (O'Brien, 1981, p. 19).

The efforts of the ELC were not conclusive. The Government then published a Prices and Incomes Bill. That threat proved effective. Between the announcement of the Bill and the ratification of the National Wage Agreement of 1970 the Government also made a variety of concessions to the ICTU, culminating in an agreement to withdraw the Bill in its entirety.

CENTRALISED COLLECTIVE BARGAINING: THE 1970s

The National Wage Agreement of 1970 inaugurated a new era in Irish industrial relations. The conventional method of wage determination had been decentralised collective bargaining. However, from 1970 to 1980 a series of eight centralised agreements were negotiated. The viability of such agreements required that the State play an increasingly crucial role as an underwriter and a compromiser.

The initial State role was modest and manipulatory. The Budgets of 1972, 1974 and January 1975 were intended to affect indirectly the level of pay settlements included in the NWAs of those years. The Government remained anxious to avoid involvement in a formal trilateral bargaining relationship despite mounting pressure from the FUE for Government involvement that would integrate pay, taxation and social welfare. The unions too were becoming concerned over the failure by Government to adjust income tax bands and allowances in pace with inflation.

In April 1975 the Minister for Finance suggested possible terms for tripartite negotiations on these issues. But the fundamental issue in his view was 'how to reconcile Government negotiations with representatives of workers and employers on matters such as taxation with the democratic and constitutional principle that Dail Eireann is supreme in these matters' (O'Brien, 1981, p. 116).

By June, however, the Government offered a major budgetary package designed to break the inflationary spiral on the condition that the NWA 1975 would be re-negotiated. The new sequence of having a Budget precede the NWA negotiations became standard. The political process and industrial relations had virtually merged. In 1977, for example, the Government offered a variety of tax concessions and commitments on employment if the proposed NWA was ratified. While the text of the resulting agreement contains no reference to the Budget, it was generally recognised that the tax concessions were integral to its acceptance (O'Brien, 1981, pp. 146–55).

Another central agreement associated with tax inducements was reached in 1978, but with only a very thin majority on the union side, and subsequently the ICTU rejected the opening of talks on a National Agreement for 1979. In the Budget in February 1979, the main tax-free allowances were substantially increased, tax bands were modified slightly, and extra public spending committed to employment creation in the public service. The initiative succeeded in renewing union interest. The Government invited the trade unions to discuss a 'National Agreement for National Development'. At a Special Delegate Conference of the ICTU, a set of policy proposals dealing with taxation, employment creation and welfare were agreed as the basis for discussions with the Government. Although the Congress executive had no mandate to enter into a wage agreement, it began a series of negotiations involving a variety of working parties. Trade union and employer representatives focused on pay, while the trade union representatives met with civil servants and Ministers in negotiations on taxation, employment, health, education, and workers' participation. The final agreement, known as the National Understanding, introduced a major 'non-pay' element into national agreements. After an initial rejection the agreement was accepted with only minor revisions by the ICTU, prompted in part by a Government threat to introduce unilateral pay guidelines.

The FUE, which had stoutly supported the concept of centralised agreements, had by 1980 begun to express dissatisfaction. Their reservations related to what they believed were the high level of days lost through strikes and the 'wrong balance' between central and local bargaining (Fogarty et al., 1981, pp. 25–35). An agreement was nevertheless concluded in which the section on non-pay items was expanded. It was the final centralised agreement: from mid-1981, wage rounds were decentralised. The structure of tripartite national agreements no longer commanded the support of the three 'partners'.

CORPORATIST SUBSTANCE OR CORPORATIST FORM?

The demise of centralised collective bargaining resulted ultimately from the inability of any of the parties to achieve their objectives under its auspices. For employers and the Government, a reduction in the level of industrial conflict was a primary objective. Many of the other limitations for them of the national agreements might have been tolerable if industrial peace had been guaranteed. It was not.

Neo-corporatist arrangements are usually understood to involve acceptance of a degree of wage restraint by the trade union movement in which the workers with the strongest labour market positions forgo short-term gains. The *quid pro quo* comes from increased employment and the redistributive impact of social policy – a substitution of political exchange for economic exchange (Cameron, 1984, pp. 173–4; Goldthorpe, 1984, p. 327). In practice, despite the increased involvement of the State in collective bargaining, the level and pattern of industrial conflict during the period of the National Agreements provides no evidence of such a substitution.

Although the terms of the NWAs consistently contained clauses favourable to the lower paid, (cash floors, cash ceilings, tapered percentage wage rises and partial indexation) a greater narrowing of differentials had actually taken place under the decentralised agreements of 1959–70 than under the NWAs (Mooney, 1978; Fogarty et al., 1981). The ICTU and FUE had limited powers to control and discipline their affiliates. Irish employers varied in the impact of wage settlements on their competitive situation. These factors produced a persistent tendency towards illegitimate, above-the-norm wage settlements. The trade unions had ensured that employers could plead inability to pay the NWA norm only under conditions so restrictive that few employers pursued this option. However, the situation with regard to above-the-norm payments was quite different:

First, the employers' side of the FUE never succeeded in getting correspondingly stringent rules concerning such increases incorporated in the NWA norms. Secondly, individual employers have sometimes been reluctant to resist unwarranted "productivity" or "anomaly" claims. Finally, employers who wished to increase wages by more than the NWA norm could usually do so without reference to, or serious fear of intervention by, any outside body (O'Brien, 1981, p. 170).

The consequence of the pattern of wage bargaining during the period of centralised collective bargaining was a change in the pattern of strikes, not a reduction in the level of industrial conflict. The changing pattern of industrial conflict over the 1960–86 period is charted in Table 8.1, which summarises the frequency and breadth of strike action. There was a dramatic increase over the 1960s in the frequency of strikes, the average number of workers involved, and the resulting man-days lost.[10] In the 1970s, the strike frequency continued to increase, but the number of workers involved and the man-days lost declined initially. The reduction in the level of industrial conflict was particularly noticeable between 1971 and 1973. The trend from 1974 was towards an increase in the frequency of strikes and, more particularly, in the extent of man-days lost.

So, although centralised bargaining did not reduce the overall level of industrial conflict, it did alter the pattern of strikes. The number of firms involved per strike declined from 3.1 in the 1960s to 1.3 in the 1970s. Disputes tended to be confined to individual workplaces and to sectional claims. The number of workers affected never returned to the levels of the 1960s and indeed the number of strikers per strike declined significantly. The balance between public sector and private sector strikes also was marked by continuity, in which the public sector experienced the greatest difficulties. But again the change in the pattern of strikes affected the form in which industrial conflict was manifested. Strikes were more frequent in the private sector but after the mid-1960s the number of workers involved and the man-days lost were consistently higher in the public sector. As we can see from Table 8.2, the

TABLE 8.1 *Strike frequency, breadth, and man-days lost per 100,000 workers, 1960–84*

	Annual average for		
	Strikes	*Workers involved*	*Man-days lost*
1960–64	6.8	1580	25 271
1965–69	10.1	3995	53 713
1970–74	14.9	3178	41 999
1975–79	14.0	3483	66 989
1980–86	11.7	4689	34 086

SOURCE   See note [10].

TABLE 8.2   *Strike frequency, breadth, and man-days lost per 100 000 workers in the public and private sectors 1960–84*

Annual average for	Strikes		Workers involved		Man-days lost	
	Public	Private	Public	Private	Public	Private
1960–69	8.2	8.4	5642	2182	52 245	36 101
1970–79	10.6	15.5	4071	2879	85 628	45 955
1980–86	11.2	11.8	11 257	1993	45 760	32 036

SOURCE   See note [10].

'workers involved' figure for the public sector was extremely high in the late 1960s while the 'man-days lost' was high, relative to the private sector in the late 1970s.

Although conflict in the public sector was greater than in the private, in an important sense it had its source in the latter. Public sector unions were likely to take their cue in regard to pay and work conditions from developments in the private sector. The importance of such external comparisons as a principle for pay determination was reinforced by a number of reviews of public sector remuneration in the 1970s. Furthermore, the desire of the Department of Public Service to control public sector pay diminished the ability of individual employers in that sector to determine pay policy and promoted a centralised and highly visible system of pay determination (McCarthy, 1979, pp. 310–6). The particular problems associated with 'special' public service claims and awards are associated with 'the active co-existence of both external and internal comparisons' (O'Brien, 1987, p. 119).

The NWAs had not led to a diminution in the extent to which individual trade unions took advantage of favourable market circumstances. Developments in relation to taxation, redistribution and employment during the 1970s were not formed out of a coherent strategy on the part of the State, to provide an environment in which the adverse consequences of distributive conflict could be contained, if not eliminated. While the State's capacity to raise and redistribute revenue increased substantially, the combination of State strategies aimed at promoting economic growth accentuated, rather than eroded, class divisions (see Chapter 4). The enhanced redistribution of income from State interventions between 1973 and 1980 is attributable mainly to rising levels of taxation and public social expenditure – greater progressivity made a negligible contribution.

Ireland is unusual in that the cost of the welfare state was borne disproportionately by the less well-to-do. This can be seen in the declining tax revenue shares provided by property, inheritance and corporate taxes on the one hand, and the five-fold increase in personal income tax, increased social insurance revenue, and the continued importance of expenditure taxes on the other. One important consequence of such a rising personal tax burden was the acute difficulty in reconciling pay outcomes pegged sufficiently low to maintain competitiveness with maintaining workers' real earnings. For example, real labour costs increased by over 30 per cent while disposable income rose by only 5 per cent in the 1973–83 period (Conniffe and Kennedy, 1984, p. 78).

Expansion in State expenditure could be accommodated through the impact of growth and inflation on taxation. But from the 1974–5 recession, a substantial portion of current government expenditure was funded by borrowing. The cost of servicing the public debt grew at an average annual rate of nearly 28 per cent between 1975 and 1983 and, on average, nearly two-fifth of the borrowings went to finance current budget deficits (Conniffe and Kennedy, 1984). Distributive conflict, far from being resolved by State expansion, was accommodated at a financial cost that ensured that the strategy would work only in the very short term.

The scale of the recent fiscal problems of the Irish State cannot be understood as deriving from interest group activity that undermined the authority of Government and Parliament (Farrell, 1986, p. 148). The decline in the influence of Parliament in Ireland, as elsewhere in Europe, seems more attributable to the expansion of the Welfare State, and to the absence of adequate instruments for controlling expenditure, than to corporatist developments (Lehmbruch, 1984, pp. 72–4). Irish parties, and the Irish Parliament indeed, have never sought more than a formal role in policy making. Corporatist policy making did not undermine the role of the Irish Parliament; such policy-making never materialised (Gallagher, 1981). The parties to the NWAs did not begin with, and never developed, a shared understanding of the relationship between wages, competitiveness, inflation and unemployment.[11] Where change occurred, as in employment creation, it was concentrated in the public sector and did not arise through the exercise of wage restraint by workers. A variety of employer–labour structures with links to the Government were established, but

they have not functioned as the principal instruments whereby private interests engage in bargaining with direct or indirect State input, to reach agreement concerning the formulation and implementation of aspects of public policy. (Hardiman, 1984, p. 84).

The label 'neo-corporatist' is clearly inappropriate to recent Irish experience. Neo-corporatist sentiments abounded, but neo-corporatist institutions did not.

INDUSTRIAL RELATIONS IN THE 1980s

The return to decentralised bargaining coincided with a rise in the unemployment rate from 6 per cent to 18 per cent between 1980 and 1986. Strike activity declined in those years so that the number of man-days lost fell to almost half the total for the previous five-year period. However, the impact of the recession has been less straightforward than these figures might suggest. It is in the private sector alone that strike frequency has declined. However, there has been a continuing decline in worker involvement in strikes in both the public and the private sector. In the latter, man-days lost during 1980–86 were at their lowest level for the period 1969–1986. Private sector strikes have continued to increase substantially in length while worker involvement has declined significantly. The increase in long drawn out strikes despite the recession is likely to be due to a variety of causes including the adoption of more uncompromising bargaining positions by employers and the increased importance of redundancy disputes as a source of industrial conflict (Kelly and Brannick, 1986, p. 87). The improvement in the public sector has been such as to remove much of the substantial differences between the sectors particularly in man-days lost.[12] By 1987 the total number of strikes had fallen to 76, the lowest level since 1963, and there had been a particularly sharp fall in unofficial strikes (Department of Labour, 1987, p. 14).

The recent pattern of conflict is related to the fact that the collapse of centralised bargaining has not involved a return to the system which pre-dated it, largely because the individual agreements concluded during the period of centralised collective bargaining made industry rates increasingly irrelevant. Bargaining is nowadays focused on individual organisations. Recent attention has been directed towards managerial strategies in those sectors of the Irish economy that are relatively 'trouble free'. A survey by the IDA (1984) for example, showed that

Irish-owned firms were no more likely than were foreign-owned firms to have experienced strike action between 1981 and 1984, but the native firms lost four times more employee work days. The difference was attributed to a 'two nations dichotomy', between the generally older Irish-owned manufacturing units in traditional industrial sectors and the newer foreign businesses established in electronics, chemicals and pharmaceuticals. It could not be explained by differences in the skill profile of the work forces found in the 'two nations'. The foreign-owned companies were also more likely to be profitable. US companies were likely to pay their workers above the wage-round norms, and to make concessions on fringe benefits such as pensions, sick pay and health insurance. The IDA report, however, emphasises the corporate policies of the 'trouble free' companies. The US companies, for example, stress the importance of 'people management'. This emphasis starts with recruitment: nearly 70 per cent of US companies use interviews and/or tests with checks of experience from more than one previous employment.[13] US companies in Ireland are strongly orientated toward employee involvement 'though of the management directed rather than power sharing variety', (IDA, 1984, p. 38). They are substantially more likely to have involved employees in local productivity and cost reduction schemes.[14] Irish unions have tended to consider such personnel practices as paternalistic and as deriving from an anti-union sentiment. Twenty per cent of US firms are currently non-unionised, compared with less than 10 per cent of Irish firms, and the unions remain unpersuaded that the presence or absence of trade unions is of less importance than a firm's willingness to invest in personnel management (Toner, 1985, p. 181; FWUI, 1986, p. 14).[15]

Employee involvement in Ireland, as elsewhere, is now seen as a key factor in successful corporate performance (Littler and Salaman, 1984). However, the difficulties should not be under-estimated. The strategy may succeed in recently established companies, where work-forces have little or no tradition of industrial work and trade union experience, and are highly dependent for jobs on a particular company. More traditional workers, such as male manual workers in Dublin, have been found to couple their positive attitude towards workers' participation with low levels of trust in management: 70 per cent of manual workers believed management will try to put one over on workers if they get the chance; almost three out of four considered that 'most managements are interested in people only for what they can produce' and almost half agreed that 'full teamwork in firms is impossible because workers and management are on opposite sides' (Whelan, 1982, pp. 39–40). Action research in Irish companies confirms that creating a climate of trust in which participative initiatives can prosper is a delicate operation (Murphy and Walsh, 1978). It is clear, however, that a defensive response by trade unions to industrial relations changes will not be sufficient. The increasing demands for flexibility in work practices will mean that trade unions need

> ... to develop a plausible concept of their own potential role in a decentralized industrial relations system in which participation by workers and interest representation by unions would be more closely than ever integrated through co-decision rights with the management of production and the concern for productivity ... (Streeck, 1987, p. 303).

From 1981 to 1987 the State reverted to a role of minimal involvement in industrial relations. The Government, however, made stringent attempts to control the growth of public service pay. These have included the most unusual step of moving a Dail motion in February 1986 in order to modify an arbitration award to the teachers. However, such efforts have not involved a modification of the institutional framework for the conduct of 'collective bargaining' in the public sector (Cox and Hughes, 1987, p. 93).

Suggestions for a return to a national approach to income determination, as part of a National Plan covering jobs, tax reform, social welfare and the public finances came from the large general unions whose membership has been most adversely affected by the recession, (Attley, 1986). The National Economic and Social Council, on which the major interest groups are represented, also stressed the importance of establishing consensus both at the national level and the level of the workplace in order that macro-economic policy should have consistency, continuity and credibility (NESC, 1986). However, the FUE in responding to such suggestions was quite explicit in rejecting wage determination at the national level. The close relationship which local level bargaining had produced between pay increases, productivity and company performance was contrasted with '... memories of bogus productivity deals and spurious relativity claims arising from sub-clauses in past national agreements ...' (FUE, 1986).

The FUE's emphasis on the individual firm echoed the 'new *laissez-faire*' prescription that government's role is to provide the institutional contexts within which market incentives and discipline can operate

(Goldthorpe, 1984, p. 338). The general unions on the other hand have highlighted Austria, Norway and Sweden as appropriate role models. The strategy pursued in those countries involved not the strengthening of the market mechanisms but finding institutional and ultimately political solutions to the declining efficiency of the market mechanism brought about by the power of organised labour (Goldthorpe, 1984, p. 325). Changing the institutional balance between the different levels of bargaining in a manner which involves a general delegation of bargaining issues to the level of the individual firm, has been identified as one of the major anti-corporatist responses by capital to the economic crisis (Streeck, 1984, p. 295).

Following Fianna Fail's return to power a national pay agreement was achieved in 1987 as part of the Programme for National Recovery. In addition to agreement on pay increases over a three and a half year period the text of the Programme contained a variety of commitments relating to tax reform, social equity and employment creation. However, the commitments were at a very general level. Furthermore, while the Government's commitment to a reduction in the number of public service employees and to reducing the Exchequer borrowing requirement are clearly stated, expenditure decisions were not part of the agenda.

While it is too early to offer an assessment of the impact for industrial relations of this agreement, an evaluation of the comparative effectiveness of firm-based personnel management strategies and centralised collective bargaining can be made by examining the reasons for the failure of neo-corporatist arrangements to develop in Ireland. Trade union multiplicity and fragmentation, the lack of class-based worker identity, and the distributional and fiscal consequences of the cross-class nature of the major political parties are all important. Any attempt to disentangle the impact of such factors may appear artificial. However, our evaluations of the prospects for Irish industrial relations will be influenced by whether we attribute primary importance to the effect which political partisanship has had on social policy or whether we emphasise the structural characteristics of the labour movement in Ireland. Our analysis leads us to agree with Cameron (1984, p. 170): high levels of industrial conflict in Ireland have derived not so much from the weakness of social democracy as from the fragmentation of the trade union movement and the absence of any institutionalised form of workers' participation at the enterprise level.[16] The exchange of labour quiescence for low levels of unemployment, which is at the heart of neo-corporatism, Cameron argues, also requires workplace schemes such as 'Work councils and co-determination schemes ... which displace unions to some extent and institutionalise precisely the kind of 'class collaboration' associated with most notions of corporatism' (Cameron, 1984, p. 170).[17] This interpretation leaves co-operation and consensus at the workplace dependent on the ability of trade unions, employers, and the State to develop an agreed set of institutions for the mediation of distributive conflict. The demise of the NWAs testified to the failure in Ireland to achieve a unified trade union strategy and a class compromise of a kind that facilitates the pursuit of shared goals. The complexity of the trade union movement and the continuing predominance of sectional interests ensures that strategies which seek to promote employee involvement and power-sharing are unlikely to serve as an adequate alternative to neo-corporatist institutions. It has been suggested that, in other countries, the success of neo-corporatist arrangements can be attributed in part to the fact that the centralised level at which bargaining occurs matches the key level of union organisation.[18] The nature of the Irish trade union movement ensures that both centralised and enterprise-based bargaining will be problematic.

CONCLUSION

In industrial relations, as in other areas, the dependent nature of the Irish economy sets strict limits to the State's autonomy.[19] The lack of State control over the consequences of industrial development also derives from a conscious choice by policy-makers to rely on the free play of market forces. The cost of the State's chosen role as the financier of the NWAs was incurred by both Fianna Fail and the Coalition as part of their efforts to create the conditions in which private enterprise would prosper. The dependent nature of the Irish economy is one of the crucial factors influencing industrial relations, not least through its impact on the structure of union and employer interest groups. In other countries vulnerability led to enhanced State capacity in the pursuit of strategies of political compensation. In offering an explanation for the failure of neo-corporatist arrangements in Ireland we outlined the influences of economic vulnerability, the representation of class interest, and the logic of electoral competition. However, the factor most likely to undermine future neo-corporatist initiatives is the continued inability of trade union and employer federations to sustain a strategy which transcends sectionalist interests.

NOTES

1. Corporatist thinking in Ireland had previously been associated with Catholic social teaching (see Chapter 2).
2. Neo-corporatism represents an attempt to re-direct the increased power of trade unions from the labour market to the political arena. However, as Goldthorpe (1984, p. 339) remarks, it is less than helpful to regard such developments as reflecting no more than the latest or 'highest' form of social control under capitalism as was argued by Panitch (1977; 1981) and Jessop (1978). Indeed, Schmitter (1982, pp. 271–8) develops the argument that corporatism may come under greatest threat from the capitalist class.
3. Panitch (1980, p. 159) notes that considerable confusion has been caused by the use of the concept of 'corporatism' to indicate variously a distinct economic system or mode of production, a State form, and a system of interest intermediation. The third use of the concept, on which we concentrate, accepts, as Crouch (1983, p. 459) puts it, that 'society and politics cannot be adequately classified according to a continuum of forms of interest intermediation alone'.
4. Horgan (1987, p. 168) observes that apart from Sweden it is hard to think of any country in which public policy has been so actively supportive of trade unions and the concept of collective bargaining for over 40 years.
5. The relevant provision of the 1937 Constitution is Article 40.6.1 in which

   the State guarantees liberty for the exercise of . . . the right of citizens to form associations and unions.

   The judgement of the Court in 1947 declared that

   both logically and practically, to deprive a person of the choice of persons with whom he will associate is not a control of the exercise of the right of association but a denial of the right altogether.

6. The proposals suggest a review of the Trade Disputes Act 'to explore actively the feasibility of giving workers a positive right to strike in place of the negative immunity from legal liability for industrial action which they now possess' and the creation of a Labour Relations Commission. The former suggestion has been developed in a more recent proposal by the Department of Labour (1986).
7. Based on the data from a sample of male employees in Dublin in the late 1970s.
8. Headey (1970), Schmitter (1974; 1979). The facilitating conditions can be linked to Olson's (1965) thesis that while common interest associations will use their strength to inhibit change hostile to their interests, this will be less true to the extent that the organisations are large in scope and small in number.
9. This neglect is related to assumptions regarding the structural advantage enjoyed by employers and the unproblematic nature of their interests

(Offe and Wiesenthal (1980)). See, however, Windmuller and Gladstone (1984).

10. The data on Irish strike statistics are drawn from two sources. Data compiled by the Central Statistics Office are published annually in the *Irish Statistical Bulletin*. The second set of data has been compiled by the Department of Industrial Relations at University College, Dublin and allows for a degree of disaggregation which is not possible with the official data. Tables 8.1 and 8.2 are taken from Kelly and Brannick (1986).

11. The FUE's position on trade disputes law provides another example of the absence of such agreement. Their position on this issue found expression in the *Report of the Commission on Industrial Relations*, 1981. The ICTU withdrew from the Commission as part of its campaign to extend the scope of the Trade Disputes Act of 1906 to workers presently excluded. In the absence of trade union representation and any detailed programme of research the ensuing report was perceived to be 'a remarkably partisan document' (Kelly and Roche, 1983; McCarthy and Van Prondynzynski, 1983) and there was fairly widespread academic agreement that the proposals of the Commission were incongruent with the Irish tradition of industrial relations. The Commission's recommendations included the establishment of a Labour Relations Court to which enforceable remedies would be available. The proposed arrangements would almost inevitably have damaged existing tripartite institutions.

12. The convergence is less obvious than it might be in the statistics in Table 8.2 because of a one-day strike in the public sector in 1985 which involved over 105 000 workers.

13. Blackburn and Mann (1979) and Oliver and Turton (1982) discuss the manner in which such screening processes emphasise characteristics such as reliability.

14. The strategy employed by the US companies clearly has much in common with that of 'bureaucratic control' identified by Edwards (1979).

15. Both aggregate trade union membership and union density have been in decline since 1980 due to a variety of factors which include unemployment and structural shifts in the economy but also, it is frequently claimed, through a hardening of management attitudes towards unions (Roche and Larraghy, 1987, pp. 33–4; Cassells, 1987, pp. 18–19).

16. See also Eric Batstone (1985) and for a conflicting interpretation Korpi and Shalev (1979, 1980).

17. Streeck (1984, p. 292) also concludes that neo-corporatism

> . . . to be more than a short lived political expedient, always need to be supported by congenial institutions of interest accommodation at the work place and these tend to be conducive not just to consensus but also to high efficiency and superior productivity.

18. Batstone (1985, pp. 56–7). Such matching is normally produced by

centralised bargaining. Japan stands out as the exception in that the match takes place at enterprise level.

19. For a discussion of the impact of structural change in a small open economy on the Government's role as 'guarantor' rather than 'short-term compensation' (Lange, 1984, p. 110) see Hardiman (1986).

9 Agriculture: Policy and Politics

The publication of the *Programme for Economic Expansion* in 1958 does not stand as a watershed for Irish agriculture in the way that it does for much of the rest of the Irish economy and society. Rather, the post-1958 period has seen the continuation of several important long-term trends in Irish farming while, at the same time, a number of developments in the 1960s and 1970s – and, crucially, entry to the EC in 1973 – have both accelerated these trends and set new ones in motion. In this chapter our central concern is to examine the link between State policy and the polarisation of Irish agriculture into two sectors: one made up of a small number of viable and, in some cases, prosperous farms, the other of very many marginalised small farms. Our secondary aim is to look at how the development of agriculture has led to a new relationship between the agricultural and non-agricultural sectors of Irish society. In both these respects we shall concentrate on the recent past, but setting such events in context will first require that we view Irish agriculture in a longer term perspective.

THE LEGACY OF THE 1800s

The present structure of Irish agriculture is rooted in events of the nineteenth century, particularly the Great Famine of mid-century, the resulting changes in demographic patterns, and the Land Acts of the late part of the century, which established the tenants of Irish land as peasant proprietors. It was in this period too that the question of the ownership of land became bound up with the question of Irish self-determination. As Lee (1973, p. 77) puts it, in writing of Parnell, 'the land question would be the engine which would draw Home Rule in its train'.

Population and the sub-division of farm tenancies had grown apace in the late eighteenth century as land increasingly came to be put under potatoes and cereals. These practices made possible the preservation of a locally acceptable standard of living on ever shrinking

184

holdings. However, after 1815, altered market conditions – an improved British market for livestock and a sharp decline in cereal prices (largely due to the relative ease with which continental corn could be imported to Britain) – made it more profitable to put land out for grazing, and the land available for the old potato–cereal mix became insufficient to support an expanding population. Thus, in this period Irish society was struggling to adjust, in demographic terms, to the altered economic climate. These adjustments took the form of curbing partibility[1] in inheritance and attempts to control population growth by late marriage. The more commercialised east of the country experienced these changes initially; gradually, however, and propelled by the famine of the 1840s and the agricultural crises of 1859–63 and the late 1870s, these practices spread through Ireland (Breen, 1984a, pp. 285–6).

The effects of the Great Famine were dramatic – a million deaths and massive emigration continuing into the late nineteenth century (Lee, 1974; Kennedy, 1973) – but also highly class-selective. Both famine and emigration disproportionately affected the class of propertyless farm labourers, cottiers and very small tenant farmers.

Between 1845 and 1851 the number of labourers and cottiers fell by 40 per cent, the number of farmers by 20 per cent. During the following 60 years the number of labourers and cottiers fell again by 40 per cent, the number of farmers by 5 per cent. Within the rural community the class balance swung sharply in favour of farmers and within the farm community it swung even more sharply in favour of bigger as against small farmers. (Lee, 1973, p. 3).

Among this newly emerging class of smallholders and middle range farmers, impartible inheritance, by one son, became the norm. It was this class which, becoming increasingly secure in their tenancies as the nineteenth century drew to a close, fought the successful 'Land War' against their landlords. By the beginning of the twentieth century the population of most rural communities had been reduced and transformed from a teeming mass of impoverished labourers, small cottiers and very small tenant farmers, into a stable, conservative, landowning peasantry, established on family farms which, for the most part, and by modern standards, are quite small.

As we noted in Chapter 1, the persistence into the late twentieth century of a large agricultural sector, made up predominantly of family farms, is one of the characteristics of European societies we describe as 'semi-peripheral'. The only other countries whose agricultural sector are of comparable relative size are Greece, Spain, Portugal and, to a lesser extent, Italy. As Table 9.1 shows, in these countries agriculture accounts for a larger share of Gross Domestic Product than in the more developed EC states and employs a much greater proportion of the work force.

TABLE 9.1 *Percentage of the labour force in agriculture, and agriculture's contribution to GNP, EC countries 1982*

	Percentage of labour force in agriculture*	Percentage of GDP arising in agriculture
Germany	5.4	2.3
France	8.1	4.5
Italy	12.1	5.7
Netherlands	4.9	3.7
Belgium	2.9	2.4
Luxembourg	4.8	2.1
United Kingdom	2.6	1.7
Ireland	16.8	12.9
Denmark	8.4	6.0
Greece	27.4	18.6
Spain	18.3	6.3
Portugal	25.9	8.2

SOURCE Eurostat *Employment and Unemployment 1985*; Sheehy and O'Connor, 1986, p. 14.
* including forestry and fishing.

LONG-TERM TRENDS IN IRISH AGRICULTURE

Adopting the date of the founding of the State as our starting point, we can identify four long-term trends which provide the background against which more recent developments can be understood. These are:
(a) little change in agricultural output and, probably, in agricultural incomes between the founding of the State and the late 1950s, followed by a twenty-year period of growth which faltered in the late 1970s;
(b) a marked decline in the numbers engaged in agricultural production;

(c) a constant decline after about 1946 in the importance of agriculture to the Irish economy as a whole; and

(d) the increasing marginalisation of farmers on smaller acreages, particularly in the western half of the country and particularly after the Second World War. This has been associated with a decline in the proportion of very small farms, but with little distribution of land.

AGRICULTURAL OUTPUT AND INCOMES

In the first half of this century, Irish agricultural output was virtually stagnant. The post-Famine period up to 1900 was dominated by two reciprocal trends in Irish agriculture – a steady decline in the area devoted to tillage and an increase in the number of cattle and sheep. At the same time there was a rapid decline in the rural population, the usual explanation for which is the declining demand for agricultural labour and the declining number of cottiers and farmers on very small acreages. After 1900 these trends continued, but at a different rate. As Crotty writes, 'from 1900 onwards, however, Irish agriculture lost the dynamic elements of structural change and did not acquire any new dynamism in respect of volume of output' (Crotty, 1966, p. 84).

Between the early twentieth century and the late 1950s, there was virtually no growth in either gross or net agricultural output (Kennedy, 1988) and we may assume that, notwithstanding the decline in the size of the agricultural work-force, there was little or no change in overall farm income in this period. This position began to alter in the late 1950s/early 1960s with accelerating output growth. Taken together with a continuing rapid decline in the agricultural labour force, this led to a rise in incomes in agriculture, so that by 1978 the incomes of workers in agriculture had, on average, come to equal – or indeed exceed – that of industrial workers. In the post-1978 period, growth has been slower and farm incomes have declined in real terms, re-establishing the gap between farming and non-farming incomes.

DECLINE IN NUMBERS ENGAGED IN AGRICULTURE

The fall in the numbers engaged in agriculture (excluding forestry and fishing) both overall and within the categories of farmers, assisting relatives (sons, daughters, brothers, sisters, etc., who worked on the farm but were often formally unpaid) and labourers, is shown in Figure 9.1. Between 1926 and 1946 the numbers declined from 645 000 to 559 000. After 1946, however, the rate of decline accelerated, so that there was a further loss of almost 200 000 over the next fifteen years, reducing the agricultural work-force to 369 000 in 1961. Since then it has virtually halved, to around 178 000 in 1981. Whereas, at the founding of the State, agricultural occupations accounted for half of the total labour force, today they account for only about a

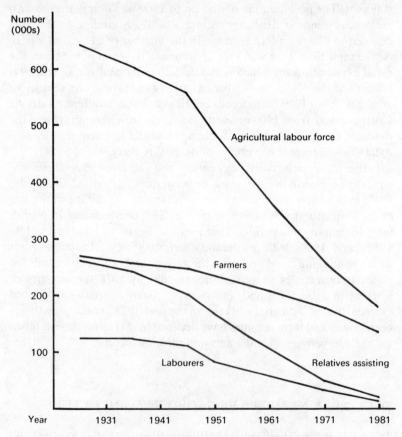

FIGURE 9.1 *Decline in the agricultural labour force and in the number of farmers, relatives assisting and farm labourers, 1926–81*

sixth, though it has been estimated that up to 40 per cent of the total labour force may depend directly or otherwise on agriculture (taking into account jobs such as those in food processing).

Figure 9.1 shows that of the main groups making up the agricultural work-force, the decline has been most marked among assisting relatives and labourers. So, over the period 1926–81, while the number of farmers has virtually halved, the number of assisting relatives has been reduced to less than 10 per cent of its 1926 figure and the number of labourers to about one-seventh of its 1926 level. Until the mid-1950s, the number of labourers and assisting relatives, taken together, exceeded the number of farmers. Thus, alongside the decline in the number of farmers, there has also been a decline in the number of additional workers each farm supports. In this respect then, the family farm, in the sense of the farm run and worked by a nuclear family, has become increasingly prominent over the twentieth century.

POST-WAR DECLINE IN THE IMPORTANCE OF AGRICULTURE TO THE ECONOMY

Currently, agricultural output constitutes about 13 per cent of Irish GDP; however, the clearest way to chart the fall of agriculture's dominance of the Irish economy is to look at the composition of Irish exports. In 1926, agriculture accounted for about three-quarters of Irish exports. After the 'Emergency', this percentage began to decline, though even by 1961 it still accounted for over 61 per cent, with industry contributing just over 30 per cent. By 1976, the position had been almost reversed: industry now produced 62 per cent of exports, agriculture 37 per cent. Presently agriculture accounts for just over 30 per cent of Irish exports.

INCREASING MARGINALISATION OF SMALL FARMERS

Arensberg and Kimball (1940) provided an extensive account of the small farm communities of the West of Ireland as they were around 1930. Their account stressed the stability and homogeneity of these communities: it is precisely farms of the type they describe which have become marginalised over the past 40 years.

Hannan (1972) has argued that, in the period up to about 1940, the small farms of the west of Ireland – the province of Connaught and the western part of Munster – were viable and were effectively reproducing themselves and their social structure: thus, Arensberg and Kimball's account of them is both 'valid and reliable'. Hannan notes, for example, that small farmers in the west were, at this time, more likely to marry than even the largest farmers of the more prosperous and commercialised east.[2] Furthermore, among those farmers who did marry, small farmers in the west were less likely to have to support unmarried brothers or sisters on the farm, because of the much greater effectiveness of the smaller western farmers in dispersing their non-inheriting children. Taking these and other indices into account, it appears that the small farm communities of the west were, during the period up to 1940, reproducing themselves somewhat more effectively than even the large farmers of the east.

In the post-Second World War period, the position reversed. Small farmers in the west are nowadays more likely to remain bachelors than are any other farm group; there has been a decline in father–son replacement ratios on these farms; and increased farm size income differentials. The result is a marginalised class of small farmers who are untouched by agricultural and land policy and who have come increasingly to rely for their support on direct social welfare payments by the State (Commins et al., 1978; Hannan, 1979; Kelleher and O'Mahony, 1984).

How large is this marginalised group, concentrated as it is (though not confined) in the western regions? One means of answering this question is to compare a figure of the minimum acreage considered viable (i.e., one capable of providing a satisfactory income at prevailing standards of living) with the size distribution of farms. Matthews (1984, p. 313) has suggested that in the 1930s 25 acres would have been the minimum needed, and 33 acres in the 1950s, while Kelleher and O'Mahony (1984, p. 6) suggest a current minimum of 50 acres. Given these figures, we see from Table 9.2 that even in the 1930s about 47 per cent of farms must be considered to have been non-viable; in the 1950s 44 per cent; and currently, about half are non-viable.[3] However, in the west, over 90 per cent of farms are now categorised as 'marginal' – that is, not considered capable of becoming commercially viable under the EC Farm Modernisation Scheme (FMS).

Table 9.2 also shows that the size distribution of Irish farms has shifted over the period since independence. In 1926 the median size of farm was 1–15 acres; by 1981 it was 50–100 acres. The decline in the percentage of farms of 30 acres or less has been offset by the

TABLE 9.2 *Percentage distribution of farmers according to farm size, selected years, 1926–81*

Farm size (acres)	1926	1936	1946	1951	1961	1971	1981
1–15	28.4	24.5	20.4	18.3	14.5	12.4	6.9
15–30	28.3	28.5	28.9	27.7	25.6	22.7	17.1
30–50	19.3	21.0	22.5	23.2	25.5	26.2	26.6
50–100	15.5	16.9	18.3	19.2	22.5	25.8	33.0
100–200	6.3	6.8	7.5	7.9	9.3	10.4	13.2
>200	2.3	2.3	2.3	2.4	2.4	2.6	3.3
Total	264 675	256 013	246 805	235 925	209 574	180 425	137 472

SOURCE *Census of Ireland* (various).

increasing preponderance of farms between 30 and 200 acres. This change in the distribution of farms, however, may conceal the fact that the number of farms in all size categories except in the 50–100 and 100–200 groups, has declined over the 1926–81 period. This decline has, of course, been most pronounced among smaller farms: the number of farmers with 15 acres or less fell by 90 per cent over the period, while those with 50–200 acres increased by 10 per cent.[4] However, over the 1970s, the number of farms in *all* size categories declined. Given the pattern of farm size decline, it would appear that there has been a considerable net loss of land held by farmers. Data for agricultural *holdings* (which may not necessarily be worked by individuals classed as farmers) show much less change in size distribution than do those for farmers. These features point to the continued existence of a considerable number of smaller holdings whose occupants are no longer classed as farmers, in the majority of cases because they are recorded as having another, main, occupation, or as retired. Two points follow from this: first, many smaller holdings are in the hands of relatively elderly occupiers and secondly, there is considerably less land mobility in Ireland than figures such as those shown in Table 9.2 might suggest. For example, Tracy (1971, p. 72) looked at the rate of farm size adjustment in eight OECD countries during the 1950s and 1960s: of those, Ireland demonstrated the least change. Thus although small farms are becoming less numerous it appears that for the most part, non-viable, marginal holdings can continue to exist from one generation to the next, often in the hands of owners whose primary occupation is not farming.

In part, the slowness of structural change can be linked to the nature of Irish land tenure and transfer. Virtually all holdings in Ireland are owned outright by the resident occupier, and over 80 per cent of land transfers are via inheritance or gift. If we further allow for land transfers that arise out of State allocations by the Land Commission, this leaves relatively little in the way of a land market. Indeed, Kelly (1982, pp. 7–8) estimated that about three per cent of the total area of crops and pasture was transferred each year and most of this was done via gift or inheritance.

These trends have not operated independently of government policy. In the following sections we look at how State policies have influenced polarisation of the agricultural sector and, later, at how the role of agricultural interests in Irish society has developed.

STATE AGRICULTURAL POLICY 1922–88: A SUMMARY

State policy towards agriculture has always had to contend with the tension arising from the conflict between intensive and extensive agriculture. The move away from intensive farming (notably tillage) towards extensive (notably cattle and, to a lesser degree, sheep) operations, meant that since the founding of the State, the balance of land usage has overwhelmingly favoured pastoral agriculture rather than cereals or other crops. At present, 90 per cent of agricultural land is under grass. Beef cattle have always (with minor interruptions) been readily exportable to Britain and the cattle trade has always been a major source of Irish exports (particularly in the early years of the State when agriculture was called upon to provide the majority of exports). Against this, however, is the structure of Irish agricultural holdings which, being predominantly small and supporting a relatively large population, were not well suited to extensive 'ranching' operations. Indeed, both recent and contemporary academic observers have argued that the trend towards extensive farming was directly responsible for the decline in the farm population (Crotty, 1966; Lee, 1973; Lyons, 1973).

State policy towards agriculture has by and large reflected these tensions, placing the emphasis in certain periods on the stimulation of exports, which furthered the trend towards extensive agriculture, while at other times seeking to promote those crops which appeared more suited to the structure of Irish agriculture.

During the 1920s and until the fall of the Cumann na nGaedheal government in 1932, efforts were made to strengthen the export potential of Irish agriculture by means of new legislation relating to the quality and standards of products. At the same time, the Department of Agriculture set up a Farm Advisory Service, and the Land Commission (established in 1923) made some attempts to alter the imbalances in the structure of land holding. In 1927 the Agricultural Credit Corporation (ACC) was set up to provide loans to farmers.

During the period of Fianna Fail government in the 1930s there was a change in policy towards protectionism and an attempt at self-sufficiency in food production.[5] This was given added urgency by the so-called 'economic war' with Britain (see Crotty, 1966, pp. 139–41, and Lyons, 1973, pp. 611–4), which began in 1932 and lasted, with decreasing severity after 1935, until 1938, in which tariffs were placed on Irish exports into Britain. This blow to the Irish cattle trade led to a decline in the cattle population and cattle prices, causing farm incomes to fall. Indeed, at this time the Government offered a bounty of two shillings and sixpence for every calf skin, to encourage the slaughter of calves and a decline in cattle numbers.

Aside from the effects of the economic war, however, it was in any case the government's policy to increase the tillage acreage and reduce the cattle herd, not only by the payment of calf skin bounties, but also by the introduction of schemes for the distribution of free beef to the unemployed and by guaranteeing the price of wheat. This policy arose out of the belief that the prevailing extensive type of agriculture was unsuited both to the structural and demographic characteristics of the sector and of the economy as a whole. The attempts to move towards more intensive, tillage-based farming would, it was hoped, slow rural population decline and ease the unemployment problem. This policy was unsuccessful; the Coal–Cattle pacts with Britain of 1935 onwards alleviated the pressure on beef producers and Irish agriculture rapidly began to re-adopt its old structure and trends.

While it was evident at the end of the decade that the decline in cattle numbers and the increased acreage of tillage during the middle years of the decade had been only a temporary phenomenon, the process of re-adjustment was halted by the Second World War. In 1940 compulsory tillage was introduced, forcing farmers to till one-eighth of their arable acreage; in 1944 this was increased to three-eighths.

After the end of the Emergency in 1948, favourable world conditions (a scarcity of food and economic policies aimed at full employment) and a desire to provide greater employment opportunities, led the government to embark on a policy of increasing State aid to agriculture. The major form of government spending on agriculture was price supports for a range of products including wheat, sugar beet, butter and pigs. Overall, tillage again declined in favour of increased cattle herds which, with the aid of subsidies, had a ready market in Britain.

The *Programme for Economic Expansion* (1958) sought to encourage the development of beef production: it noted that beef and dairy produce were the two agricultural commodities which Ireland, by virtue of her climate and geography, was best suited to providing. In the absence of a foreign (that is, British) market for butter, any hopes for increased export earnings from agriculture rested with the further development of the cattle industry. To some extent the prospects for dairy exports were improved in the mid-1960s as a result of an Anglo-Irish trade agreement under which Britain agreed to remove import quotas on Irish butter.

The most salient event for Irish agriculture in the post-1950 period was entry to the EC in 1973, the economic consequences of which were chiefly three-fold. First, a number of commodities – initially, cereals, milk products and beef – were given guaranteed prices through the system of intervention buying. Second, entry into the EC lessened the dependence of Irish agriculture on the British market. For example, in 1970, 75 per cent of Irish dairy exports went to the UK; by 1983 this had fallen to 42 per cent, (Sheehy and O'Connor, 1985, pp. 67–73). Third, since Irish prices were much lower than EC prices for all the supported products, Irish farmers enjoyed both the benefit of support prices and, during a five-year transition period into the EC, price rises in Ireland which were greater than among the six 'old' members of the Community. The results were a large increase in farm incomes and in land prices. The latter reached a peak in 1979: between 1970 and 1979 land prices increased fourteen-fold in nominal terms, or almost five-fold in real terms. Since then, however, they have declined, so that in 1983 the real price of land was only 25 per cent greater than it had been in 1970 (Sheehy and O'Connor, 1985, p. 146).

We can isolate two features of State policy which have had particular significance in shaping the polarisation of Irish agriculture. First, between the late 1930s and the mid-1960s there was an increasing reliance on cattle to provide agricultural exports which, in turn, encouraged extensive agriculture of a type unsuited in many respects to the structure of Irish farm holdings. Second, the major policy instrument was price supports. For example, a quarter of total State expenditure on agriculture during the 1950s and 1960s went to price subsidies and, indeed, it is indisputable that the major exchequer effect of EC entry was to shift the increasingly onerous burden of price support from the Irish to the European taxpayer (Matthews, 1981).

PRICE SUPPORT POLICIES AND THEIR EFFECTS

Many features characteristic of agricultural modernisation and development tend to increase income inequalities within the farm sector, unless government policy dictates otherwise. For example, technological developments tend to reduce the marginal costs of production and to increase the scale of operations. Large farms benefit most from this process because they can more easily adjust their scale of output to an optimal level and also because the fixed costs of new techniques are often too high to make it worthwhile for smaller producers to adopt them. Even if technological innovation occurs in small farm products, the emergence of associated economies of scale will lead to the development of much larger and more efficient production units which, in turn, will drive these products off small farms. In Ireland such has been the case with pigs and poultry, both of which were, until the late 1950s/early 1960s, small farm products within mixed farming but which are now produced in large specialised units (Matthews, 1981, p. 121).

Relative product price changes accompanying modernisation tend to change the distribution of income arising in agriculture if the 'income multiplier' (the ratio of gross revenue to farm income) differs between farms of different sizes, depending also on the actual pattern of price changes across the various products of large and small farms. In addition to the immediate effects so arising on farm incomes, price shifts may also cause changes in the income distribution if farms of different sizes show different abilities to adjust to new sets of prices.

Because the income multiplier is more favourable among large farmers (Matthews, 1981, p. 125), a unit price increase for products will benefit the largest farmers to a greater extend than the smaller, though conversely a fall in prices will tend to hurt the large farmer more than the smaller. However, the post-war period has been one of generally rising prices for Irish agricultural products (in part due, of course, to government price support policy).

Over the post-war period, price support has been a major aspect of Irish agricultural policy. In 1983, 65 per cent of expenditure on Irish agriculture by the Irish government and the EC went on product price support (Sheehy and O'Connor, 1985, p. 263). Price supports were first introduced in the 1930s for cereals, dairy produce and sugar beet, in order to encourage the restructuring of production. In the 1950s, support was extended to other products, but the aim at this time appears to have been not so much to restructure production in a major way as to support farm incomes and close the gap between the incomes of the farm and non-farm sector (Lyons, 1973, p. 627). Since price increases disproportionately benefit the larger producer (all other things being equal), it follows that a government policy of price support will lead to the same result unless the commodities which receive such support are those of the smaller rather than the larger farms. In Ireland, cereals and older store cattle have been typical of the larger farms, sheep and younger store cattle of the smaller farms, together with, until recently, poultry and pigs. Dairying was traditionally found on farms of all sizes, though recently there has been a trend towards larger production units which can take advantage of technological developments in dairying.

Those farm commodities which have benefited most from government and, latterly, EC price supports have been dairy products, beef and cereals. Poultry and sheep have been less favourably treated. Hence, in general, the allocation of price supports across products has been biased towards those products requiring large acreages and/or capital-intensive operations. As a result, the allocation of price supports has strengthened rather than offset the regressivity of the mechanism. The policy had some clearly deleterious effects. For example, price support for wheat in the 1950s led to overproduction and probably acted to reduce the acreage allotted to other crops and cereals such as oats or potatoes. Combined with measures designed to maintain the price of barley (e.g. the control of imports of barley and maize) this led to greatly increased food prices for pig and poultry producers, thus directly penalising the smaller farmer who relied more heavily on these commodities (Lyons, 1973, p. 626).

As several authors (Crotty, 1966; Lyons, 1973; Hannan and Breen, 1987a) have pointed out, although one of the central goals of farm price support has been to help equalise farm and non-farm incomes, one of its central consequences has been to widen the gap in income and wealth between large and small farmers. It has been estimated, for example, that the top 17 per cent of farmers (having over 100 acres) captured roughly 40 per cent of price support expenditure (Matthews, 1981).

It is, however, not only price support policy which has tended to favour the larger producer. For example, under the EC Farm Modernisation Scheme, the most generous grants are available to farms classed as having 'Development' status – those capable of becoming viable given development aid. This excludes the majority of Irish farms – particularly those of the West – which are too small to aspire to commercial viability. Matthews (1981, p. 129) concluded that the trend in the recent past has been towards a concentration of investment in the better-off counties, suggesting that the distribution of grant-aid favours more prosperous farmers.

State interest subsidies on loans to farmers are regressive, for the simple reason that the utilisation of farm credit is very uneven across farm sizes (Matthews, 1981, p. 135). By the mid-1970s, 90 per cent of farm credit went to the upper third of farms of 50 acres and over: virtually no credit went to the bottom 42 per cent of farms with under 30 acres.

STATE POLICY AND SMALL FARMS

Given the increasing polarisation of Irish agriculture and the growing recognition of the problems of small farm size, the State introduced policies which, initially, were aimed at seeking to promote output growth on small farms. This phase of policy commenced with the *Second Programme for Economic Expansion* in 1964, and included such schemes as the Small Farm (Incentive Bonus) Scheme, the 'Pilot Areas Scheme' (under which in pilot areas of the 12 western counties development schemes were centred on units of 200–400 farms: see *Second Programme*, 1964, p. 105) and some price support schemes which graded subsidies according to the size of the farmer's enterprise (Scully, 1971; Commins et al., 1978; Kelleher and O'Mahony, 1984).

The *Third Programme for Economic and Social Development 1969–72*, heralded a change in policy, acknowledging that agricultural development alone could not lead to viability for the bulk of small farms. Instead, a decision was made to maintain those small farmers on their land via two mechanisms (*Third Programme*, 1969, pp. 44–5). The first of these was the provision of off-farm employment, chiefly through industrial development, and following the rejection of the Buchanan Report of 1968, a policy was adopted of dispersing new industry throughout the country, rather than concentrating it in a small number of centres.[6] The second was the provision of direct income supports, chief among which was and remains the Small-holders Assistance Scheme (SHA). This was introduced in 1966 but has undergone major reviews since. Under the scheme, farmers whose acreage valuation was of a particularly low level – generally under 30 acres in the West of Ireland – received a weekly social welfare payment somewhat lower than that received by the long-term unem-ployed. Since 1983, the amount payable depends on a means test. Despite some anomalies, this scheme is of great benefit to the smaller, poorer farmers. Data from the 1980 Household Budget Survey indicates that 36 per cent of the gross income on farms of under 30 acres came from this and other sources of direct State transfers (such as pensions), and that 60 per cent of the households in that category had more than 30 per cent of gross income from such State transfer sources. Both these percentages are greater than those applicable to households from unskilled manual backgrounds.[7]

In the years following the publication of the *Third Programme*, policies aimed at developing the small farm sector have disappeared. Since entry to the EC, farm development has been carried out via the FMS, which, as we have seen, finances only viable or potentially viable farmers.

An alternative policy would have been to encourage small farmers to give up their land and effect structural reform by creating a reduced number of larger, and therefore more viable, holdings. For a number of reasons, such policies, although in existence, have proved virtually useless. For example, the Farm Retirement Scheme introduced in 1967 was availed of by only 38 farmers during the lifetime of the scheme. The present EC Farm Retirement Scheme has met with more success, but the individual farmer will generally be better off retaining his or her farm and obtaining additional income support from the SHA or the old age pension than under the terms of the Retirement Schemes. More generally, Irish policy in the area of land restructuring has been restricted by the nature of land tenure (outright ownership), the rights of property holders and the high level of attachment to land ownership deriving from the circumstances of the last century and the importance accorded to the possession of land as a source of status within the community.

AGRICULTURAL POLARISATION

The recent history of State – and latterly EC – policies for agriculture in Ireland is, at its simplest, one of growing dichotomisation between measures that seek to stimulate and/or reward commercial agricultural production and those that simply attempt to maintain the income of poorer farmers at or around the poverty level.

The most revealing index of the polarisation process operating within Irish agriculture is the divergence in farm incomes. Increased output and income have been concentrated in the large, specialised dairying, tillage or beef enterprises in the South and East. As a result, economic inequalities have increased, so that the farming sector now comprises some of the poorest, but also a minority of the richest, families in Ireland (Rottman et al., 1982); indeed, variation in incomes is greater in the farming than in the non-farming sector (Cox et al., 1982; Kelleher and O'Mahony, 1984).

The change in income associated with different farm sizes is shown in Table 9.3. The picture it presents is straightforward: farm income and farm size are related and the rate of growth in income is likewise related to farm size. In particular, it is worth noting the very rapid divergence of incomes after 1972.

About 25 per cent of farmers are part-time (Hannan and Breen, 1987a, p. 14). The availability of off-farm employment depends upon proximity to industrial locations. Where these industrial centres have developed, they appear to have had positive effects on local rural

TABLE 9.3 *Index changes in family farm income per farm, 1955–83 (full-time farmers*)*

| Year | Farm size (acres) | | | | | |
	5–15	*15–30*	*30–50*	*50–100*	*100–200*	*200+*
1955–58	100	100	100	100	100	100
1966–67	73	64	97	103	103	112
1968–69	129	131	155	171	176	177
1972	199	200	253	279	327	338
1975	293	298	429	381	477	529
1978	1124	600	815	856	893	943
1981	n.a.	664	878	817	786	850
1983	773	744	1042	1211	1288	1639

SOURCES CSO *National Farm Survey*, 1955–56/1957–58; An Foras Taluntais *Farm Management Survey* (various)
n.a. not available.
* data for 1955–58 and 1966–67 are for all farmers; remaining years for full-time farmers.

communities. Between 1961 and 1966, for example, 70 per cent of mainly open country rural districts declined in population. This had fallen to 57 per cent for the period 1966–71. But between 1971 and 1981 only 18 per cent of such districts declined in population. This appears to be mainly accounted for by the dispersed nature of industrialisation that occurred in the 1970s rather than any growth in farm prosperity – given the continued outflow of population from farming in the 1970s. Only those places remote from towns and developing industrial centres declined in population in the 1970s.

However, the majority of low income farmers, lacking off-farm employment, depend upon direct cash payments from the State to meet their income needs. This policy has had some clearly undesirable effects – particularly in rewarding 'land hoarding' behaviour among a smallholding class which attaches enormous value to land both as a symbol and for security. A serious attempt to integrate social welfare, rural industrial, land transfer and small farm development policy is urgently needed (see Commins et al., 1978). The prospects for this, however, are less encouraging. As Kelleher and O'Mahony (1984, p. 173) note:

> State intervention functions in such a way as to reproduce the very conditions which call for State support in the first place . . . current trends in agricultural development, agricultural advisory work and land policy do not suggest that any amelioration of marginal farming and its associated problems can be expected in the immediate future.

The category of marginal farmers contains a disproportionate share of elderly and/or unmarried land holders. As smaller farms became less viable in the post-war period, so the privilege of farm inheritance became an obligation, one which frequently fell on that son who remained after his siblings had migrated. Women, for their part, generally preferred migration to marriage into these farms, and thus their operators are nowadays frequently elderly bachelors. Although heirs can usually be found for such farms, particularly among nephews and nieces, the physical absence of a future heir from the farm means that the owner his little incentive to work his land.

A high proportion – 43 per cent – of male farmers (as defined in the 1981 Census) are aged 55 or above, and in the poorer province of Connaught this rises to 48 per cent. Of these, around a third have never married, and nowadays the marriage prospects of farmers are highly correlated with farm size (Hannan, 1979). The existence of such a large share of agricultural land in the hands of old owners presents obvious difficulties when seeking to increase agricultural output. In addition, these farmers are unlikely to have any off-farm employment, since they lack not only the incentive to develop their farms, but also those attributes that would make them attractive to potential employers. Such farmers are

> out of touch or are ill-disposed to adopt the most basic modern farm practices. In many ways they have more pressing concerns in terms of ill-health, social isolation and meagre levels of living. Their marginal status in agriculture is matched by an equal exclusion from the basic standards of modern living (Kelleher and O'Hara, 1978, p. 68).

The consequences of such marginalisation for the social structure of local communities is reported in some recent ethnographies, notably that of Brody (1974). Brody presents a picture of rural communities on the western seaboard in which the traditional forms of life among small farmers have given way to demoralisation and despair. While it is not possible to generalise from this study to all or even the majority of communities in the west, Brody's work nevertheless presents a telling portrait of the disintegration of at least some sections of the small farm sector. Against this must be set the effects of policies which have acted to revitalise many previously declining rural communities. We have already referred to the reduction in the number of rural districts recording a decline in population, and this appears to have been due to the provision of off-farm employment, both directly through industrial location, and indirectly via a growth in service employment. By 1984 in only one region of the country (the west) did the agricultural labour force exceed 30 per cent of the total employed labour force.

STATE POLICY OR EC POLICY?

Just as the burden of financing the agricultural sector has been shifted to the EC, so the Irish Government's direct control over agricultural policies pursued in Ireland has diminished, and the Government's capacity to make policy changes can nowadays be exercised only through the EC and within the restrictions of the Common Agricultural Policy. On the other hand, there is little to suggest that, even had that State been able to dictate policy directly, its broad pattern over the post-1973 period would have been greatly different. The policies pursued by the Irish Government up to 1973 were largely in accord with those subsequently pursued by the EC. In particular, the failure of EC schemes to tackle successfully the problems of marginal farmers mirrors the failure of earlier Irish policies. Indeed, with the advent of the *Third Programme*, some four years before EC entry, the burden of dealing with the problems of marginal farms effectively passed from the realm of agricultural policy and into those of social welfare and industrial policy.

THE POLITICS OF FARMING

In the Irish Free State the interests of the farmers and of the nation are, at least *prima facie*, identical, and the best utilisation of the resources of the country is that which maximises the prosperity of the farming classes (O'Brien, 1936, p. 356).

Such a view was held widely for much of the period after independence. During this time, the agricultural sector occupied the great majority of the labour force, and provided the bulk of exports. Despite the subsequent decline in the importance of agriculture to the economy, increased government spending on the sector, together with the State's adoption of a more 'corporatist' approach, led to the politicisation of agriculture. Expenditure on farming is viewed in terms of the redistribution of income and wealth from the non-farm to the farm sector, and this has given rise to antagonism centring, in recent years, on the issue of farmer taxation. Farmers have also become more involved, both formally and informally, in the corporatist arrangements of the Irish State. In all these areas, the farmers' case has been presented via the two major farming organisations, the Irish Creamery Milk Suppliers' Association (ICMSA) and the Irish (formerly National) Farmers' Association (IFA).

Manning (1979, pp. 51–2) has described the birth and demise of a number of short-lived and generally unsuccessful farmers' political parties in the period since 1922, the most recent being Clann na Talmhan, which participated in the inter-party governments of the late 1940s and early 1950s, but ceased to exist in the mid-1960s. Of much greater significance was the formation, in 1944, of the Young Farmers'

Clubs (later Macra na Feirme), with their emphasis on farm education and development and, out of them, the ICMSA in 1950 and the IFA in 1955. The former organisation, as its name indicated, was set up to protect and further the interests of dairy farmers; the latter is a much larger body representing farmers regardless of the commodity they produce. There have been numerous attempts to effect a merger between these two bodies, all unsuccessful, and in general relations between the two have been poor and occasionally acrimonious.

These organisations have sought to promote farmers' interests over a wide range of areas, but their primary concern has always been with farm incomes. As the then President of the IFA, Juan Greene, expressed it:

Agriculture is entitled to remunerate both capital and labour input at rates reasonably equivalent to average current national earnings in other enterprises. (NFA, 1964, p. 7).

As successive farmers' leaders have argued, average farm incomes have been lower than average non-farm incomes throughout the period, with the exception of one or two years in the late 1970s. This situation was initially highlighted by the farmers' organisations in the 1950s, but in the 1960s their cries became more strident, largely because, following the failure in 1961 of Ireland's initial attempt to enter the EC (which would have afforded access to protected European markets), farmers perceived a marked worsening in their relative economic position (Matthews, 1982, p. 244). The increased prosperity of Ireland in the 1960s was, at least in the eyes of the farmers, confined to the non-farm sector. In addition, farmers held 'an equally strong conviction ... that the bureaucrats in Dublin simply didn't understand or care enough about their problems, or were too remote to do anything about them' (Manning, 1979, p. 54).

These feelings led in 1966 to an IFA-led campaign of marches and civil disobedience, which persisted well into 1967. Manning (1979, p. 57) argues that, as a result 'government realised that it could not afford not to consult fully with the farmers while the farmers got an accurate measure of their own strength'.

Equally, however, these demonstrations occurred at a period during which the efforts of the Exchequer (via price support policies and other measures) to maintain farm incomes 'threatened to overwhelm the financial capacity of the non-farm sector' (Matthews, 1982, p. 245) which was being called upon to fund these policies. Such farmer militancy coming at a time during which there had developed substantial redistribution from the non-farm to the farm sector, was fertile ground for the development of conflict.

Although regular Government consultation with the IFA in the formulation of policy was promised as early as 1964, it did not occur until after the 1966–67 disturbances (Manning 1979). Farmers' organisations were not represented on the National Industrial and Economic Council, one of the corporatist institutions established in the 1960s, but they were represented on its successor, the National Economic and Social Council, set up in 1973. However, farmer representatives do not appear to have played an active role in this body except where farm interests were directly involved, nor were they partners to the various National Wage Agreements of the 1970s. Nevertheless, the farm organisations have wielded a great deal of influence through their direct relationship with the Department of Agriculture.

The most salient issues on which the IFA in particular has campaigned have related to incomes: specifically farm taxation and EC policies. In regard to the latter, Irish Ministers of Agriculture have come under severe pressure from the farmer organisations to oppose those reforms of the Common Agricultural Policy (CAP) which would lead either to restrictions on production (such as milk quotas) or to more limited (more recently, zero or negative) price increases. In some instances, IFA demands have not met with success, as with their call for a currency devaluation in the early 1980s, and their demand that relief following the disastrous summer of 1985 should take the form of cash payments. In other cases, the Irish Minister for Agriculture, with a rampant IFA at his back, has met with success, as in the partial exemption afforded to Irish dairy farmers from the 1984 EC schemes to limit milk production.

In relation to farmer taxation, the IFA has been very successful. Farmers – except the very largest and those with off-farm earnings – pay no income tax, and following a legal case in 1982, in which the valuation used as the basis for levying rates (property tax) was found to be unconstitutional, farmers have not paid rates.

The favourable position of farmers with regard to income tax derives from the traditionally low level of farm incomes and also from difficulties in agreeing a basis on which farmers should be taxed. In recent time, with rising incomes, farmers have, as Sheehy (1974, p. 99) notes, 'repeatedly proclaimed that they are willing to pay their fair share towards the running of the country, yet each tax proposal seems to be greeted by unqualified opposition'. This has naturally fuelled resentment on the part of the non-farm sector, particularly among PAYE workers, who see themselves as bearing a disproportionately large share of the taxation burden.

Some indication of the degree of success enjoyed by the farming organisations in this area is given by the somewhat surprising finding that, on average, farmers on all sizes of farm are net beneficiaries of the State's taxation and transfer policies. Table 9.4 shows disposable

TABLE 9.4   *Standardised direct and disposable income and their ratio, according to class category, 1973 and 1980*

Class category	Direct*	1973 Income disposable†	(b) as % of (a)	Direct*	1980 Income disposable†	(b) as % of (a)
	(a)	(b)		(a)	(b)	
Large proprietors	215	205	96	177	160	90
Small proprietors	106	104	98	122	120	98
Large farmers (100 + acres)	177	178	101	118	127	108
Medium farmers (50– 100 acres)	126	129	102	94	103	110
Small farmers (30–50 acres)	80	88	110	71	83	117
Marginal farmers (under 30 acres)	51	66	129	42	66	157
Higher professionals	202	173	86	195	160	82
Lower professionals	156	134	86	138	120	87
Intermediate non-manual	127	116	91	130	116	89
Skilled manual	107	101	94	107	103	96
Service workers	98	95	97	94	94	100
Semi-skilled manual	91	91	100	95	97	102
Unskilled manual	69	79	114	56	73	130
Residual	24	41	171	27	46	170
National	100	100	100	100	100	96

SOURCE   All data originally from Household Budget Surveys 1973 and 1980.
            1973 Table from Rottman and Hannan *et al.* (1982, p. 77).
          * Direct incomes is expressed as a percentage of overall direct income.
          † Disposable income is expressed as a percentage of overall disposable income.

income (that is, income after tax plus the effect of State benefits) as a percentage of direct incomes (income before tax and without State benefits) for the years 1973 and 1980.[8] For most non-farm households, except the semi-skilled or unskilled, disposable income is less than direct: that is, these households are net losers under the taxation and benefit schemes. On the other hand, all farm households are net beneficiaries. This is very striking in the case of the very smallest farmers whose direct income is, anyway, very low (42 per cent of the national average in 1980). However, even those farmers with 100 or more acres whose incomes are greater than the national average, are also net beneficiaries, whereas all other households with above average direct income were net losers – in some cases substantially so.

The strength of the farmers' organisations – particularly the IFA – derives from their organisation and the unity of their members. The economic and political (in terms of votes) muscles of the farm sector are rarely directly in evidence, though they are doubtless considerations taken into account by ministers and politicians. Manning (1979, pp. 50, 57) has drawn attention to the nature of the IFA as an organisation. Starting in the late 1960s, it developed into

'one of the most effective and sophisticated pressure groups of its kind in Europe. It had adapted to the changed and pressurized conditions of the EC better than any other Irish organisation. Its research, expertise and public relations is as good, if not better, than most government departments.

One outstanding question is how the IFA can present a united front when, as we saw earlier, Irish agriculture is becoming polarised between a small, in some cases wealthy, sector of commercial producers and a large, marginalised rural 'lumpen-bourgeoisie' of non-viable farmers. The question is all the more puzzling when we consider that the central issues taken up by the IFA – the maintenance of product prices and farm taxation – if successful, are likely to accelerate this polarisation (in the case of price increases) or to have little relevance to smaller farmers (in the case of farmer taxation, given that marginal farmers are unlikely to have to pay any form of tax). The ability of the IFA to negate internal differences among farmers has been a feature since its inception. This question has not been researched in Ireland, and we can only sketch some suggestions as to why farmers see themselves as having common policy interests which can best be articulated by the IFA. Doubless the conditions under which the IFA developed – the low farm incomes of the 1950s, and the sense of farmers being left behind in the booming 1960s – helped forge unity within the farming community. Furthermore, the ideology of the family farm is still pervasive. Virtually all farms in Ireland are family farms in the sense that landowners are usually resident on their land, and the position of the farm family is central in the 'rural fundamentalism' which, as Commins (1986, pp. 52–3) has argued, has shaped the perception of farming for most of this century and earlier. So not only is the family-owned farm seen as the basic agricultural production unit, but it is imbued with a moral and aesthetic value: as the Catholic Bishop of Cork, Dr Lucey, put it, in his minority report to the *Commission on Emigration* (1955, pp. 335–6, quoted by Commins, 1986), 'the rural home always has been, and is still, the best place to raise a family'.

The IFA emphasises the family farm, both through the widely read newspaper, *The Farmers' Journal* and in the pronouncements of its leaders (who refer, for example, to *family farm* incomes). This ideology negates the fact that, on the one hand, 38 per cent of all farmers aged over 55 with less than 50 acres are unmarried and are extremely unlikely ever to be in a position to put Bishop Lucey's assertion into practice, and on the other, that a number of large farmers, far from being solely dependent on their farm income, have interests extending into the worlds of commerce and industry. Despite this, the image, and the values and attitudes it invokes, of the farm family, provide a powerful rallying point for the farmer organisation.

Finally, and, perhaps of chief importance, are other deeply in-grained values and attitudes – the perception that all farmers acquired their land only through the struggles of their forebears in the Land War – a struggle which, possibly more so in retrospect than contemporaneously, came to be viewed as an integral part of the long search for Irish independence. Likewise, the local standing traditionally associated with the position of farmer is still a potent force. Particularly in the West of Ireland, the role of farmer/proprietor conferred on the individual a much prized autonomy, status and independence that no other occupation could. Furthermore, because it was precisely in this area that large farms were few, the small farmer in the West was acutely conscious of farmer/non-farmer distinctions, but not of differentiations within the farmer class. Given these considerations, it may not be surprising that these small farmers prefer to identify themselves primarily as 'farmers' rather than as, say, marginalised farmers who require particular policies to help them.

NOTES

1. Partibility is the term given to inheritance by more than one heir: in the Irish case, inheritance of farms by several children led to a continuing subdivision of tenancies. Impartible inheritance, on the other hand, ensured that holdings were passed intact to one heir.
2. There are major differences between the agricultural sectors in the east and west of the country. Generally speaking, in the west (the province of Connaught, the three counties of Ulster and the western counties of Munster) farms are predominantly small and the quality of land is poor. In the east (east Munster and Leinster) farms are larger and the land is of much higher quality.
3. Using the Irish standards, about 45 per cent of Irish farms are considered 'viable'. Under the more stringent EC criteria, employed as part of the Farm Modernisation Scheme, only 31 per cent were considered viable or potentially viable in 1982 (Commins, 1983; Kelleher and O'Mahony, 1984).
4. The decline in assisting relatives and labourers was greatest on the smallest farms. For example, on farms of 50 acres or less, labourers and assisting relatives, taken together, declined in number by over 90 per cent between 1926 and 1981.
5. This strand of Fianna Fail policy has featured in nationalist philosophy as Bew and Patterson (1982, p. 2) note; 'In 1932 Fianna Fail took office as a party of radical reform with a very real 'progressive' image. In the countryside it stood for a generalised agrarian radicalism – the roots of which went back to at least the Irish Land League of 1879–82'.
6. The Buchanan Report (*Regional Development in Ireland: A Summary*, prepared by Colin Buchanan and Partners) of 1968, reviewing Irish regional industrialisation policy, recommended that the previous policy of widespread geographical dispersal of new industry should give way to a locational policy based on the centralisation of new industry in nine regional growth centres, one of which was Dublin. While the recommendation was apparently received favourably by civil servants, TDs of the Fianna Fail party reacted vehemently against it and as a consequence the new policy was not adopted.
7. The comparable figures are 28 and 51 per cent.
8. 1980 was a particularly poor year for farmers, as a comparison of their direct income with that of non-farmer groups reveals. We have, therefore, included data for the previous Household Budget Survey of 1973. The latter was a relatively good year for farm incomes and should redress the imbalance which the use of the 1980 figures alone would induce.

10 The Ebbing Tide

In the preceding nine chapters we have sought to present an account of the relationship between State policy and the class structure of present day Ireland. In doing so we have concentrated on how that relationship has been shaped, and how it has been reflected in particular areas within Ireland's economy and social structure. Our analysis is intended to contribute to the growing body of work which seeks to improve our understanding of the circumstances which encourage the pursuit of autonomous goals by the State and the conditions which affect its capacity to pursue such goals successfully (Evans et al., 1985, p. 351).[1]

The Irish State is currently confronted with a crisis not only of unemployment, but also of national indebtedness. Irish society is one in which the State, directly and indirectly, has come to play a central role in underpinning the distribution of economic opportunities – perhaps indexed most clearly by the fact that total State expenditure now comes to 60 per cent of GNP. Despite the enormously bloated role of the state as an economic intermediary, it has been monumentally unsuccessful either in ensuring sustained economic growth or in moderating inegalitarian tendencies in the class system. It is our intention to apply the argument developed in this book to provide an account of the origins of the crisis confronting the State, and also to shed some light on how the Irish State might be expected to respond to it.

THE TRANSFORMATION OF IRISH SOCIETY

The Irish State, prior to the 1950s, enjoyed considerable autonomy as a consequence of a segmented bourgeoisie, a locality-centred political system, and a stable administrative apparatus. On the other hand, the capacity of the State was limited by, among other factors, restrictions on its role as a direct provider of services and a low level of taxation. The move towards State activism involved a two-stage transformation. The first phase, stretching from the 'Emergency' to the late 1950s, was associated with growing conflict between Church and State, political instability and realignment, a changing élite, and a profound economic crisis. The second phase involved the addition of outward-looking economic policies from the late 1950s onward. A modernising élite from within the Civil Service provided the crucial momentum.[2]

For both the Civil Service and Fianna Fail the strategy pursued required a redefinition of Irish nationalism which focused on the use to which independence would be put for the people's benefit. The benefits of economic developments were conceptualised in national rather than class terms. The 'politics of productivity' deflected attention away from the need to construct mechanisms aimed at resolving issues of allocation and finance. During the 1950s and 1960s Irish society was cast in its modern day mould: the problems of the 1980s are, by and large, traceable to decisions – about industrial policy, taxation policy, and so forth – that were made in the first 10–15 years following the watershed year 1958.

What were these crucial decisions? Perhaps the central decision lies in the manner in which industrial development was pursued in Ireland. This has relied upon the attraction to Ireland of foreign-based multinational manufacturing companies and, as we discussed at some length in Chapter 7, the Irish State has both expended considerable sums and incurred considerable losses of potential revenue (in, for example, choosing to offer very generous tax concessions) in order to provide incentives to attract these firms. Despite such high levels of actual expenditure (and of income foregone), the State's involvement in industrial development has been indirect. Primacy was accorded to free enterprise: so, rather than investing in State industry or entering into partnership arrangements with private industry, the Irish State chose to try to provide a climate in which industries would be attracted to Ireland. The advantage of such a policy is manifest: the foreign manufacturing industries were 'ready made' and potential large scale employers: a policy of fostering native industry (which, in any case was seen to have performed poorly during the long period of protectionism) would have entailed a much longer lag before the reaping of any returns. However, the disadvantages of this policy are now equally manifest, particularly in two areas. First, the high costs to the Exchequer of this policy go beyond questions of the financing of incentives and the foregoing of revenue to include the losses entailed in permitting the free repatriation of profits on the part of multinationals. Since these are subject to no restrictions and to a very low rate of corporation income tax, the particular policy of industrial development pursued cannot, under these circumstances, ever become 'self financing' (in the sense of the tax yield from companies' profits being used to offset further investment in industrial development). Taken together with what we know of the growth rates of newly established foreign based companies in Ireland, which usually display growth in their employee numbers for five years, remaining static or declining afterwards (O'Hearn, 1987), the implications for industrial policy are clear. Given a growing labour force, reliance on current industrial policy will require an ever increasing level of expenditure in order to attract further location by new multinationals in order to create new jobs.

Secondly, the pursuit of industrial growth by these particular means has placed severe limits on the autonomy of the State in this area. The level of overseas investment by mutinationals depends heavily upon the condition of the world economy and the prospects for international trade. When these prospects diminish and the world economy enters a recession (as in the mid-1970s and again in the late seventies and eighties) the level of such foreign investment diminishes. A country like Ireland, which occupies a dependent position in seeking to attract these firms, can do relatively little under such circumstances, except possibly seek to offer larger incentives to those firms willing to locate in the country. As a consequence, the kind of industrial policy pursued by the Irish State is likely to lead to considerable difficulties if the overall level of overseas investment by multinationals should decline[3] – difficulties which are exacerbated where, as in the Irish case, the labour force is growing rapidly.

Such was the situation faced by the Irish State in the recessions of the 1970s and 1980s, when the inflow of new manufacturing jobs fell at the same time as the loss of existing ones increased. Given an under-developed native industrial base (which itself was adversely affected by the recession), a declining agricultural sector, and only a limited capacity for the creation of jobs in the private services sector, an expansion of public sector job creation appeared, in the 1970s, to be the only means of providing jobs. This policy, however, was funded not by increasing taxation or reducing expenditure in other areas of the budget, but by recourse to Government borrowing on a large scale.

IRISH PUBLIC DEBT AND DISTRIBUTIONAL CONFLICT

In retrospect, the recourse to large scale borrowing to provide jobs in the 1970s can be seen as symptomatic of failure: but what exactly was the nature of this failure, and how did it come about?

We have argued that successive Irish governments since 1958 sought to negate distributional conflict through growth. Hence the significance of the 1960s catchphrase 'the rising tide that lifts all boats'. The attempts on the part of Government to accommodate conflicting interests led to an increasing role for the State in the day to day workings of society and to an inevitable increase in public expenditure. The success of such a policy, although at best only partial, depended crucially on the continuation of economic growth, both domestically and internationally. We have already examined the consequences of the failure of growth in the international economy for industrial and job creation policy in Ireland. More generally, until the mid-1970s the capacity of the State to undertake its role as accommodator of conflicts was made possible through the impact of economic growth and, in the later period, through inflation and increased taxation. However, once this growth slackened, as it did in the mid-1970s and subsequently, the State was led to attempt to retain its capacity to act via recourse to borrowing. Perhaps paradoxically, the longer term consequence of this has been in recent years a dramatically diminished autonomy, in that, as the debt burden has grown, policy options have narrowed to a virtual impasse.

The attempt on the part of successive Irish governments to accommodate conflicting interests in a politically acceptable manner should not be taken to mean that an equitable solution was achieved. On the contrary, the logic of industrial and agricultural development led to an increasing bifurcation of the class structure between, on the one hand, the urban middle and upper working class and the better off farmers, and on the other, the unskilled working class and marginal farmers. Changes in the tax system in the last twenty years have been particularly favourable to large property owners, large farmers, and those drawing income from investments in property.

At the same time that taxation change has been beneficial to the interests of family-owned property, the State has substantially expanded expenditure on Welfare State programmes in education, health, housing and social welfare. In education this growth in expenditure has been primarily directed towards the benefit of the middle class, particularly the employee middle class who have been most severely affected by the increasing tax burdern.

The Welfare State emerged in Ireland in the 1960s with a secure Fianna Fail government expanding State provision in education and health.[4] The latter increased under the pressure to raise Irish health and social welfare services up to European – and particularly UK – standards. The philosophy underlying State expansion in education came directly from the OECD and, clothed in a 'human capital' development logic, found a ready ear at that time of economic growth. The development of areas such as health and social welfare has to be understood in the context of a party political system in which the two major political parties – with around 80 per cent of the total vote – did not reflect or seek to mediate class forces. Fianna Fail and Fine Gael were largely cross-class alliances, operating on a broad populist basis in which inter-party competition was founded less on current ideological differences than on an appeal to traditional loyalties, coupled with an attempt to offer rewards to as wide a section of the electorate as possible. The proportional representation voting system requires a party to get around 50 per cent of the vote to achieve a governing majority. Such a result has become increasingly difficult to obtain as, with increasing economic differentiation, class fractioning has increased. In six successive elections since 1973 Fianna Fail and Fine Gael have alternated in government. The former has on two occasions operated as a minority government, while the latter has entered into coalition arrangements with the Labour party. The intensification of competition for office between broad 'catch-all' political opponents, exacerbated by the intra-party competition encouraged by the electoral system, contributed to a remarkable expansion in public expenditure accompanied by the active maintenance of political ideologies which deny the importance of class conflict.

THE ILLUSION OF CAPACITY

From the late 1950s the choice of goals by the State was greatly circumscribed but both its revenue generation powers and the scope of its expenditure were greatly enhanced. However, the increase in public expenditure should not be equated with ability to manage the economy. Capacity refers not just to the sources and amounts of State revenue, but to the authority and organisational means to deploy resources (Skocpol, 1985, p. 17). While the foundation of ministerial responsibility exercised through government departments was recognised to be inadequate, the expanded role of the State did not translate into the necessary institutional arrangements for problem solving or analysis. The State's capacity – so formidable on paper – on closer examination proves to be illusory.

A variety of new advisory forums comprising independent experts, civil servants and representatives of the main interest groups, were established. However, none developed into genuinely neo-corporatist structures serving the function of interest intermediation. Despite the increased involvement of the State in industrial relations, the level and pattern of industrial conflict provided no evidence of the substitution of political exchange for economic exchange. The dependent nature of the Irish economy and the strategy of indirect employment creation provided obstacles to such development. Furthermore, the pattern of Irish industrialisation, through its impact on the diversity of interests represented by central associations of unions and employers, contributed to a diminution in the strategic capacity of the peak organisations.[5]

'Strategic capacity', however, is not simply a reflection of such structural characteristics. In other countries openness and vulnerability have led to enhanced, rather than diminished, State capacity. The 'social partners' in Ireland failed to develop agreement on a common strategy on pay, taxation, redistribution and employment, and the pursuit of sectionalist interests continued to predominate. This failure cannot be attributed simply to a lack of expertise; neo-corporatist arrangements, while making considerable use of experts, always impose political limits on the range of technical solutions that can be considered (Lehmbruch, 1984, p. 78).

A more complete explanation requires that we take into account the way in which the timing and characteristics of State intervention affect the structure of interest groups. The role of the State in Ireland as a partner in National Wage Agreements was accompanied by a variety of measures aimed at enhancing the power of the ICTU. Reliance on the discipline of the market was not a feasible political option because of the power of organised labour and the 'non-ideological' character of party politics. More fundamentally, State activities helped shape the definition of interests. State policy can create and sustain, as well as serve, vested interest groups. The Irish trade union movement has lacked the capacity to create a definition of interests in terms of a class-based analysis of inequalities. In contrast the IFA has managed to maintain a united front despite objective polarisation. In Ireland a combination of State strategies aimed at promoting economic development has an impact on interest group formation which encouraged divisiveness rather than coherence.

The Irish experience illustrates the need, in considering the relationship between politics and the development of the Welfare State, to go beyond the issue of expenditure and consider the control, financing and distribution of social benefits. This approach views such expenditure as part of the set of State interventions capable of altering life chances. '. . . both social and economic issues speak to the same issue: namely how the fruits and costs of growth, or the burdens of stagnation are to be distributed.' (Shalev, 1983a, p. 319).

State action in Ireland altered the distribution of occupational opportunities but without exercising a great deal of influence over which individuals have access to such opportunities. Those in the marginal categories had little opportunity to transfer to the expanding categories. The restrictions on the mobility opportunities of their children ensured that in today's class structure one-quarter of the gainfully occupied are in positions which depend for their viability on State social welfare schemes.

While social expenditure grew more rapidly than other areas of expenditure until the early 1980s, the implications of the replacement of a minimalist State by a Welfare State depends on how it is financed. The State's capacity to raise and redistribute revenue increased substantially but the combination of State strategies in some respects accentuated, rather than eroded, class divisions. The expansion of the Welfare State produced relatively little in the way of class abatement. The cost of rising public social expenditure was disproportionately borne by the less well-to-do, as a consequence of the decline in revenue shares from property, inheritance and corporate taxes. Until the mid-1970s expansion in public expenditure was accommodated primarily through the impact of growth on inflation and taxation. From that point onwards borrowing played an increasing role. The cost of this strategy ensured that it could not be sustained in the long term.

The alternatives – a reduction in public expenditure and/or a broadening of the tax base to include realistic wealth, inheritance, property and corporate taxes on manufacturing – were not pursued until 1987. In some areas, such as industrial policy, low taxation was an integral part of the development strategy. Elsewhere the political difficulties were perceived as too great. Election platforms have most frequently been designed to maximise cross-class voting and minimise the political cost of making 'hard decisions'. Opposition to policy changes is minimised by as far as possible obfuscating the full class-implications of policy changes. In such circumstances senior civil servants have become most unlikely to develop an autonomous capacity to plan effectively and to act rationally on the basis of such planning.

This situation was exacerbated (perhaps one should say encouraged) by the absence of policy evaluation in many areas of government. The 'comparative logic' by which Irish public services were expanded to match those of other north European countries led to an often uncritical incorporation of programmes of expenditure taken particularly from Britain. Growing State expenditure encouraged this, while providing no motivation for the development of the regular evaluation and monitoring of policies. As an example, in the Department of Education the planning and development units, after an active period in the 1960s, were allowed to wither, while the national inspectorate, at both the primary and post-primary level, has reduced in size almost in inverse relationship to the growth in pupil numbers. Under such circumstances – where attempts at 'rational planning' and critical assessment are deliberately avoided – the major factor dictating policy is political expediency.

A further illustration of this can be found in the establishment of a plethora of semi-State and State sponsored bodies whose setting up has permitted perceived problems to be tackled on a relatively *ad hoc* basis outside the formal structure of government. Such a policy has led to subsequent difficulties – as in the manpower area where, until 1988, a number of government departments and semi-autonomous semi-State bodies, acting largely independently of each other, administered a range of overlapping programmes. The administrative procedures of these agencies were each unique thus making inter-agency or inter-programme comparisons virtually impossible, and the fact of having so many different bodies operating in this field led to a diffusion of power which rendered large scale changes of policy difficult to bring about, and induced considerable rivalry between agencies.

The development of specific manpower programmes since the mid 1970s presents a good example of how political expediency has triumphed over other considerations. The guiding force in the development of job creation and training programmes in this area has been the perceived need of the Government to be seen to be 'doing something' about the problem. As a consequence, the agencies administering this policy have come under considerable pressure to enrol individuals in what have often been ill thought out programmes. The priority has been placed on numbers – the number of temporary jobs created, the number of training places filled and, most crucially, the number removed from the unemployment register. Evaluations of these schemes have been markedly absent and, in at least two instances in which pilot projects were established to investigate the feasibility of a new programme, the programme itself was introduced either before the pilot phase had been completed or the evaluation produced.

The limited capacity of the State, we have argued, is influenced by the social bases of political partisanship and the structure, modes of organisation, and representation of class interests. An additional influence is the fact that in many areas of social expenditure the State's intervention came relatively late in the day so that frequently the State was not initiating a service but, rather, was taking over or augmenting an already well developed framework of provision. Given the pre-eminent position of the Roman Catholic Church in Ireland, it is hardly surprising that it, in the absence of the State, had been responsible for establishing and administering systems of health care and education. Thus, when the State sought to establish a modern Welfare State, it was required to take over – to some degree – the existing structures. This inevitably meant that compromises to safeguard Church interests had to be made; but perhaps more significantly, it placed the State in the position of financier of the services over which it exercised relatively little control. Thus, educational policy provides a most striking illustration of the failure of a shift of the financial burden of services onto the State to lead to an increase in the degree of control it exercises. The educational system is one in which the State provides the bulk of the finance while owning and exercising a managerial function over only a small proportion of educational institutions. Moreover, the failure to develop 'organisational mechanisms' necessary to make State capacity a reality goes beyond the question of ownership. The absence of a central monitoring and policy development body indicates an extra-ordinary degree of institutionalisation of traditional schooling arrange-ments, such that what schools do is widely accepted as natural and given (Hannan, 1987).

Equality of opportunity, despite being a goal of State policy, has never been actively pursued by the State. The State, either at local or central level, has not accepted responsibility for the way schools are operated. State policy indeed has colluded in the development of locally stratified schooling provision by 'filling in the gaps' left by selective provision. The structure of the educational system ensured that the deleterious effects of such arrangements were not projected as issues requiring policy debate. Any dissatisfaction present is publicly voiceless and unorganised.[6]

The Irish case provides a particularly good example of the manner in which '... State interventions in economic life can, over time, lead to a diminution of State autonomy and to reduction of any capacity the State may have for coherent action' (Evans et al., 1985, p.354).

Economic development produced a particular balance between insti-tutions and between classes which was underwritten at State expense.

The State has been willing to adjust taxation and expenditure policies to defuse distributional conflict even when these settlements were against the public interest. Bluntly, the State has tended to give in rather than develop an overall strategy of development. The peculiar and shifting balance of class interests served by the two main political parties therefore has acted rather to obscure any underlying tendency to serve particular class interests in any medium- to long-term sense, such as, for instance, the long-term decline in the tax take from large property owners at the same time as the level of benefits they receive from the Welfare State has been increasing. The underwriting of that precarious class balancing act has been provided first by inaccessibly tortuous taxation arrangements and latterly by borrowing.

CONCLUSION: THE CURRENT CRISIS

The crisis that faces the Irish State has two major components – a very high rate of unemployment and a very large national public debt. Faced with these two components of crisis, the State is at once urged to intervene in the unemployment crisis while being pressured to reduce the level of debt. The existence of either one component vastly increases the difficulties of, and circumscribes the State's freedom of action in, addressing the other.

The election campaign of 1987 and the policies of the subsequent Fianna Fail minority government have shown that a reduction in the debt will be the first priority – to be achieved via cuts in public expenditure. The vast majority of seats in Dail Eireann are now held by candidates of parties which either advocated such policies during the election campaign (Fine Gael and the Progressive Democrats) or which adopted them immediately after coming to power (Fianna Fail). Between them, these three parties have 146 of the 166 Dail seats, thus ensuring that there will be little parliamentary opposition to what appears likely to be the broad thrust of government policy. Furthermore, faced with the political unlikelihood of any appreciable broadening or deepening of the tax base, cuts in public expenditure appear to enjoy a good deal of popular support. In pursuing the goal of reducing the public debt through expenditure cuts, Fianna Fail has responded to the fragmentation of the administrative system by centralising decision making in the hands of the Department of Finance, so re-establishing Finance's primacy within the administrative structure of the State.

While accepting that there is no scope for appreciably reducing the debt crisis through the broadening of the tax base (though the equity arguments for doing this seem to us undeniable), the reduction of public expenditure presents difficulties of extraordinary degree. At its simplest the reason for this may be stated as follows: Irish society is itself the product of public expenditure, and such expenditure supports an unusually high proportion of the Irish class structure. The State holds a position as the financier of Irish society, underpinning, by its taxation and expenditure policies, a wide range of positions.

Of course, it can be argued that this is true of all societies and all States: but what is striking in the Irish case is the very direct nature of the link between public *expenditure* and the viability of class positions. This is perhaps most evident in the case of those who rely directly on the State for their income – on the one hand are those, like the unemployed, the disabled, the aged, deserted wives, unmarried mothers and marginalised farmers, who are wholly or partially dependent upon social welfare payments. On the other hand are the direct employees of the State – public servants, defined to include workers in central and local government, semi-State and State sponsored bodies, health board employees, teachers and so on. Beyond these groups are those who are contracted by the State to provide services – such as medical practitioners under the General Medical Scheme and consultants employed by government departments. Beyond them, both industry and agriculture rely heavily on subsidies, tax expenditures and a favourable taxation schedule. We have already remarked how the pursuit of industrial policy requires large and continuing government expenditure. More generally, of course, the position of those who own or hold all forms of property has been underwritten by the State's very lenient taxation policy towards them.

The extent to which the State underpins the class structure can be gauged via some straightforward statistics. Of the population of three and a half million, roughly one and one quarter million are in full-time education or under school age. Of the remaining two and a quarter million, 1.3 million are in the labour force, of which around 1.05 million are at work. Of this latter figure, between a quarter and one third are employed in the broadly defined public sector (Ross, 1986, pp. 302–6). Just less than a further million people are not in the labour force nor in full-time education. The number of recipients of social welfare payments (including unemployment compensation, old age pension, disability benefits, and so on) is approximately three quarters of a million, with the total number of beneficiaries of such payments numbering over 1.3 million (Report of the Commission on Social

Welfare, 1986, pp. 56–60). Figures such as these show the pervasiveness of the direct financing of Irish society by public expenditure.

The class basis of Irish politics was more evident in the 1987 election than at any time in the previous twenty years (Laver et al., 1987, p. 112). The emergence of the Progressive Democrats who have been described as the 'first child of the recession' (Mair, 1987b, p. 37) changed the pattern of electoral competition. Their espousal of tax cuts, privatisation and fiscal rectitude ensured that their appeal was predominantly to the bourgeois and middle class voters. Despite the origins of the party in divisions in Fianna Fail their gains among these groups were mainly at the expense of Fine Gael. The decline in Fianna Fail middle class support was much less but was sufficient to weaken its claim to be a genuine catch-all party.

A policy which concentrates primarily on reducing public expenditure is likely to erode Fianna Fail's working class and small farmer base and push the party into more intense competition with Fine Gael and the Progressive Democrats for the 'increasingly fickle middle class voters' (Laver et al., 1987, p. 139).

An alternative strategy, and one which would hold out the possibility of Fianna Fail becoming once again *the* 'catchall' party, would be to use the agreement on the Programme for National Recovery as a basis for making progress along the lines recommended by the National Economic and Social Council. The Programme for National Recovery is an agreement between Government, the trade unions and employer organisations on the direction which policy should take in the face of the twin problems of unemployment and public debt. Such a strategy would involve control of public expenditure; the acceleration of output growth and consequently employment growth; and the removal of the inequities inherent in the taxation and public expenditure systems, and in the broad issues of access and opportunity. In this manner it might be hoped to generate the consensus necessary to provide sufficient acceptance of the sacrifices needed for the achievement of a more rapid and sustainable rate of growth and the correction of the chronic imbalances in the public finances (NESC, 1986, pp. 303–21).

However, recent evidence suggests that while economic growth will be important in correcting the debt problem (insofar as it will act to reduce the ratio of outstanding debt to Gross National Product) its effects on employment will be less direct. In 1987, despite an export-led growth rate in GNP of four per cent, both the volume of personal consumer expenditure and the numbers at work declined. Profit repatriation by multinationals accounts in part for this unusual situation, but the single most important factor is the level of capital outflows from the country.[7] Such trends suggest that addressing the unemployment problem will have to await the solution to the debt problem. Until such time as the public finances are reckoned to be healthy enough to permit the Government to undertake policies which, directly or otherwise, will generate jobs, the unemployed will have to bear with their lot.

The question which remains is whether the experiences of the 1980s have made a form of political exchange such as the Programme for National Recovery more likely to succeed than the National Wage Agreements and National Understanding of the 1970s. Any such arrangement is unlikely to take a genuinely neo-corporatist form. The structural characteristics of labour and capital in Ireland create serious obstacles to the development of an agreed set of institutions for the mediation of distributive conflict. However, the predominance of sectionalist interests and in particular the inability of the trade union movement to sustain a definition of interests in terms of a class-based analysis of inequalities is itself a consequence of the strategies pursued by successive governments and especially by Fianna Fail.[8]

Both Fianna Fail and Coalition governments have sought to attract and maintain cross-class support. In the late 1970s and early 1980s this entailed an increasingly precarious political and fiscal balancing act, an integral part of which was the obfuscation of distributional issues. In the face of the current crises this is a role which any government will find it difficult, not to say impossible, to play. As a result it seems clear that in future – whatever political options are taken – the underlying interests served by the role of State will start to become much more visible.

NOTES

1. Following Skocpol (1985, p. 14) we have viewed 'State autonomy' not as a fixed structural attribute but as an historically variable quality.
2. The Irish experience is consistent with the argument that linkages of states with transnational structures and international flows of communication through organisations such as the World Bank and the OECD may encourage collectivities of State officials to develop new strategies in periods of crisis (Skocpol, 1985, p. 9).
3. Or if the country's share of total overseas investment should decline. In this respect the Industrial Development Authority has faced increasing pressure in the competition for foreign industrial investment from within the EC from agencies such as the Scottish and Welsh Development Authorities, and seems likely to meet further severe competition from the more recent EC member states – Greece, Spain and Portugal.

4. The expansion of the Welfare State in Ireland is not consistent with a 'logic of capital' formulation; neither does it fit the social democratic model of 'power resources' on the corporatist model both of which construe welfare expenditure as part of an exercise aimed aimed at constructing mechanisms for the achievement of class compromise. It does, however, provide support for the conclusion that class conflict is reflected in the party system as a whole (Castles, 1982; Shalev, 1983b).

5. The difficulties experienced by the State in developing such arrangements illustrate the value of a 'relational perspective' which takes into account the complementary and conflicting relationships of State and societal actions (Skocpol, 1985, p. 20).

6. 'States matter, not simply because of the goal-oriented activities of State officials. They matter because their organisational configurations, along with their overall patterns of activity, affect political culture, encourage some kinds of group formation and collective political actions (but not others) and make possible the raising of certain political issues but not others' (Skocpol, 1985, p. 21).

7. Over half the growth in the economy in 1986 and 1987 appears to have been invested overseas (Baker and Scott 1988, p. 28).

8. So, for example, during the 1970s the trade unions found it easier to make progress on short term issues such as wage gains rather than on the restructuring of the tax system or the reduction of expenditure-based inequalities.

References

Arensberg, C. A. (1937) *The Irish Countryman* (New York: Macmillan).
Arensberg, C. A. and S. T. Kimball (1940) *Family and Community in Ireland* (Cambridge, Mass.: Harvard University Press, 2nd edn 1968).
Armingeon, K., 'Formation and Stability of Neo-Corporatist Incomes Policies: A Comparative Analysis', *European Sociological Review*, 2, (2), pp. 138–47.
Attley, W. (1986) 'Need for a Return to National Planning', Address to a meeting on jobs and tax reform, Western Area of the FWUI.
Bacon, P., J. Durkan and J. O'Leary (1982) *The Irish Economy: Policy and Performance 1972-1981* (Dublin: Economic and Social Research Institute).
Bacon, P., J. Durkan and S. Scott (1983) *Quarterly Economic Commentary*, May (Dublin: Economic and Social Research Institute).
Bairoch, P. (1981) 'The Main Trends in National Economic Disparities since the Industrial Revolution', in P. Bairoch and M. Levy-Leboyer (eds), *Disparities in Economic Development since the Industrial Revolution* (London: Macmillan).
Baker, T. J. and S. Scott (1988) *Quarterly Economic Commentary*, April (Dublin: Economic and Social Research Institute).
Baker, T., S. Scott and L. Hayes (1985) *Quarterly Economic Commentary*, July (Dublin: Economic and Social Research Institute).
Barrington, T. J. (1982) 'Whatever Happened to Irish Government?', in F. Litton (ed.), *Unequal Achievement: The Irish Experience 1957–82* (Dublin: Institute of Public Administration).
Batstone, E. (1985) 'International Variations in Strike Activity', *European Sociological Review*, 1, (1), pp. 46–64.
Bax, M. (1976) *Harpstrings and Confessions: Machine-Style Politics in the Irish Republic* (Assen: Van Garcum).
Benjamin, R. and R. Duvall (1985) 'The Capitalist State in Context', in R. Benjamin and R. Duvall (eds), *The Democratic State* (Manhattan: University Press of Kansas).
Berger, P. (1967) *The Sacred Canopy* (New York: Doubleday).
Bew, P. and H. Patterson (1982) *Sean Lemass and the Making of Modern Ireland: 1945–66* (Dublin: Gill and Macmillan).
Blackburn, R. M. and M. Mann (1979) *The Working Class in the Labour Market* (London: Macmillan).
Blackwell, J. (1982) 'Government, Economy and Society', in F. Litton (ed.) *Unequal Achievement: The Irish Experience 1957–1982.* (Dublin: Institute of Public Administration).
Blackwell, J. (1986) *Women in the Labour Force* (Dublin: Employment Equality Agency).
Blaug, M. (ed.). (1968) *Economics of Education* (Harmondsworth: Penguin).
Bornstein, S. (1984) 'State and Unions: From Postwar Settlement to Contemporary Stalemate', in Stephen Bornstein, David Held and Joel Krieger (eds), *The State in Capitalist Europe: A Casebook* (London: George Allen and Unwin).

223

Boylan, T. A. (1985) 'Versions of Community and Economic Change: Consensus or Conflict?', in M. A. G. O Tuathaigh (ed.), *Community, Culture and Conflict* (Galway: Galway University Press).

Breen, R. (1984a) 'Dowry Payments and the Irish Case', *Comparative Studies in Society and History*, 26, (2), pp. 280–96.

Breen, R. (1984b) 'Irish Educational Policy: Past Performance and Future Prospects' in *Public Social Expenditure – Value for Money?* (Dublin: Economic and Social Research Institute).

Breen, R. (1984c) *Education and the Labour Market: Work and Unemployment among Recent Cohorts of Irish School Leavers* (Dublin: Economic and Social Research Institute) Paper No. 119.

Breen, R. (1985) 'The Sociology of Youth Unemployment', *Administration*, 33, (2), pp. 167–86.

Breen, R. and C. T. Whelan (1986) 'Vertical Mobility and Class Inheritance in the British Isles', *British Journal of Sociology*, 36 (2), pp. 175–92.

Bristow, J. (1980) 'Economics', *Economic and Social Review*, Speical Tenth Anniversary Issue, January.

Brody, H. (1974) *Inishkillane: Change and Decline in the West of Ireland* (London: Allen Lane).

Brown, T. (1985) *Ireland: A Social and Cultural History, 1922–85* (London: Fontana).

Buchanan, C. and Partners (1968) *Regional Development in Ireland: A Summary* (Dublin: An Foras Forbartha).

Cameron, D. (1978) 'The Expansion of the Public Economy: a Comparative Analysis', *American Political Science Review*, 72, pp. 1243–61.

Cameron, D. (1984) 'Social Democracy, Corporatism, Labour Quiescence and the Representation of Economic Interests in Advanced Capitalist society', in J. Goldthorpe (ed.), *Order and Conflict in Contemporary Capitalism: Studies in the Political Economy of Western European Nations* (Oxford: Clarendon Press).

Cardiff, P. (1982) 'Reform: What Needs to be Done', in H. Pollock (ed.), *Reform of Industrial Relations* (Dublin: O'Brien Press).

Carty, R. K. (1981) *Party and Parish Pump: Electoral Politics in Ireland* (Waterloo, Canada: Wilfried Laurier University Press).

Cassells, P. (1987) 'The Organisation of Trade Unions in Ireland,' in *Industrial Relations in Ireland: Contemporary Issues and Developments* (Dublin: Department of Industrial Relations, University College, Dublin).

Castles, F. G. (1982) 'The Impact of Parties on Public Expenditure', in F. G. Castles (ed.) *The Impact of Parties* (Beverly Hills, Calif.: Sage).

Central Statistics Office (CSO), (various). Age by Duration Analysis of the Live Register (mimeo).

Central Statistics Office (1985) *Population and Labour Force Projections, 1986–1991* (Dublin: Stationery Office, pl. 3117).

Chubb, B. (1970) *The Government and Politics of Ireland* (Oxford: Oxford University Press).

Clancy, P. (1982) *Participation in Higher Education: A National Survey* (Dublin: Higher Education Authority).

Collins, C. A. (1985) 'Clientelism and Careerism in Irish Local Government:

The Persecution of Civil Servants Revisited', *The Economic and Social Review*, 16, (4), pp. 273–86.

Commins, P. (1982) 'Land Policies and Agricultural Development' in P. J. Drudy (ed.) *Ireland: Land, Politics and People* (Cambridge: Cambridge University Press).

Commins, P. (1983) 'The Land Question: Is Leasing the Answer?' in *Adjustment and Structural Problems in the Agricultural Sector*, Papers of the Agricultural Institute, Economic and Rural Welfare Annual Conference 1983, Dublin.

Commins, P. (1986) 'Rural Social Change', in P. Clancy, S. Drudy, K. Lynch and L. O'Dowd (eds), *Ireland: A Sociological Profile* (Dublin: Institute of Public Administration), pp. 47–69.

Commins, P., P. Cox and J. Curry (1978) *Rural Areas: Change and Development* (Dublin: National Economic and Social Council).

Commission on Social Welfare (1986) *Report* (Dublin: Stationery Office) Pl. 3851.

Comprehensive Public Expenditure Programmes (1985) (Dublin: Government Publications Office) Pl. 3364.

Conniffe, D. and K. A. Kennedy (eds) (1984) *Employment and Unemployment Policy for Ireland* (Dublin: Economic and Social Research Institute).

Cox, B. and J. Hughes (1987) 'Industrial Relations in the Public Sector', in *Industrial Relations in Ireland: Contemporary Issues and Developments* (Dublin: Department of Industrial Relations, University College, Dublin).

Cox, P., J. Higgins and B. Kearney (1982) *Farm Incomes: Analysis and Policy* (Dublin: National Economic and Social Council).

Craft, M. (1970) 'Economy, Ideology and Educational Development in Ireland', *Administration*, 18, (4), pp. 363–74.

Crotty, R. (1966) *Irish Agricultural Production* (Cork: Cork University Press).

Crouch, C. (1983) 'Pluralism and Neo-Corporatism: A Rejoinder', *Political Studies*, 31, (3), pp. 453–60.

Cullen, L. M. (1972/76) *An Economic History of Ireland Since 1660* (London: B. T. Batsford).

Curran, J. M. (1980) *The Birth of the Irish Free State 1921–1923* (Alabama, University of Alabama Press).

Dail Eireann (1919) *Democratic Programme*, Minutes and Proceedings, 21 January.

Danaher, G., P. Frain and J. Sexton (1985) *Manpower Policy in Ireland* (Dublin: National Economic and Social council) Report No. 82.

Department of Education (various years) *Statistical Report* (Dublin: Stationery Office).

Department of Labour (1983) *Discussion Document on Industrial Relations Reform: Laws, Institutions, Parties, Problems* (Dublin: Department of Labour).

Department of Labour (1985) *Economic Status of School Leavers 1984* (Dublin: Department of Labour).

Department of Labour (1986) *Outline of Principal Provisions of Proposed New Trade Dispute and Industrial Relations Legislation* (Dublin: Department of Labour).

Department of Labour (1987) *Annual Report* (Dublin).

Dignan, Most Rev. J. (1945) Social Security: Outlines of a Scheme of National Health Insurance (Sligo).

Donaldson, L. (1965) *Development Planning in Ireland* (New York: Praeger).

Downey, L. (1983) 'Role of ACOT in Rural Development', Paper to Agricultural Science Association Conference (Kilkenny).

Duncan, W. (1979) *The Case for Divorce in the Irish Republic: A Report Commissioned by the Irish Council for Civil Liberties* (Dublin: Irish Council for Civil Liberties).

Economic Development (1958) (Dublin: Stationery Office).

Economist Intelligence Unit (1963). *Studies on Immigration from the Commonwealth* (London: Economist Intelligence Unit).

Edwards, R. (1979) *Contested Terrain: The Transformation of the Workplace in the Twentieth Century* (London: Heinemann).

Elvin, L. (1981) *The Educational Systems in the European Community: A Guide* (Windsor: NFER–Nelson).

Erikson, R. and J. Goldthorpe (1987) 'Communality and Variation in Social Fluidity in Industrial Nations, part II: The Model of Core Social Fluidity Applied', *European Sociological Review*, 3 (2), pp. 54–77.

Erikson, R., J. Goldthorpe and L. Portocarero (1982) 'Social Fluidity in Industrial Nations', *British Journal of Sociology*, 33, 3, pp. 1–34.

Eurostat (1980) *Basic Statistics of the Community* (Luxembourg: Statistical Office of the European Communities.

Eurostat, 1985. *Employment and Unemployment 1985*, Luxembourg: Statistical Office of the European Communities).

Evans, P. B., D. Rueschemeyer, and T. Skocpol (1985) 'On the Road Towards a More Adequate Understanding of the State', in P. B. Evans, D. Rueschemeyer, and T. Skocpol (eds) *Bringing the State Back In* (Cambridge: Cambridge University Press).

Fanning, R. (1978) *The Irish Department of Finance 1922–58* (Dublin: Institute of Public Administration).

Fanning, R. (1983) *Independent Ireland* (Dublin: Helicon).

Farm Management Surveys (various years) (Dublin: An Foras Taluntais).

Farrell, B. (1982) *Sean Lemass* (Dublin: Gill and Macmillan).

Farrell, B. (1986) 'Politics and Change', in K. A. Kennedy (ed.) *Ireland in Transition* (Cork: Mercier Press).

Federated Union of Employers (1986) A Joint Effort? FUE bulletin, November.

Federated Workers Union of Ireland (1986) *Industrial Democracy Report* (Dublin).

Fine-Davis, M. (1983) *Women and Work in Ireland: A Social Psychological Perspective* (Dublin: Council for the Status of Women).

Fitzpatrick, D., (1977) *Politics and Irish Life: 1913–21* (Dublin: Gill and Macmillan).

Fitzpatrick, J. and J. Kelly (eds) (1985) *Perspectives on Irish Industry* (Dublin: Irish Management Institute).

Fogarty, M. (1982) 'The Irish Economy: An Outside View' in *The Economic and Social State of the Nation* (Dublin: Economic and Social Research Institute).

Fogarty, M., L. Ryan and J. Lee (1984) *Irish Values and Attitudes: The Irish*

References 227

Report of the European Value Systems Study (Dublin: Dominican Publications).

Fogarty, M. P., D. Egan and W. L. Ryan (1981) *Pay Policy for the 1980s* (Dublin: Federated Union of Employers).

Frank, A. G. (1967) *Capitalism and Underdevelopment in Latin America* (New York: Monthly Review Press).

Gallagher, M. (1976) *Electoral Support for Irish Political Parties, 1927–1973* (London: Sage).

Gallagher, M. (1981) 'Societal Change and Party Adaptation in the Republic of Ireland 1960–81', *European Journal of Political Research*, 9, (3), pp. 269–85.

Garvin, T. (1978) 'The Destiny of the Soldiers: Tradition and Modernity in the Politics of de Valera's Ireland', *Political Studies*, 26, (3), pp. 328–47.

Garvin, T. (1981) *The Evolution of Irish Nationalist Politics* (Dublin: Gill and Macmillan).

Garvin, T. (1982) 'Change and The Political System', in F. Litton (ed.) *Unequal Achievement: The Irish Experience 1957–1962* (Dublin: Institute of Public Administration).

Geary, R. C. (1935/36) 'The Future Population of Saorstat Eireann and some observations on population statistics', *Journal of the Statistical and Social Inquiry Society of Ireland*, 15, pp. 15–36.

Giddens, A. (1973) *The Class Structure of the Advanced Societies* (London: Hutchinson).

Goldthorpe, J. (1983) 'Woman and Class Analysis: In Defence of the Conventional View', *Sociology*, 17, (4), pp. 465–88.

Goldthorpe, J. (1984) 'The End of Convergence: Corporatist and Dualist Tendencies in Modern Western Society', in J. Goldthorpe (ed.) *Order and Conflict in Contemporary Capitalism: Studies in the Political Economy of Western European Nations* (Oxford: Clarendon Press).

Goldthorpe, J. and C. Payne (1986) 'Trends in Intergenerational Class Mobility in England and Wales 1972–1983, *Sociology*, 20, (1) pp. 1–24.

Gould, F. (1981) 'The Growth of Public Expenditure in Ireland, 1947–77', *Administration*, 29 (2), pp. 115–35.

Greaney, V. and T. Kellaghan (1984) *Equality of Opportunity in Irish Schools* (Dublin: Educational Company).

Hajnal, J. (1965) 'European Marriage Patterns in Perspective', in D. Glass and D. Eversley (eds) *Population in History* (London: Edward Arnold).

Hall, P. (1984) 'Patterns of Economic Policy: An Organizational Approach', in S. Bornstein, D. Held and J. Krieger (eds) *The State in Capitalist Europe: A Casebook* (Cambridge, Mass.: Harvard University Press).

Hannan, D. F. (1970) *Rural Exodus: A Study of the Forces Influencing the Large-Scale Migration of Irish Rural Youth.* (London: Geoffrey Chapman).

Hannan, D. F. (1972) 'Kinship, Neighbourhood and Social Change in Irish Rural Communities', *The Economic and Social Review*, 3, (2), pp. 163–88.

Hannan, D. F. (1979) *Displacement and Development: Class, Kinship and Social Change in Irish Rural Communities,* (Dublin: Economic and Social Research Institute) Paper No. 96.

Hannan, D. F. (1987) *Schooling Decisions: The Origins and Consequences of Selection and Streaming in Irish Post-Primary Schools* (Dublin: Economic and Social Research Institute) Paper No. 136.

Hannan, D. F. and R. Breen (1987a) 'Family Farming in Ireland' in B. Galeski and E. Wilkening (eds) *Family Farming in Europe and America* (Boulder: Westview Press).

Hannan, D. F. and R. Breen (1987b) 'Schools and Gender Roles' in M. Cullen (ed.) *Girls Don't do Honours: Irish Women in Education in the 19th and 20th Centuries* (Dublin: Womens Education Bureau).

Hannan, D. F., R. Breen, B. Murray, D. Watson, N. Hardiman, and K. O'Higgins (1983) *Schooling and Sex Roles: Sex Differences in Subject Provision and Student Choice in Irish Post-Primary Schools* (Dublin: Economic and Social Research Institute) Paper no. 113.

Hannan, D. F. and N. Hardiman (1978) Peasant Proprietorship and Changes in Irish Marriage Roles in the Late Nineteenth Century. (Dublin: Economic and Social Research Institute) Seminar Paper.

Hannan, D. F. and L. A. Katsiaouni (1977) *Traditional Families?* (Dublin: Economic and Social Research Institute) Paper No. 87.

Hardiman, N. (1984) 'Corporatism in Ireland: An Exchange of Views', *Administration*, 32, (1), pp. 76–87

Hardiman, N. (1986) Centralized Collective Bargaining: Trade Union and Government in the Republic of Ireland 1970–1980. D. Phil. Thesis, University of Oxford.

Headey, B. (1970) 'Trade Unions and National Wage Policies', *Journal of Politics*, 32, (2), pp. 407–39.

Heald, D. (1983) *Public Expenditure* (Oxford: Martin Robertson).

Heclo, H. (1974) *Modern Social Politics in Britain and Sweden* (New Haven, Conn.: Yale University Press).

Hecter, M. (1975) *Internal Colonialism: The Celtic Fringe in British National Development, 1536–1966* (London: Routledge and Kegan Paul).

Hensey, B. (1982) 'The Health Services and Their Administration', in F. Litton (ed.) *Unequal Achievement: The Irish Experience 1957–82* (Dublin: Institute of Public Administration).

Honohan, P. (1985) 'Is Ireland a Small Open Economy?' *Administration*, 29 (4), pp. 356–75.

Horgan, J. (1987) 'The Future of Collective Bargaining', in *Industrial Relations In Ireland: Contemporary Issues and Developments* (Dublin: Department of Industrial Relations, University College Dublin).

Hout, M. and A. Jackson (1986) 'Dimensions of Occupational Mobility in the Republic of Ireland', *European Sociological Review* 2, (2), pp. 114–37.

Hout, M. and A. Raftery (1985) 'Does Irish Education Approach the Meritocratic Ideal? A Logistic Analysis', *Economic and Social Review*, 16, 2, pp. 115–40.

Hughes, J. G. and B. Walsh (1976) 'Migration Flows Between Ireland, the United Kingdom, and the Rest of the World, 1961–1971', *European Demographic Information Bulletin* 7, (4), pp. 125–49.

Humphreys, P. C. (1983) *Public Service Employment: An Examination of Strategies in Ireland and Other European Countries.* (Dublin: Institute of Public Administration).

Hurley, D. G. and Alan McQuaid (1985) *Department of Finance Data Bank of Economic Time Series. Part 1: National Accounts Data (adjusted)* (Dublin: Department of Finance) Research Paper.

ICE Report (1975) (Final Report of the Committee on the Form and Functions of the Intermediate Certificate Examination) (Dublin: Stationery Office).

Industrial Development Authority (1984) *Survey of Employee/Industrial Relations in Irish Private Sector Manufacturing Industry* (Dublin: IDA).

Investment in Education (1965) (Dublin: Stationery Office).

Jessop, B. (1978) 'Capitalism and Democracy: The Best Possible Shell', in *Studies in the Political Economy of Western European Nations* (Oxford: Clarendon Press).

Johnson, D. (1985) *The Interwar Economy of Ireland* (Dublin: Dundalgan Press).

Karabel, J. and A. H. Halsey (1977) 'Educational Research: A Review and an Interpretation', in J. Karabel and A. H. Halsey (eds) *Power and Ideology in Education* (Oxford: Oxford University Press).

Katsiaouni, O. (1977/78) 'Planning in a Small Economy: The Republic of Ireland', *Journal of the Statistical and Social Inquiry Society of Ireland*, 23, (5), pp. 217–75.

Katzenstein, P. (1984) *Corporatism and Change: Austria, Switzerland and the Politics of Industry* (Ithaca: Cornell University Press).

Katzenstein, P. (1985) *Small States in World Markets: Industrial Policy in Europe* (Ithaca: Cornell University Press).

Kelleher, C. and P. O'Hara (1978) *Adjustment Problems of Low Income Farmers* (Dublin: An Foras Taluntais).

Kelleher, C. and A. O'Mahony (1984) *Marginalisation in Irish Agriculture* (Dublin: An Foras Taluntais).

Kelly, A. and T. Brannick (1983) 'The Pattern of Strike Activity in Ireland 1969–1979, Some Preliminary Observations', *Journal of Irish Business and Administrative Research*, 5 (1), pp. 65–77.

Kelly, A. and T. Brannick (1985) 'The Strike Proneness of Public Sector Organisations', *The Economic and Social Review* 16, (4), pp. 251–73.

Kelly, A. and T. Brannick (1986) 'The Changing Contours of Irish Strike Patterns: 1960–84', *Journal of Irish Business and Administrative Research*, 8, (1), pp. 77–88.

Kelly, A. and W. Roche (1983) 'Institutional Reform in Irish Industrial Relations', *Studies*, Autumn, pp. 221–30.

Kelly, P. W. (1982) *Agricultural Land – Tenure and Transfer* (Dublin: An Foras Taluntais).

Kennedy, F. (1971) The Growth and Allocation of Public Social Expenditure in Ireland since 1947, Ph.D. Thesis submitted to the National University of Ireland, (Dublin: Central Statistics Office).

Kennedy, F. (1975) *Public Social Expenditure in Ireland*, (Dublin: Economic and Social Research Institute) Broadsheet No. 11.

Kennedy, F. (1981) 'Poverty and Changes in the Socio-Economic Environment in Ireland 1971–1981', in P. Berwick and M. Burns (ed.) *Conference on Poverty 1981* (Dublin: Council for Social Welfare).

Kennedy, F. (1986) 'The Family in Transition', in K. A. Kennedy (ed.) *Ireland in Transition: Economic and Social Change* (Dublin: Mercier Press).

Kennedy, K. A. (1971) *Productivity and Industrial Growth: The Irish Experience* (Oxford: Clarendon Press).

Kennedy, K. A. (1988) *The Economic Development of Ireland in the Twentieth Century* (London: Routledge & Kegan Paul)

Kennedy, K. A. and B. Dowling (1975) *Economic Growth in Ireland: The Experience Since 1947* (Dublin: Gill and Macmillan).

Kennedy, R. (1973) *The Irish: Emigration, Marriage and Fertility* (Berkeley: University of California Press).

King, D. S. (1986) 'The Public Sector Growth and State Autonomy in Western Europe: The Changing Role and Scope of the State in Ireland since 1950', *West European Politics*, 9, (1) pp. 81–96.

Kirwan, F. X. (1982) 'Recent Anglo-Irish Migration – the Evidence of the British Labour Force Surveys', *Economic and Social Review* 13, (3) pp. 191–204.

Kohn, L. (1932) *The Constitution of the Irish Free State*, (London: George Allen and Unwin.

Komito, L. (1984) 'Irish Clientelism: A Reappraisal', *Economic and Social Review*, 16, (4), pp. 173–94.

Korpi, W. (1978) *The Working Class in Welfare Capitalism: Work Unions and Politics in Sweden* (London: Routledge & Kegan Paul).

Korpi, W. (1983) *The Democratic Class Struggle* (London: Routledge & Kegan Paul).

Korpi, W. (1985) 'Economic Growth and the Welfare State: Leaky Bucket or Irrigation System', *European Sociological Review*, 1 (2) pp. 97–118.

Korpi, W. and M. Shalev (1979) 'Strikes, Industrial Relations and Class Conflict in Capitalist Societies', *British Journal of Sociology*, 30, (2), pp. 164–87.

Korpi, W. and M. Shalev (1980) 'Strikes, Power and Politics in Western Nations, 1900–1976, in Maurice Zeitlin (ed.) *Political Power and Social Theory*, 1.

Lange, P. (1984) 'Unions, Workers and Wage Regulation: The Rational Bases of Consent', in J. Goldthorpe (ed.) *Order and Conflict in Contemporary Capitalism: Studies in the Political Economy of Western European Nations* (Oxford: Clarendon Press).

Laver, M. (1986) 'Ireland: Politics with some Social Bases', *Economic and Social Review*, 17 (3), pp. 107–31.

Laver, M., M. Marsh and R. Sinnott (1987) 'Patterns of Party Support', in Laver M., P. Mair and R. Sinnot, *How Ireland Voted: The Irish General Election 1987*, (Dublin: Poolbeg Press).

Lee, J. J. (1973) *The Modernisation of Ireland* (Dublin: Gill and Macmillan).

Le Grand, Julian (1982) *The Strategy of Equality: Redistribution and the Social Services* (London: George Allen and Unwin).

Lehmbruch, G. (1977) 'Consociational Democracy, Class Conflict and the Neo-Corporatism', in P. Schmitter and G. Lehmbruch (eds) (1979) *Trends Towards Corporatist Intermediation* (Beverly Hills: Sage).

Lehmbruch, G. (1984) 'Concertation and the Structure of Corporatist Networks', in J. Goldthorpe (ed.) *Order and Conflict in Contemporary Capitalism: Studies in the Political Economy of Western European Nations.* (Oxford: Clarendon Press).

Lehmbruch, G. and P. Schmitter (eds) (1982) *Patterns of Corporatist Policy Making* (Beverly Hills: Sage).

Lijphart, A. (1968) *The Politics of Accommodation: Pluralism and Democracy in The Netherlands* (Berkeley: University of California Press).

Littlejohn, G., B. Smart, J. Wakeford and N. Yuval-Davic (eds) (1978) *Power and State* (London: Croom Helm).

Littler, C. and G. Salaman (1984) *Class at Work* (London: B. T. Batsford).

Longford, Earl of and T. P. O'Neill (1970) *Eamon de Valera* (Dublin: Gill and Macmillan).

Lyons, F. S. L. (1973) *Ireland Since the Famine* (London: Fontana; revised edition 1979).

Maguire, M. (1984) 'Social Expenditure in Ireland and Other European OECD Countries: Past Trends and Prospective Developments' in *Public Social Expenditure: Value for Money?* (Dublin: Economic and Social Research Institute).

Mahon, E. (1987) 'Womens Rights and Catholicism in Ireland', *New Left Review*, 166, pp. 53–77.

Maier, C. S. (1978) 'The Politics of Productivity: Foundations of American International Economy Policy after World War II', in P. J. Katzenstein (ed.) *Between Power and Plenty: Foreign Economy Policies of Advanced Industrial States* (Madison: University of Wisconsin Press).

Mair, P. (1987a) *The Changing Irish Party System*, (London: Frances Pinter).

Mair, P. (1987b) 'Policy Competition', in M. Laver, P. Mair and R. Sinnott, *How Ireland Voted: The Irish General Election 1987* (Dublin: Poolbeg Press).

Mann, M. (1986) 'A Crisis in Stratification Theory? Persons, Households/ Families/Lineages, Genders, Classes and Nations', in R. Crompton and M. Mann (eds.), *Gender and Stratification* (Cambridge: Polity Press).

Manning, M. (1979) 'The Farmers', in J. J. Lee (ed.) *Ireland 1945–70* (Dublin: Gill and Macmillan).

Marceau, J. (1977) *Class and Status in France: Economic Change and Social Immobility, 1945–1975* (Oxford: Oxford University Press).

Marshall, T. U. (1950) *Citizenship and Social Class*, (Cambridge: Cambridge University Press).

Matthews, A. (1981) 'The Changing Distribution of Income in Irish Agriculture', in *Proceedings of the Agricultural Economics Society of Ireland* pp. 114–42.

Matthews, A. (1982) 'The State and Irish Agriculture, 1950–1980' in P. J. Drudy (ed.) *Ireland: Land, Politics and People* (Cambridge: Cambridge University Press).

Matthews, A. (1984) 'Agriculture' in J. W. O'Hagan (ed.) *The Economy of Ireland* (Dublin: Irish Management Institute).

McCarthy, C. 1968 *The Distasteful Challenge*, (Dublin: Institute of Public Administration).

McCarthy, C. (1973) *The Decade of Upheaval* (Dublin: Institute of Public Administration).

McCarthy, C. (1977) *Trade Unions in Ireland, 1894–1960* (Dublin: Institute of Public Administration).

McCarthy, C. (1979) 'Industrial Relations, Some Strategies for Change', *Administration*, 27, (3), pp. 294–321.

McCarthy, C. (1980) 'The Development of Irish Trade Unions', in Donal

Nevin (ed.) *Trade Unions and Change in Irish Society* (Dublin: Mercier/ RTE).

McCarthy, C. and F. Van Prondynzynski (1983) 'The Reform of Industrial Relations', *Administration*, 31, pp. 220–59.

McCarthy, W., J. O'Brien and V. Dowd (1975) *Wage Inflation and Wage Leadership: A Study of the Role of Key Wage Bargains in the Irish System of Collective Bargaining* (Dublin: Economic and Social Research Institute) Paper No. 79.

McCormack, D. (1979) 'Policy Making in a Small Open Economy – Some Aspects of Irish Experience', *Central Bank of Ireland Quarterly*, Winter.

McDowell, R. B. (1964) *The Irish Administration: 1801–1914* (London: Routledge & Kegan Paul).

McMahon, B. (1985) 'A Sense of Identity in the Irish Legal System', in J. Lee (ed.) *Ireland: Towards a Sense of Place* (Cork: Cork University Press).

Meenan, J. (1967) 'From Free-Trade to Self-Sufficiency', in F. McManus (ed.) *The Years of the Great Test 1926–39* (Cork: Mercier Press).

Meenan, J. (1970) *The Irish Economy Since 1922* (Liverpool: Liverpool University Press).

Meenan, J. (1980) *George O'Brien: A Biographical Memoir* (Dublin: Gill and Macmillan).

Meenan, J. 1982. 'The historical perspective', in *The Economic and Social State of the Nation* (Dublin: Economic and Social Research Institute).

Messenger, J. (1969) *Inis Beag Isle of Ireland* (New York: Holt, Rinehart and Winston).

Mooney, P. (1978) 'Incomes Policy', in B. Dowling and J. Durkan (eds) *Irish Economic Policy* (Dublin: Economic and Social Research Institute).

Moore, B. (1966) *The Social Origins of Dictatorship and Democracy* (Harmondsworth: Penguin).

Morrissey, M. (1986) 'The Politics of Economic Mangement in Ireland 1958–70', *Irish Political Studies*, 1, pp. 79–96.

Mouzelis, N. (1978a) *Modern Greece: Facets of Underdevelopment* (London: Macmillan).

Mouzelis, N. (1978b) 'Capitalism and the Development of the Greek State', in R. Scase (ed.) *The State in Western Europe* (London: Croom Helm).

Mulcahy, D. G. (1981) *Curriculum and Policy in Irish Post-Primary Education* (Dublin: Institute of Public Administration).

Murphy, D. (1983) *Education: The Implications of Demographic Change* (Dublin: National Economic and Social Council).

Murphy, D. (1984) 'The Impact of State Taxes and Benefits on Irish Household Incomes 1973–1980', *Journal of the Statistical and Social Inquiry Society of Ireland* 25 (1) pp. 55–120, 23 February.

Murphy, J. A. (1975) *Ireland in the Twentieth Century* (Dublin: Gill and Macmillan).

Murphy, T. and D. Walsh (1978) *National Survey of New Forms of Work Organisation* (Dublin: Irish Productivity Centre).

National Economic and Social Council (1975) *Income Distribution: A Preliminary Report* (Dublin: Stationery Office) Report No. 11.

National Economic and Social Council (1983) *Economic and Social Policy*

1983: Aims and Recommendations (Dublin: National Economic and Social Council) Report No. 75.

National Economic and Social Council (1986) *A Strategy for Economic Development* (Dublin: National Economic and Social Council) Report No. 83.

National Farmers' Association (1964) *Farm Income and Agricultural Development* (Dublin: NFA).

National Industrial and Economic Council (1965) *Report on Economic Planning* (Dublin: National Industrial and Economic Council) Report No. 8.

National Insustrial and Economic Council (1970) *Report on Incomes and Prices Policy* (Dublin: National Industrial and Economic Council) Report No. 27.

Norton, D. (1974) *Problems in Economic Planning and Policy Formation in Ireland* (Dublin: Economic and Social Research Institute) Broadsheet No. 12.

Norton, D. (1980) *Economic Analysis for an Open Economy* (Dublin: Irish Management Institute).

O'Brien, G. (1936) 'Patrick Hogan, Minister for Agriculture, 1922–1932', *Studies*, 25, (100), pp. 353–68.

O'Brien, G. (1962) 'The Economic Progress of Ireland: 1912–1962', *Studies*, 51, (201), pp. 9–26.

O'Brien, J. (1981) *A Study of National Wage Agreements in Ireland* (Dublin: Economic and Social Research Institute) Paper No. 104.

O'Donnell, R., (1979) 'Economic Dependence and National Development', in A. Spencer (ed.) *Proceedings of the Fifth Annual Conference, Sociological Association of Ireland* (Belfast: Queen's University of Belfast).

O'Hearn, D. (1987) 'Estimates of New Foreign Manufacturing Employment in Ireland (1956–1972)', *The Economic and Social Review*, 18 (3), pp. 173–88.

O'Higgins, M. (1984) 'Income Redistribution and Social Policies during a Recession', Paper read to the Conference on *The Future of the Welfare State*, (Maastricht, Netherlands) 19–21 December.

O'Leary, J. (1986) 'Service Sector Employment Trends in the Republic of Ireland', Paper presented to Irish Congress of Trades Unions Economic Conference, Dublin. May 1986.

O'Mahony, M. (1983) 'The Length of Spells of Unemployment in Ireland', *Economic and Social Review*, 14, (2), pp. 119–35.

O'Malley, E. (1980) *Industrial Policy and Development: A Survey of the Literature from the Early 1960s*, (Dublin: National Economic and Social Council) Report No. 56.

O'Malley, E. (1985) 'The Problem of Late Industrialisation and the Experience of the Republic of Ireland', *Cambridge Journal of Economics*, 9, (2), pp. 145–54.

O'Malley, E. (1986) 'State Initiatives in Industrial Development', Unpublished paper.

OECD (1984) *Improving Youth Employment Opportunities: Policies for Ireland and Portugal* (Paris: OECD).

Offe, C. and H. Wiesenthal (1980) 'Two Logics of Collective Action: Theoretical Notes on Social Class and Organizational Form', in Maurice Zeitlin (ed.) *Political Power and Social Theory*, 1.

Oliver, J. and J. Turton (1982) 'Is There a Shortage of Skilled Labour?' *British Journal of Industrial Relations*, 20, (2), pp. 195–200.

Olson, M. (1965) *The Logic of Collective Action*, (Cambridge, Mass.: Harvard University Press).

Orridge, A. (1983) 'The Blueshirts and the 'Economic War': A Study of Ireland in the Context of Dependency Theory', *Political Studies*, 31, (3), pp. 351–69.

Panitch, L. (1977) 'The Development of Corporatism in Liberal Democracies', *Comparative Political Studies* 10, reprinted in P. Schmitter and G. Lehmbruch, *Trends Towards Corporatist Intermediation* (Beverly Hills: Sage).

Panitch, L. (1980) 'Recent Theorizations of Corporatism. Reflections on a Growth Industry', *British Journal of Sociology* 31, (2), pp. 159–85.

Panitch, L. (1981) 'The Limits of Corporatism', *New Left Review* 125, pp. 21–44.

Poggi, G. (1978) *The Development of the Modern State: A Sociological Introduction* (Stanford: Stanford University Press).

Poulantzas, N. (1973) *Political Power and Social Class* (London: New Left Books).

Programme For Economic Expansion (1958) (Dublin: Stationery Office).

Przeworski, H. and M. Wallerstein (1982) 'The Structure of Class Conflict in Democratic Capitalist Societies', *American Political Science Review* 76, pp. 215–37.

Pyne, P. (1969) 'The Third Sinn Fein Party 1923–1926: Part I', *Economic and Social Review* 1, (2), pp. 229–57.

Randles, E. (1975) *Post-Primary Education in Ireland, 1957–1970* (Dublin: Veritas).

Report Of The Commission Of Inquiry On Industrial Relations (1981) (Dublin: Government Publications Office) pl. 114.

Report Of The Commission On Social Welfare (1986) (Dublin: Government Publications Office) pl. 3851.

Robinson, M. (1986) 'Women, Work and Equality', Tenth Countess Markievicz Memorial Lecture (Dublin: Irish Association for Industrial Relations).

Roche, W. (1982) 'Social Partnership and Political Control: State Strategy and Industrial Relations in Ireland', in M. Kelly, L. O'Dowd and J. Wickham (eds) *Power, Conflict and Inequality* (Dublin: Turoe Press).

Roche, W. and J. Larraghy (1987) 'The Trend of Unionisation in the Republic', in *Industrial Relations in Ireland: Contemporary Issues and Developments* (Dublin: Department of Industrial Relations).

Ross, M. (1978) 'Comprehensive Regional Policy', in B. Dowling and J. Durkan (eds) *Irish Economic Policy: A Review of Major Issues* (Dublin: Economic and Social Research Institute).

Ross, M. (1986) *Employment in the Public Domain in Recent Decades* (Dublin: Economic and Social Research Institute) Paper No. 127.

Rottman, D. and D. F. Hannan (1981) 'Fiscal Welfare and Inflation: Winners and Losers', Paper presented at a conference on The Irish Economy and Society in the 1980s (Dublin: Economic and Social Research Institute).

Rottman, D. B., D. F. Hannan N. Hardiman N and M. M. Wiley (1982) *The Distribution of Income in the Republic of Ireland: A Study in Social Class and Family Cycle Inequalities* (Dublin: Economic and Social Research Institute) Paper No. 109.

Rottman, D. B., D. F. Hannan and P. J. O'Connell (1984) 'The Redistributive Effects of Social Expenditure and Taxation in the Republic of Ireland: An Evaluation of Welfare State Policies', Paper prepared for the Conference on The Future of the Welfare State (Maastricht, Netherlands) 19–21 December.

Rottman, D. and P. J. O'Connell (1982) 'The Changing Social Structure of Ireland', in F. Litton (ed.) *Unequal Achievement: The Irish Experience 1957–1982* (Dublin: Institute of Public Administration).

Rueschemeyer, D. and P. B. Evans (1985) 'The State and Economic Transformation: Toward an Analysis of the Conditions Underlying Effective Intervention', in P. Evans, D. Rueschemeyer and T. Skocpol (eds) *Bringing the State Back In* (Cambridge: Cambridge University Press).

Rumpf, E. and A. C. Hepburn (1977) *Nationalism and Socialism in Twentieth-Century Ireland* (Liverpool: Liverpool University Press).

Sacks, P. (1976) *The Donegal Mafia* (New Haven: Yale University Press).

Sandford, C. and O. Morrissey (1985) *The Irish Wealth Tax: A Case Study in Economics and Politics* (Dublin: Economic and Social Research Institute) Paper No. 123.

Saunders, P. (1984) *Evidence on Income Distribution by Governments* Working Paper No. 11 (Paris: OECD).

Schmitter, P. (1974) 'Still the Century of Corporatism', *Review of Politics* 36. Reprinted in P. Schmitter and G. Lehmbruch (eds) (1979) *Trends Towards Corporatist Intermediation* (Beverly Hills: Sage).

Schmitter, P. (1977) 'Modes of Interest Intermediation and Models of Societal Change in Western Europe', *Comparative Political Studies* 10. Reprinted in P. Schmitter and G. Lehmbruch (eds) (1979) *Trends Towards Corporatist Intermediation* (Beverly Hills: Sage).

Schmitter, P. (1982) 'Reflections on Where the Theory of Neo-Corporatism has Gone and Where the Praxis of Neo-Corporatism may be Going', in G. Lehmbruch and P. Schmitter (eds) *Patterns of Corporatist Policy Making* (Beverly Hills: Sage).

Schmitter, P. and G. Lehmbruch (eds) (1979) *Trends Towards Corporatist Intermediation* Beverly Hills: Sage.

Schregle, J. (1975) 'Restructuring of the Irish Trade Union Movement', mimeo submitted to the ICTU (Geneva: International Labour Organisation).

Schultz, T. W. (1961) 'Investment in Human Capital', *American Economic Review*, 51, 1, pp. 1–17.

Scully, J. (1971) *Agriculture in the West of Ireland: A Study of the Low Farm Income Problem* (Dublin: Stationery Office).

Second Programme for Economic Expansion (1964) (Dublin: Stationery Office).

Sexton, J. J. (1982) 'Sectoral Changes in the Labour Force over the Period 1961–1980', *Quarterly Economic Commentary, August 1982* (Dublin: Economic and Social Research Institute) pp. 36–46.

Sexton, J. J., B. J. Whelan and J. A. Williams (1988) Transition from School to Work and Early Labour Market Experience (Dublin: Economic and Social Research Institute) Paper No. 141.

Shalev, M., (1983a) 'The Social Democratic Model and Beyond: Two Generations of Comparative Research and the Welfare State', *Comparative Social Research* 6, pp. 315–51.

Shalev, M. (1983b) 'Class Politics and the Western State', in Spiro, S. E. and E. Yuchtman-Yarr (eds) *Evaluating the Welfare State: Social and Political Perspectives* (New York: Academic Press).

Sheehan, J. 1982. 'Education, Education Policy and Poverty' in L. Joyce and A. McCashin (eds) *Poverty and Social Policy* (Dublin: Institute of Public Administration) pp. 63–74.

Sheehy, S. J. (1974) 'Taxation – The Farmers' Fair Share', in *Whither Ireland?* (Dublin: Irish Farmers' Association).

Sheehy, S. J. and R. O'Connor (1985) *Economics of Irish Agriculture* (Dublin: Institute of Public Administration).

Sinnott, R. (1978) 'The Electorate' in M. R. Pennman (ed.) *Ireland at the Polls: The Dail Election of 1977* (Washington D.C.: American Enterprise Institute).

Sinnott, R. (1984) 'Interpretations of the Irish Party System', *European Journal of Political Research*, 12 (3), pp. 289–307.

Skocpol, T. (1985) 'Bringing the State Back In: Strategies of Analysis in Current Research', in Evans, P. B., D. Rueschemeyer and T. Skocpol (eds) *Bringing the State Back In* (Cambridge: Cambridge University Press).

Skocpol, T. and E. Amenta (1985) 'Did Capitalists Shape Social Security: Comment on Quadagno, ASR, October 1984', *American Sociological Review*, 50 (August), pp. 572–5.

Skocpol, T. and E. K. Trimberger (1977/78) 'Revolutions and the World – Historical Development of Capitalism', *Berkeley Journal of Sociology* 22, pp. 101–3.

Snyder, D. and E. Kick (1979) 'Structural Position in the World System and Economic Growth 1955–70: A Multiple Network Analysis in Transnational Interactions', *American Journal of Sociology*, 84, (5), pp. 1096–1126.

Spain, H. (1968) 'Agricultural Education and Extension in Ireland', Paper to Agricultural Adjustment Conference, Dublin.

Stanton, R. (1979) 'Foreign Investment and Host-Country Politics: The Irish Case', in D. Seers, B. Schaffer and M. Kijunen (eds) *Underdeveloped Europe: Studies In Core-Periphery Relations* (London: Harvester Press).

Stark, T. (1977) *The Distribution of Income in Eight Countries, Background Report No. 4* (London: HMSO) Royal Commission on the Distribution of Income and Wealth.

Streeck, W. (1984) 'Neo-Corporatist Industrial Relations and the Economic Crisis in West Germany', in J. Goldthorpe (ed.) *Order and Conflict in Contemporary Capitalism* (Oxford: Oxford University Press).

Streeck, W. (1987) 'The Uncertainties of Management and the Management of Uncertainty: Employers, Labour Relations and Industrial Adjustment In the 1980s', *Work, Employment and Society* 1, (3), pp. 281–308.

Summers, R. and A. Heston (1984) 'Improved International Comparisons of Real Product and its Composition, 1950–1980', *Review of Income and Wealth* 30, (2), pp. 207–62.

Sweeney, J. (1974) 'Foreign Companies in Ireland', *Studies* pp. 273–86.

Telesis Consultancy Group (1982) *A Review of Industrial Policy* (Dublin: National Economic and Social Council) Report No. 64.

Third Programme For Economic and Social Development 1969–72 (1969) (Dublin: Stationery Office).

Toner, B. (1985) 'The Unionisation and Productivity Debate: An Employee Opinion Survey in Ireland' *British Journal of Industrial Relations* 23 (2), pp. 179–202.

Tracy, M. A. (1971) 'Agricultural Policies and the Adjustment Problem', in I. F. Baillie and S. J. Sheehy (eds) *Irish Agriculture in a Changing World* (Edinburgh: Oliver and Boyd).

Tussing, A. D. (1978) *Irish Educational Expenditures – Past, Present and Future* (Dublin: Economic and Social Research Institute), Paper No. 92.

Uusitalo, M. (1985) 'Redistribution and Equality in the Welfare State: An Effort to Interpret the Major Findings of Research on the Redistributive Effects of the Welfare State' *European Sociological Review*, 1 (2), pp. 162–76.

Wallerstein, I. (1974) 'The Rise and Future Demise of the World Capitalist System: Concepts for Comparative Analysis' *Comparative Studies in Society and History* 16 (4), pp. 387–415.

Wallerstein, I. (1975) *The Modern World System: Capitalist Agriculture and the origins of the European Economy in the Sixteenth Century* (New York: Academic Press).

Walsh, B. M. (1968) *Some Irish Population Problems Reconsidered* (Dublin: Economic and Social Research Institute) Paper No. 42.

Walsh, B. M. (1970) *Migration to the United Kingdom from Ireland: 1961–66* (Dublin: Economic and Social Institute) Memorandum Series No. 70.

Walsh, B. M. (1979) 'Economic Growth and Development, 1945–70' in J. J. Lee (ed.) *Ireland 1945–70* (Dublin: Gill and Macmillan) pp. 27–37.

Walsh, B. M. (1980) 'Recent Demographic Changes in the Republic of Ireland', *Population Trends*, 21 (Autumn), pp. 3–9.

Walsh, B. M. (1984) 'Marriage in the Twentieth Century', in H. Cosgrave (ed.) *Marriage in Ireland* (Dublin: College Press).

Walsh, B. M. (1985) 'Youth Unemployment: The Economic Background', *Administration*, 33, 2, pp. 151–66.

Walsh, B. M., assisted by A. O'Toole (1973) *Women and Employment in Ireland: Results of a National Survey* (Dublin: Economic and Social Research Institute) Paper No. 69.

Weede, E. (1980) 'Beyond Misspecification in Sociological Analyses of Income Inequality', *American Sociological Review*, 45, (3), pp. 497–501.

Weede, E. and J. Kummer (1985) 'Some Criticisms of Recent Work on World System Status, Inequality, and Democracy', *International Journal of Comparative Sociology*, 26, (3–4), pp. 132–48.

Whelan, B. J. and J. G. Hughes (1976) A Survey of Returned and Intending Emigrants in Ireland. (Dublin: Economic and Social Research Institute) draft report.

Whelan, C. T. (1980) *Employment Conditions and Job Satisfaction: The Distribution, Perception and Evaluation of Job Rewards* (Dublin: Economic and Social Research Institute) Paper No. 101.

Whelan, C. T. (1982) *Worker Priorities, Trust in Management and Prospects for Workers' Participation* (Dublin: Economic and Social Research Institute) Paper No. 111.

Whelan, C. T. and B. J. Whelan. (1984) *Social Mobility in the Republic of*

Ireland: A Comparative Perspective, (Dublin: Economic and Social Research Institute) Paper No. 116.

Whelan, C. T. and B. J. Whelan (1985) 'Equality of Opportunity in Irish Schools: A Reassessment' *Economic and Social Review*, 16, (2), pp.103–14.

Whitaker, T. K. (1986) 'Economic Development, 1958–1985' in K. A. Kennedy (ed.) *Ireland in Transition* (Cork: Mercier Press).

White Paper (1963) *Closing the Gap (Incomes and Output)* (Government Publications Office) Pl. 6959.

Whyte, J. (1980) *Church and State in Modern Ireland 1923–1970* 2nd edn (Dublin: Gill and Macmillan).

Wickham, A. (1980) 'National Educational Systems and the International Context: The Case of Ireland', *Comparative Education Review* 6, 4, pp. 323–37.

Windmuller, J. and H. Gladstone (eds) (1984) *Employers' Associations and Industrial Relations* (Oxford: Clarendon Press).

Wright, E. and L. Perrone (1977) 'Marxist Class Categories and Income Inequality', *American Sociological Review*, 42, (1), pp. 32–55.

Zeitlin, J. (1985) 'Shop Floor Bargaining and the State: A Contradictory Relationship', in S. Tolliday and J. Zeitlin (eds), *Shop Floor Bargaining and the State: Historical and Comparative Perspectives* (Cambridge: Cambridge University Press).

Index

All entries refer to Ireland except where otherwise indicated.